I SAW HIM
STANDING THERE

I Saw Him Standing There

Spiderwize
Remus House
Coltsfoot Drive
Woodston
Peterborough
PE2 9BF

www.spiderwize.com

A CIP catalogue record for this book is available from the British Library.

The views expressed in this work are solely those of the author and do not necessarily reflect the views of the publisher, and the publisher hereby disclaims any responsibility for them.

Cover - Painting by Mike Powell of first sighting and encounter with John Lennon (15.11.1992) 'IT WAS YOU'

I SAW HIM STANDING THERE

Mike Powell

I SAW HIM STANDING THERE

Introduction

I suppose most people writing a book, who have never done so before, start with a blank piece of paper and spend some time just staring at it, as if it's the enemy. It is daunting. It is certainly not what I am used to. This is going to require discipline on a scale I have never experienced before. This is the first time since I was 16 years old doing my CSEs and O Levels that I have ever 'put pen to paper'. I suddenly feel now at my tender age, which is somewhere in my fifties, I must engage my brain and use the grey matter to recall events in my life that have happened to me. I am hoping that I get into the 'groove' of writing, quickly, and will be hoping that the 'Pavlovian Theory' really does work. They reckon that if you do something repetitively for more than 21 days, it becomes second nature, in fact, habit.

We shall see.

I guess fiction writing would probably be an easier option as it doesn't matter whatever exciting and far-fetched fictitious ramblings of a story one decides to make up. The reader may then select the book based on what the cover looks like, a five minute browse, the title, the film, the celebrity, or the author's name which is famously synonymous with, say, thrillers or whatever.

However, I had no choice in the matter.

This book had to be done.

Thy will be done.

This is my story.

It is Friday 30th March 2012, 8.30pm at The Pavillion Theatre, Rhyl, North Wales.

On stage is a Liverpool boy, Mike (Mickey) Powell with his band.

He has just totally captivated the audience with songs, stories and art at this special 'one-off' concert called 'JOHN LENNON AND ME'.

Among the 500 or so audience are 20 of Mike's friends from the local running club, all of whom have no previous knowledge that he has anything whatsoever to do with music, let alone that he has recorded, written songs and can even sing.

He then finishes his last song, a stormin' rock track, given to him by John Lennon. The crowd erupts to tumultuous applause once more.

Deadly silence ensues as Mike quietly pays homage to John Lennon and thanks his mum, dad and God for helping him, that day he prayed to them on 8th November 1992.

Mike looks up to the heavens with eyes closed and murmurs, 'John, I hope I have done your music justice, I promise to do my best to get this music all around the world.'

He then opens his eyes and gives a heartfelt thanks to everyone for coming to the show.

The crowd erupts once more. (Mike dreams of giving a similar concert in New York City, in Madison Square Garden – 'for all America to sit up and take notice of this John Lennon music'.)

Growing Up
48 Years Earlier

It was 1964 and a 9-year-old Liverpool kid called Mickey Powell kicked a ball against the coal merchants' gates at the top of the little terraced street in Anfield, Liverpool, where he lived.

At the same time, a 24-year-old Liverpool kid had just led his group onto the Ed Sullivan show in the USA and caused a furore.

It was John Lennon, and his band was called The Beatles.

LYRICS FROM 'IN THE BEGINNING' © Mike Powell 2000

In the beginning, when life was new, as a kid, you took what life threw at you
Then something happens, you grow up, supposed to be a man, and all that stuff

Do you remember, on the street, you'd run errands, hello to everyone you meet
In the beginning, in the beginning, in the beginning
Cast your mind back to that day
When the sun always shone and the rain came out to play
When the sun went in, the moon came out to stay
And when the moon was up to a dream you'd float away
Oh for the simple things in life - oh for the simple things in life – oh for the simple things in life
In the beginning it was all you could do, to stop and help someone, if they needed help from you, men would whistle all the time, mum would sing, nursery rhymes
Five pound note, was as big as a letter, the letter you wrote, to a girl you met her
Holidays, caravan, on the beach, hand in hand
In the beginning, in the beginning, in the beginning
Cast your mind back to that day
When the sun always shone and the rain came out to play
When the sun went in, the moon came out to stay
And when the moon was up to a dream you'd float away
Oh for the simple things in life, oh for the simple things in life, oh for the simple things in life

1

The Marriage

I remember distinctly the evening the woman, who would eventually become my wife and the mother of my two beautiful children, entered my life.

It was around late September 1983 on a Friday night, around 9.30pm in Chester. I was with 'the lads', namely Steve Ashy, Little Macca, Mike Alli, Frank Pasinski, Tich, Shunty, The Dog, No-neck, and a few others of our crowd who frequented the Golden Eagle in Chester. This was my local even when I lived in Buckley some 10 miles away!

Within the 'Eagle' was a happening corner (which was ours – the lads' very own territory) affectionately called the 'boys' pen'. We would meet there and discuss the latest news, women, football, food, Weinholt's steak pies, etc. The landlord was a diamond called Ed. We would encourage him to book a 'turn' known as Billy May – Billy was wicked on the guitar and would play Purple Haze with his teeth. It was a great evening's entertainment particularly when one is, erm, how shall I put it, slightly inebriated! We would cast our eyes over the latest girlfriend of whichever mate had dropped or been dropped by their previous girlfriend. It was weird but I suppose we were the kiddies in town. There were always girls around, jockeying for a seat in the 'pen'. Because with this bunch of highly charged lads there was always an excitement that people/girls wanted to be around. We played for the pub football team. We did some sponsored charity drinking, which we were very good at, and on one occasion raised over £1,500. We had after-hours drinking whenever we were there. We were a great bunch of real mates.

I had just come out of a seven year relationship with a lovely girl called Jean, and to cut a long story short, had sold my house in Buckley and bought the house I had got for Jean in Handbridge. We went our separate ways and I ended up buying and moving into 36 Pyecroft St, Handbridge.

I was aged 28 and I had bought a V12 E-Type Jaguar from the sale of the Buckley house, as well as having my company car that I referred to as the 'repmobile'. The other lads' ages varied from 24ish to 34ish. There was a good mix in the group of reps, accountants, engineers (British Aerospace) and other assorted employed and self-employed people. There were no wrong'uns in there, and the crack was good!

So back to the story. It was about 9.30pm on a Friday evening and me and the boys were all standing in the boys' pen corner. This 'vision' walked into the Golden Eagle. She had a skin-tight red catsuit on and masses of blonde hair, a gorgeous figure and a stunning, beautiful face. The zipper of the catsuit was only unzipped about six inches from her neck, but it was tasteful, sexy and provocative.

I was hooked that instant; I think my legs went like jelly. Then when I finally refocused on the room I noticed she was with a friend of mine called Jeff Green. I went cold all over and felt sick to the stomach, and immediately turned right around and looked the other way to blot her out of my mind.

She was with a friend of mine and it's always been an unwritten rule – certainly for me – that you do not entertain anyone who is married or with a friend. You don't encourage any form of friendly dialogue, particularly if you fancied them, or, as was the case in some instances, they fancied you. Never! I've seen more men in fights over women that have thrown themselves at their boyfriend's best mate, or when their actions have been misconstrued as such. One of my dad's favourite sayings comes to mind – 'Don't tempt fate'.

So I didn't tempt fate.
But the temptress fated me.
Half an hour or so went by and I had put to the back of my mind the vision I had seen. I was able to do this with a couple more pints of alcohol and talking to the lads about anything they wanted to talk about. I swear I didn't look back once.

I felt a tug on my back jean pocket and heard the words, 'Yves Saint Lauren eh!' The voice was female and was warm and I detected it had a slightly upper class, well bred, confident manner about it.

Earlier in the year I had won a competition with my company – J.A. Sharwood & Co. Speciality Foods. I was the country's top salesman and over a six month target period three top prizes were up for grabs. I won them all! I won a video player (unlike now, this was then a brand new, state of the art invention), £1000 bonus, and a fortnight's holiday for two in Hong Kong. The competition was based around introducing a new Chinese food product range into the UK. Out of 30 reps I left them all for dead. Anyway, the aforementioned Yves Saint Lauren jeans I had bought in a backstreet of Kowloon for the equivalent of 50p. I'd watched them being made.

Not having a clue who on earth it was tugging at my jeans, I instinctively said, "50p in Hong Kong."
As I turned around to see who it was I froze. It was the vision and she said, "Hong Kong eh!" She introduced herself by saying, "My name's Karen, what's yours?"
I wanted the earth to swallow me and her to go away, as she was with my mate. I said, "My name's Mike," and I called to the other lads to gee them up into going to our next port of call, a classy nightclub in Northgate Street. The club had sumptuous deep leather chesterfields, and was owned by a small stylish Italian who wore the best suits money could buy.
We said our goodbyes abruptly and all the way to the nightclub the lads were talking about this girl called Karen. I didn't give an opinion, and went into the club and got wasted.

The next day, mid Saturday morning, I was walking through town with Steve, my best friend in Chester. I was still feeling slightly 'muggy' from the night before. I think we had just come from the riverfront, where we had watched the rowing club lasses row their stuff whilst having breakfast on this tranquil, sunny day.
We walked up to Eastgate Street and just past the Chester Grosvenor hotel we literally bumped into Karen and Steve started talking to her. He said, "We're going back to Mike's for a coffee, do you want to come?"
She said, "Yes," and immediately I felt really awkward because of the feelings I had for her.
At some point Steve went to the bathroom upstairs and Karen said, "Why don't you want to talk to me?"
I said to her, "You are my friend's girlfriend and I don't want to get

involved, or upset him."

She laughed out loud and said, "I've known Jeff for years; he's just a good mate." I then asked her if she was sleeping with him and she said it was a very casual affair, not going anywhere. "I only see Jeff every few weeks."

To which I said, "Sorry, I can't be friends with you, I want you too much."

Steve entered the room and the conversation changed to some Athena posters and catalogues I had on my table.

I had left Sharwood's, headhunted by my former Sales Director, Gerry Sloane, joined Athena, and started purveying fine art – or flogging posters, depending on your point of view. Karen had asked me if I could get her a poster from the catalogue. Out of decency I said I could. She took my phone number and said she would phone me next week to see whether I had got the poster.

A few days went by and I got the call. I said I'd got the poster, so she arranged to pick it up from my house the following evening. When she arrived she looked like a million dollars. We had a coffee and with my razor sharp Scouse wit, she was soon hysterically laughing at my daft jokes. After about half an hour I made an excuse and said I was meeting someone up town. She offered to pay for the poster, which I refused and she left saying hopefully, "I'll see you again." It has to be said, at that moment I was fighting a losing battle with myself. I wanted so much to hold her, stare into those deep brown hypnotic eyes and melt into a gentle kiss that would last forever. That said, the front door closed behind her and I was relieved; I was off the hook. Or so I thought.

I got a call from her two days later saying she couldn't stop thinking about me and she had to see me (my thoughts exactly!). She had finished with Jeff.

I said, "Sorry, I don't think so. I know Jeff, he's a good'un, but he is no idiot. He's not going to roll over, lie down and die for someone else to swan in and take his girl." She laughed again saying it was just a very casual affair, and that Jeff wouldn't have a problem with it at all. I got another phone call after the weekend. It was Karen saying she had spoken to Jeff and he understood. He was cut up about it, but said, "Mike's a great guy, I wish you all the best."

I wasn't convinced, and told her so.

Another day or so went by. She phoned me and said that she had spoken to Jeff over the way I felt, and that Jeff was calling to see me to explain everything was OK, and that he didn't have a problem with us getting together.

Sure enough, Jeff called to my house, we talked and he was humble and assured me, "Mike, Karen's a gorgeous lovely girl. She's well out my league. We have only been seeing each other every few weeks, but that's the way she wanted to play it. I wanted more, but realised very early on that wasn't going to happen. Really Mike, it's OK."

I said, "Are you absolutely sure about this Jeff? If you say no, then I swear I won't go anywhere near her." Suffice to say, he convinced me it was OK. Then we shook hands and I wished him all the best and he left.

I phoned Karen shortly afterwards and explained how the meeting had gone. We were both terribly excited about the prospect of seeing each other right away, but we arranged it for the following night. The apprehension was colossal, but the night arrived. I opened the front door and we kissed. The kiss was just as I had envisaged it, as I described before. Her eyes, those lips, that body, that mind. It was slow, sensuous, long, amazing, knockout, and it did seem to go on forever. We walked into town from my house and had a couple of jars before going back to mine.

How did I feel walking with her that first night? I felt like I was King Kong. I was proud, ecstatic, happy, excited, floating, strong, dynamic, and definitely in love. We went straight to bed and consummated our love affair. It felt as if I had never ever made love before that night.

It was exquisite and took me to a higher place where I wanted to stay. I'm sure she felt the same. The way she gave herself to me melted my heart and my mind.

From then on every day seemed an absolute joy. We would take simple pleasures like a walk in the park hand in hand, telling each other stories and past experiences we'd had. Morning, noon and night we always had something to say. Even when we didn't talk, it was magical. We would take each other to our special haunts, areas that we liked to visit, and share the experiences. For instance, I took Karen to Arisaig in the Western Isles. She took me to her parents' former home, the smallholding in Tarvin where she enjoyed so much of her childhood. As we revisited these and other places it was like a walk down memory lane that we both shared. We had a special night (Friday) when we would walk the 50 metres to our local pub in Hoole and have a drink and a meal. We would go into the snug and find a quiet corner where we would giggle and of course, snuggle. We would snuggle in the snug! I am sure we would probably have given the impression of love-struck kids. Only we weren't kids, we were in our late 20s. Our friends would come to visit, or we would visit them, and a great time was always had by all. We soon had quite a busy social life together, as opposed to separately. The nightclubs and bars in Chester where we would go out 'on the town' seemed to take on a new meaning and excitement. It felt like together, me and Karen were where it was at. It felt like it was meant to be. We were together for the whole time, except when I used to do my circuit training every Tuesday and Thursday nights for an hour or so at Queensferry Leisure Centre, Deeside.

We were engaged within six months and married within one year.

When Karen and I decided to marry, I put my house in Pyecroft Street, Handbridge, up for sale. I sold it soon after the marriage, but had basically been living with her from the outset in Claude Road, Hoole. A neat terraced house with a backyard that was south facing, which was soon tidied and whitewashed and we spent many happy hours in this suntrap. We had discussed children and Karen was anxious to start a family soon. I agreed, and then we discussed the possibility of a house with a garden for when 'the children' came along.

Soon we were looking in all the estate agents' windows in Chester, and found a lovely 30s' semidetached house in Durban Avenue in a leafy suburb called Christleton. It cost £32,000 and had been extended, virtually doubled in size by the owner. It had an enormous garden and inside was like a show home, the guy having changed the complete specification of the house. He was a builder who claimed to me that he had spent too much time and money on her, saying 'never again'! We moved in within months of the marriage, and sold Karen's house in Claude Road.

The marriage was in a catholic church in Upton, Chester. It was on the 26th May 1984. The priest's name was FATHER JOHN LENNON.

At 6am on the morning of the wedding I was running around Chester walls on my own. It was cold but I was warm and heady with expectation about the wedding. I remember thinking, from today, my life is going to change. When I got back to my cosy little terraced house I had a cup of tea and a bath.

Then I destroyed my past.

I had, over the years, dated and gone out with lots of girls. I had collected lots of photographs, lots of letters, lots of sentimental keepsakes from girls mainly from the UK, but also from around the world. I had two black bin bags full of my past. Full of love letters, photos, knick-knacks and other assorted items! Probably the earliest love letters I can remember in the bin bags came from Linda McCullock from Formby. Linda was a very mature 17-year-old, and had ample of everything. She was a great girl; we were always walking on the beach hand in hand and laughing together when we weren't up to mischief! I had kept these letters since I was 16 years old. The day of my wedding I was 29 years old, so you can imagine there was a lot of stuff I had collected. Linda, by the way, was almost Latin in appearance and came from a family who were wealthy and owned a chain of betting shops throughout Merseyside. (She is the girl I mention in the song 'In the Beginning'.)

Then there was Gary Glitter's babysitter Paula, who lived in Sheffield, and whose dad owned his own Sheffield Steel foundry. They lived in Eccleshall and were very well to do and she was an absolute little minx! There was Snezana, a doctor from Yugoslavia. She looked just like an 18-year-old Jackie Kennedy. Etc. etc. etc. I destroyed my past. I threw the bin bags and all their contents into the rubbish bin at the bottom of my backyard. The bins were emptied on a Thursday, so my past was just lying in the bin, waiting for its ultimate fate. 14 years of history waiting to be dumped on the council tip.

The wedding was a success, but I was on pins the whole time. My younger brother let me down. He was pissed and swearing like a trooper on the top table. This only added to my edgy state, but after calling him out to the loo I had words with him and he calmed down a bit.

They say if you want to know what your girl will turn out like, look at her mother.

Karen's mum Jean looked down her nose at people, particularly me, and in my opinion was sanctimonious. It was something that I just had to put up with. She came from the South Wales Valleys and married a fighter pilot. Ashley 'Ash' Norman Goodhew had been an RAF Flight Lieutenant and had seen action in Aden and Egypt. He went on to become the chief test pilot for British Airways and literally wrote the manual on the 737 jets that, at the time, BA were ordering. They had a son younger than Karen called Phillip. He was an actor who went on to write a couple of films. He also starred in Crossroads the soap opera, and did a few TV adverts like Timotei and Gillette.

Initially after retiring from the RAF, Ash became a captain with Eagle Airways, operating from Liverpool Airport. British Airways took over this company and Ash became the youngest ever Captain of BA at 28 years of age. They lived near Heathrow in a mock Tudor spread after being promoted within BA from his base in Liverpool, moving down from their smallholding in Tarvin, Cheshire.

Eventually, Ash retired and bought a nice new house in Abergavenny where Jean, his wife, had been brought up.

Ash hailed from Oxford and had always wanted to fly from when he was a young boy, ever since the first time he saw an aircraft in the skies over Oxford. He was a giant among men, in every sense and I adored him. I think that she, the wife, aspired to the upper class life and in some way to me , seemed cosseted by her loving husband.

I know she thought Karen married beneath herself. Isn't it ironic? Isn't life ironic?

She always dictated everything, and everyone had to put up with it. She always looked down her nose at people as if she was unquestionably in the right, and far superior to whoever she was speaking 'at'. She revelled in talking down to people, particularly Karen. Very early on in the marriage I realised she had a horrendous effect on Karen. Karen was scared of her and used to tremble whilst talking to her on the phone. When the in-laws came to stay for a weekend, we, Karen and I, would spend eight hours cleaning the house. Everything had to be just right for Jean; Karen made sure she couldn't be criticised by her mother. You could see the judgemental old woman weighing up everything to make sure it was in order, clean, the right recipe for the meal etc. It was horrendous, but I put up with it for the love of my wife. Many, many times I promised I'd sort it out if she would just let me, if she had supported her husband who wanted to support her. I had planned what I would do. I'd drive down to Abergavenny and deliver her the ultimatum she so badly deserved. "If you want to see your grandchildren ever again, you will behave like a normal human being towards Karen." I was ready to read her the riot act. All Karen had to say to me was, "OK, do it."

But Karen was just too frightened of her and thought, illogically, it couldn't be done, so she'd rather persevere with the persecution and, I guess, endure a lifelong, painful, Catholic suffering.

The only way to deal with bullies and stop the persecution, is to stand up to them. That's what I wanted to do.

The only time I made the mother cry was after an eight hour housecleaning-prior-to-visit session. We were shattered and Karen and I had fallen out over this very subject. I think I said, "This is the last time I am doing this for your mother." This always caused tension between me and Karen, she just wouldn't stand up and face her demons, or should I say, her demon. Anyway, I was having a coffee and had put the television on with my feet up on the coffee table. Jean and Ashley came through the front door. Jean walked through to the snug where I was, walked straight past me and turned the television off and said, and I quote, "We'll have that off for a start."

I couldn't believe it and I leant forward and said softly, "Jean... this is my house, do you hear..." and screamed with every sinew in my body, "this is my fucking house!" At the same time as screaming at her I had clenched my fist and smashed it down onto the coffee table, twice, which shattered the vase and the cup.

She burst out crying, ran into the kitchen and said to Ashley, "I want to go home." But Ash refused and I was pleasantly surprised. In fact he came in and we had our usual friendly banter. I did say to Ash, "Who in God's name does she think she is coming into my house and turning off the TV that I was in the middle of watching?" He looked up to the ceiling and shook his head. We understood each other, more than the others realised. He had great strength of character; he deserved a medal. We then had a beer. We were OK, me and Ash, but as you can imagine the weekend wasn't really a success (understatement of the year!). On these occasions our two children were, as always, as good as gold. They'd play in the big lounge, all day, while we played the whirling dervishes, cleaning the house for that dreadful woman. Extra time we could and should have had with our very own angels.

Hindsight's a great thing but foresight is king.

It must be said, over the years we were married, Karen myself and the children all had many brilliant times together. It actually felt like we were a team, a winning team. We did love each other; we always said that together we could overcome anything. We both gave each other great support and comfort in the knowledge that we'd be there for each other, always. We both felt the same. We were each other's friend, lover and married spouse. A fantastic force was blossoming between us as we relished the future, together.

2

The Children

Timothy Michael Powell. Born on 11th October 1985.

Stephanie Louise Powell. Born on 8th November 1988.

I was present at the births of both my children, Tim and Stephie.
These two events in my life eclipse everything that has ever, or will ever happen to me. They are the finest and most beautiful moments of my life and I thank God for them. Nothing comes close, and I pity the father who was never present at the birth of his child or children. It is beyond compare. It is an earth shattering moment, when you watch your own flesh and blood created and brought into this world. It humbles you to ashes. It reduced a grown man to uncontrollable tears. It introduced this grown man to heaven on earth.

Timothy Michael Powell

The birth of our first-born was always going to be special. We had no idea whether it was going to be a girl or boy.
Karen had suggested that we try for a baby that would fall in the winter months, so she would have the school summer holidays as well as maternity leave. It was a good idea, and that's what we did. She was a primary school teacher and worked in a local Catholic primary school.
She was always a fit woman, sporty, but hated the competitive environment in which she was brought up within the horsey upper class 'Tarvin set'. During her pregnancy she swam virtually every day. During the pregnancy I prayed virtually every day. "Please God make our baby healthy. Whatever it is, whether a boy or girl, please make it healthy." I was being subjected to a kind of pressure/pain almost to ensure the baby would be alright. It was instinctive and it was beyond my control.
Nine months later I took Karen to the Countess of Chester Hospital in readiness for the birth. Her blood pressure was through the roof. The doctors were concerned and had arranged for her to have a caesarean section. She had requested an epidural, which means that the mother's

top half is compos mentis, but below the waist and through the subsequent birth there is no feeling or pain. Well, the doctor injected her lower spine four times, but it just wasn't working. She could feel the pain. (I heard the doctor say that Karen's spine was very solid, with little room to get the needle into the required area.) He gave her a fifth and final injection and the theatre was prepared for the delivery. I think that with all the swimming she was like a honed athlete, and that was why the doctor had difficulty injecting.

So I was sitting at the head of the bed holding her hand in readiness for the moment when the doctor's knife went into her stomach.

It did and Karen let out a searing scream. Immediately the doctor said, "Put her out." Now I don't know what they did, but she became unconscious within a second or so and the doctor proceeded.

A minute later he pulled out a bloodied creature from her stomach. I remember the huge cord, the blood and then this little creature crying its first vocals into its brave new world.

Instinctively I walked to the foot of the bed to see my baby. I saw it was clearly a boy, although the doctor then said to me, "It's a boy." He handed me this bloodied little wonder. I remember blood was everywhere, but I was holding our very own baby. I looked towards Karen who was still out, but to my shock I saw her stomach sliced right open. I could see all her vital organs and worried if she would be alright. This cut was right across her stomach, and the size of the opening, which was loose and baggy, you could have fitted a football into. I suppose I shouldn't have seen this sight, but all was well and the doctors scurried me out of the theatre in order to put Karen back together again. I didn't have the luxury of holding the baby for too long, as there was still major surgery to perform. However, it was long enough for me to see him looking at me in wonderment, and me to see him. How on earth could anyone hurt these little creatures? They are totally dependent. It is a huge responsibility and one I looked forward to with relish.

I then went into an empty waiting room and cried and cried my eyes out. I thanked God for our miracle; somehow I knew Tim was going to be OK. The vice-like pressures that had been in place on my brain for those past nine months were removed, lifted, gone. Another miracle I thought.

Timothy Michael Powell, born into the world on 11th October 1985, was the most beautiful thing I had ever seen in my life. His head and face were perfection. There were no marks anywhere on him as he didn't have to struggle through the normal canal route, so nothing was squashed. He was perfect. And I am intensely proud to say he has developed into a wonderful, intelligent, witty and creative human being. I am enormously proud of my boy and I would be happy to stand his ground against the whole wide world, so much does he mean to me. I love him more than life itself. God bless our Tim.

We played happily in the garden of Durban Avenue with Tim, and he used to play with his toys and paddling pool, and we'd walk around the village, and I'd carry him in a seated rucksack with a balloon tied to it, or sometimes in the pushchair. Everything was new to him. He had an incredible eye for detail and would spot something, say on the floor, and really focus on it.

Our friends Heather and Allen would visit with their child Fiona and a party atmosphere would ensue. Fiona was born within a month of Tim and they became inseparable friends. Allen and I would pop over to the local, 'for the last pint' at 9.30pm, and the girls would stay and have a glass of wine and chatter, both sets of proud parents enjoying the moment.

Stephanie Louise Powell

Just over two years later Karen suggested having another baby and so we had a similar conversation to the one before Tim was born, about the prospect of having another baby. I was happy, and agreed with Karen that the timing should be the same as was with Tim, in the winter months, etc.

We decided to move house yet again and found a gem of a house in Mold. The house in Greenside Mold had been on the market for some time. It needed everything doing to it and we bought it for £80,000. It was a bargain, given the size and potential. It was a huge early 70s' detached four bedroom house, with a separate double garage and a huge corner plot. It had a large lounge and a smaller lounge we called 'the snug'. It had a dining room, w/c downstairs, and four bedrooms and a bathroom and w/c upstairs. Outside there were thirty 25 foot conifers overgrown, taking up all the space in the garden. We got them cut down and I planted thirty more Golden Leylandi - slower growing with a light green, prettier plant – that we could keep well trimmed and under control. First job was to start on cleaning and decorating. We cleaned everywhere and I decided to work on one room at a time, complete it, shut the door, and start on the next room, and so on until the house was done. I started on 'the snug'. It had a low long veneered type sideboard in it with drawers in. When we opened one of the drawers it was obvious the family cat used to live in there; the smell was obscene. We threw that out and I peeled the old carpet up, stripped the old wallpaper off, filled the holes in the walls and painted and glossed the woodwork and soon the room was like new. New paint, new carpets, new curtains, and our comfy leather sofas fitted in a treat. Perfect!

We sold Durban Avenue for £59,000, virtually doubling what we had paid for it, and moved into Greenside when Karen was heavily pregnant. The nine months that followed were similar to the first pregnancy. Karen swam for England. I prayed to God and throughout all of this we nurtured Timothy. When Tim was born, Karen breastfed our very own little angel while I looked on, mesmerised. We were so very happy and now we were looking forward to creating another miracle, another baby, and a little friend for our Tim.

This time around Karen's blood pressure was fine. Her waters broke and everything was a bit surreal. Her bag for the hospital was already packed and in the car. I phoned the hospital and said we would be probably about 15 minutes. There was a sense of calm about the whole proceedings. I think it was about 3pm when I took Karen in. Her parents were staying with us, specifically to look after Tim.

About 7pm that evening, after a couple hours of labour pains, Karen was ready to give birth to our second child. Again, those past nine months, it seemed my apprehension knew no bounds, and allowed no let up of the pressure in my head.

I was holding her hand. I was at the side of the bed this time and it was a normal delivery.

She was sweating profusely and breathing fast, regular and hard. She knew what she was doing. She was fighting for both of us to bring this creature into the world and she wanted to bring it in now. I was willing the same.

Then out came this tiny head, bloodied but visible. Tiny, I thought, compared to Tim's head. A few minutes later the rest of the body just flew out and held onto life through its umbilical cord. I saw it come out. It was a baby girl. "It's a girl. It's our own baby girl."

Karen's head fell back on the pillow and she was presented with our little girl to cuddle. This baby was looking all around and taking note of the light and the surroundings. Karen hadn't had chance to hold Tim when he was born because she was unconscious. So this time it was lovely to see their bond form instantly.

Then I kissed Karen and held our baby. She, the baby, was calm and just looking at me as if I was from another planet. Remember everything, everything, every day is new to this baby and she already wanted to see what was going on in her brave new world.

I kissed her forehead. She was my angel and our very own beautiful baby girl.

I went for a walk down the corridor and out into the hospital grounds on a surprisingly warm evening. I passed people as I went. Tears were just falling from my eyes. My pain was lifted once more and I thanked God again. I was deliriously happy. Why was I crying? Why wasn't I telling everyone I met that I'd just become a father again, or I'd just had a beautiful baby daughter? It's because it was a moment that I wanted to savour. It was an intensely personal moment. I took time on my own in the hospital grounds. It was quiet and in that moment I believed that dreams really can come true. Just like the song in the film Pinocchio: 'When you wish upon a star, makes no difference who you are... your dreams come true.'

Stephanie Louise Powell was born into the world on 8th November 1988. As soon as I saw Steph's face coming out of her mother, she had a calm aura around her. She still carries that aura to this day. It seems to me as if she knows 'things' that give her the confidence to just be quietly at peace with herself, our little girl. When she first looked at me she seemed to have some sort of 'knowledge', as if she'd been here before. She also seemed to have an inner peace and contentment. That might sound garbage to anyone reading this, but, if you meet her, you'll know why I say this. She was our very own little angel. Not so little anymore. Ahh, but she is still daddy's little girl. She is blossoming into a woman, beautiful woman, with a beautiful mind and a heavenly soul. Stephanie has made my life complete. I love her, as with Tim, more than life itself.

I am all consumed with the pride I have for my baby girl. She makes me feel so happy when I talk to her on the phone or see her. We still act daft together, she's got a great sense of humour, and I bet even now she'd still love to play the 'name game'. We used to play this game in Broadbottom, when she was only eight years old: Steph, Tim and me. We'd walk alongside one of the oldest stretches of railway line in the country, the Manchester to Glossop line, and we would play the 'name game'. The name game went like this: Steph – I went to the shop and bought an apple; Tim – I went to the shop and bought an apple and a banana; me – I went to the shop and bought an apple, a banana, and a cup... and so on right through the alphabet. That was the 'name game'!

As the song *'In the Beginning'* says: 'Oh for the simple things in life!'

Tim and Steph

3

The Break Up

Most marriages go through difficult periods from time to time. It is something that happens. It is a fact of life. We are, after all said and done, only human. Something you come to understand. I think it is more a case of sharing yourself with another person, and subsequently, giving them an equal amount of space in your brain, whereas before you only had to think of yourself. You have to make compromises all the way. But that's OK. You hope that you will grow and flourish together, along with your children. You hope that life will take you, with your lover, into old age and beyond. At some stage, in-between, you envisage bouncing a baby grandson or daughter on your knee and joyously recalling the good old times when you got married and started out with nothing.

It's a learning curve, where mistakes are made along the way but the answer is to learn from them, and of course compromise. We fell hopelessly in love, we married, and the object of this union, that we were both free to choose and which we did, was to be married for the duration. For me, it meant once only, forever, for richer, for poorer, in sickness and in health, so help me God.

Karen was a primary school teacher who had great empathy with her pupils. She was good at what she did in the classroom and her school was all the better for it. She got her Honours Degree in Psychology, and decided teaching was what she wanted to do. There was friction at the school with a slightly misguided head who, occasionally, would walk along the corridors, drinking from a can. There were also school funds going missing from the petty cash, which brought even more pressure to bear on all the staff, particularly the secretary. All in all, the atmosphere was not good. The teachers felt unable to face their masters i.e. the governors over the Head's behaviour. They felt sorry for him and he made their lives an absolute hell. I asked Karen if she wanted me to go and speak to the head, specifically for the way he was treating her. It was appalling. She said no, but I did give Karen unstinting support. Eventually the head was transferred somewhere well away from the school and got off with his tyranny, scot-free. What is it they say? Power corrupts; absolute power corrupts absolutely.

Back to the story.

So one evening, Karen had talked to me about wanting to become an educational psychologist. She said it would require going to university in Manchester to gain the required Master's Degree, and the course was 14 months long. She said that she may be able to get funding from the education authority, which meant that she would still get paid her teaching salary throughout the duration of the university course. It also meant, she pointed out to me, that whilst she was commuting back and forth to Manchester every day, I would have to look after the kids for virtually the whole time she was on the course. It was going to be very intensive indeed. No question, without a thought, I said, "If this is what you want, we will do it."

So came the induction day at Manchester University, and Karen was excited at the prospect of meeting the other students that would be on her course. She would learn more about the psychology degree and relish not having to go into school with the added benefit of getting paid for 14 months for the privilege. Who wouldn't be happy?

She arrived home about 4pm and told me with great enthusiasm all about how the day had gone, saying, "There are only 12 people on the course and you'll never guess, one of them is just like you. He was a footballer with Everton Football Club, he was a roofer, he's a teacher, he's got hair just like yours and he only lived a few streets away from where you lived in Liverpool."

I knew in my heart, I knew. I thought, 'oh no, no, I just know there is no one on this earth like me,' and I knew that this John Banks had made such an impression on her that she would fall for him. I knew it as I know night follows day. I knew it. I just knew it.

I tried to play it cool and asked her was he married? She said he was, and that he had four kids. They lived in Melling near Aintree, a nice suburb 15 minutes out of Liverpool. The conversation went onto what books she needed for the course and how the first day of the course was on the following Monday.

Monday teatime arrived and so did Karen. She came home about 6pm and said each day she would be home at a similar time, a sort of set timing that we'd work to, to help me organise the food, kids' bedtime, washing etc.

Tuesday came and went and Wednesday did the same.

Then Thursday morning arrived.

I was busy seeing to the kids, with breakfast, preparing lunch for Tim, Steph's clothing, books and so on. Everything was on autopilot for the school and nursery runs. This was before even thinking about my work ahead for the day.

Then as I was going from the dining room through the hall to the kitchen I realised something. I had passed Karen about half a dozen times and she was still standing in front of the hall mirror. I looked at her and she looked a million dollars. She was wearing a flowing skirt and a blouse. She had put make up on, something she hadn't done before. Not the normal jeans and top she had worn the previous few days. I remember thinking – you don't go and sit in a college lecture room like that. It's obvious, or at least it was to me. What to do? Perhaps I'd exaggerated the situation, don't prejudge, wait and see. Keep an open mind.

Trust your woman, your lover, your life.

Then Thursday evening arrived. But Karen didn't. She got home at about 8pm.

She looked a bit flummoxed and told me John's car wouldn't start and she had to help him. Her hands looked as if she had been under a car bonnet, oily, but hold on a second, we are talking about Karen here. She doesn't even know how to put water into the windscreen bottle. It didn't make sense. The fact was that I was going out of my mind with worry, thinking she might have been in an accident. She did apologise, as she thought she should, but it wasn't heartfelt so I was concerned even more. Then she went up and had a bath, something she never does as she always prefers to shower.

The same pattern of events was to unfold over the next three weeks. Every Thursday it would be 'we're all going for a pizza', or 'we're all going for a drink to discuss so and so', etc. This meant that she would arrive home, usually about 8.30pm and always go straight into the bathroom and have a bath! Hmmm, strange behaviour, I pondered.

Now at this time I had my own business and was able to adjust my working hours to suit. I didn't have an option, what with two young children, but that's what was agreed and I was happy to do it.

At the time Tim was at primary school and Steph was at the childminder's. The childminder was a lovely, warm, wholesome, sensitive woman called Sue. We had been recommended to Sue for childminding from our friends. When Tim was a baby she had looked after him, just as she was doing with Stephanie.

It meant me shrinking my normal working day to drop Tim at school, then Steph at the childminder's and continuing on to work. Then I would finish work about 2.30pm to pick Tim up from school at 3pm, then Steph from Sue's. It usually meant me making the food for all of the family. I would feed the kids and when Karen came in we would have our food before I would put the kids to bed and read them their favourite story. She was focussed on the degree and would give the kids a cuddle and kiss before locking herself away in the computer room till maybe 11pm or later each night.

This was our normal life for 14 months, and I have to say I didn't complain once. I loved being with the kids and I loved the idea of helping Karen achieve what she had always wanted.

The following week was the same as the previous weeks, and the Thursday was virtually identical – Karen got in at 8.30pm and said, "Oh we've all been for a curry," and promptly went to the bathroom.

Now I am nothing if not tenacious.

That day I had looked at the student list that was on our notice board and thought, if Karen's late home tonight I will find out just what is going on. I took down John's address and telephone number.

I nipped up to the bathroom and told Karen that I had to go out and see someone about business. She looked shocked and asked how long I was going to be. I said I didn't know and that if I was late she wasn't to wait up.

I got in the car and drove from the house, towards where I didn't know. I picked up my mobile phone, which was then the size of a house brick. My heart thumping to get the extra oxygen to my lungs, I proceeded to phone John Banks' home. A quiet gentle woman answered and I said in my broadest Scouse, Liverpool accent, "Orright luv, is John about? I'm a mate of his, just got back from abroad."

She said, "He's at university and stays over in residences every

Thursday."

She asked where I was phoning from and I said I was on the M6. She said if I wanted she'd give me his address and telephone number and maybe I could call and see him and have a pint or stay over. "Great!" I said and drove like a scalded cat to see my adversary, currently residing in the halls of residence near Didsbury, Thursday nights only!

There was no point in phoning him. I would just arrive and face him.

I knocked on the door. No answer. I knocked louder. There was still no answer.

A neighbouring student came out of his room and said that John had probably gone for a pint and that he should be back soon. By now it was 10.30pm.

He arrived and I confronted him saying, "Are you John Banks?"

He said, "Yes," and started to unlock his door. He said to me, "You must be Mike."

We went in and the first thing I saw on his bedside table was the Tesco bag of food and fruit I had prepared for Karen that day.

He asked me if I wanted a cup of tea.

I asked him if he was having an affair with my wife.

He took a long pause and said, "We love each other, we want to be together and I'm sorry for the hurt this is going to cause. Have you travelled far?"

I said, "But what about your wife and your four children, and our two children?"

He couldn't give me an answer and tried to start talking to me as if we were old friends...

It's the type of talk that bullshitters and fantasists, and, I have since come to learn, some psychologists, believe they can say to patients or clients so that they believe that what they are being told is the truth. You know – we are on your side, we're the good guys, we want to do the right thing and sort this out, etc. etc. The trouble is, this is real life. Not some annual collective psychological theorists symposium of 'don't I sound good wankers', patting each other on the back.

But in reality, these are the very ones that fuck up their own personal lives with absurd statements like 'my wife doesn't understand me'. They in turn pal up with like-minded lightweights who listen to, re-deliver, and buy the bullshit. What makes it worse is that these elitists don't know any more than the next man or woman. So much of psychology is theory, and it is how you pitch your argument that matters. It's got nothing to do with actualities and real life and everything to do with how good you are at being seen to be jumping through the right hoops and saying the right things that, of course, your peers will applaud you for. Common sense is what is required, although on this degree course, clearly not a pre-requisite.

After the university course was over Karen was to become an educational psychologist and dealt with all classes of people in some horrendous situations. Her job was to assess and try to sort out the children's psychological problems – wetting the bed, pooing on the kitchen floor, abused and sometimes silent children. Her job was trying to sort out the root cause of that family's problem.

When all along it was Karen who was to cause her own family to suffer by creating this self-inflicted meltdown. How couldn't she see that?

Caused by what? Love? Lust? Excitement? Let's try and find out shall we?

I got up and left his room in the middle of his attempted rendition to pacify the injured party, namely me, by sarcastically saying to him, "Save the bullshit for your wife and kids."

I got home shortly after midnight to find Karen nervously pacing up and down the kitchen.

I said we needed to sit down and talk. She sat at the breakfast bar and said, "Oh my God, what's the matter, what is it, tell me, what's the matter?"

I said, "Karen you are having an affair."

She denied it outright. "Never! No! Never!" You would have sworn, you would have bet your life she was telling the truth.

At which point I said, "Just be honest with me, I'm not an ogre, just tell me the truth as I have always told you the truth. That's all I ask."

Well, 20 minutes later she was still swearing that she was not having an affair. I kept pushing and pushing her to at least come clean when suddenly I heard the words fall from her lips in slow motion, "I think you need to see a doctor. You are imagining it, are you alright? I think you need to see a doctor."

I questioned, "I need to see a doctor?"

To which she emphatically shouted, "Yes! Yes! You do need to see a doctor!"

I was pacing around the kitchen when at that deciding moment I thought enough was enough. I looked at her straight between the eyes and said two words to her. "John Banks."

She went into a catatonic state and focussed on the worktop, whilst I was walking around the room waving my hands in the air, much the way an evangelist does, and I began to say, "Oh Lordy, I have seen the light. Lordy, Lordy, I have seen the light."

A further 10 minutes went by and I could see her, still staring into the marbled effect worktop that she hoped would swallow her up from this inquisition. She was drowning in guilt and her self-preservation was catatonically induced.

Then her inevitable tears and recriminations flowed.

I asked again and again, "Why? Tell me why. Have you gone off me?"

Eventually she summoned up the courage to speak and said it wasn't meant to happen, it just did. "He – John – just reminded me of you. I suppose it was the excitement of the moment. I'm so sorry. I promise it will never happen again."

I said this 'moment' had gone on for the past month. She didn't deny this so I guess it must have done. I then explained what John had said to me about how much in love they both were. She looked shocked and said, "In love? We're not in love! It was just a bit of excitement, that's all."

I said, "John doesn't think so, phone him up now and explain to him the situation, and what you propose to do about it."

She said, "It's far too late tonight," and that she would see him tomorrow morning and explain to him it was over, face to face. I still couldn't believe he hadn't bothered to phone her after I had left his room to, at the very least, warn her that I had just seen him and that they had been rumbled. When I mentioned it to her she seemed somewhat put out, and hadn't thought about it that way.

The following night she arrived home at the normal time and told me she had seen John, and that she had told him it was finished and it was all over between them.

Then a kind of normality reigned over the Powell household for a further three months.

But it was short lived.

I found out a further three times over the following 11 months that they had started the affair again, and again, and again. This repetition, looking back, felt like Chris Tarrant (from Who Wants to be a Millionaire) was saying to Karen, "You had an affair. You still have an affair," the same way as he says, "you have £32,000, and you've still got £32,000."

Every time I found out it was through pure gut feeling followed by a string of circumstances.

The circumstances were unbelievable and weirder than any fiction could ever be. But apart from coincidences, they left themselves wide open. I won't go into all these coincidences. Suffice to say these affairs were rumbled, on average, about every three months. They started up again like clockwork. One such occasion I was to find out in the most cruel of ways, which came to light playing with my children in our big lounge. Around April 1994, my day-to-day life consisted of dropping the kids off at school, going through the motions of work, seeing customers around the North West of England, and answering my mobile phone. It was weird at home where I would play with the kids, feed them and read them bedtime stories. It was surreal, as if nothing was happening to the family. The only difference was that Karen and I didn't talk, only through our solicitors. The kids knew something was up as we both slept in different bedrooms but we never argued, so at least the children didn't suffer that indignity as well.

One Friday morning I was getting the kids ready for school and both Tim and Steph were in the big lounge with me dancing around and playing some music. Their sandwiches were packed and we had a few minutes to spare for a laugh. Steph had asked me to put the music on and picked up the microphone. We had a microphone linked up so that the kids could sing along, like karaoke, and I would tape them and they would titter when they heard it played back. Not unlike my father had done with his children/family. We were having such a good time that we had forgotten about the time. Karen popped her head around the corner and said, "It's 10 to nine, you don't want to be late." I thought that she herself was also late, but made no comment. With that I rushed the kids out and turned the record turntable to off. I thought nothing more about it then I dropped the kids off and went on my way to work. I picked them up at 3pm and as soon as they got in the car, Stephanie asked, "Can we play some music and sing when we get home Dad?" Tim asked the same.

I said, "OK," and the three of us sang in the car happily on the way home with the expectation of us dancing and singing and generally fooling around. Steph went over to the music stack system with me and I noticed it was switched on, all of it apart from the turntable. I noticed that the cassette that we had put in that morning had run right to the end. It must have continued running on when we left in the morning. I told the kids this and put a record on whilst waiting for the tape to rewind to where we left off this morning. I had Steph and Tim kneeling by my side as I found the position of the tape. As I was about to press record, a noise came out of the speakers. It was the noise of Karen's voice saying we were late for school. You could clearly hear us rushing out and the lounge door closing, then silence. But seconds later and after I had driven off with the kids, the lounge door could be heard opening. I then heard Karen's voice on the walkabout phone, dialling some number and muttering something to herself. I wondered why she should come into the big lounge to make a phone call. Remember that this room was the room we had previously only used for special occasions. I knew soon I would have to leave the house, and started enjoying this lounge with my children every chance I got. That's why I was in there. But why was she in there? A sixth sense made me change the tape for another one and I recorded Tim and Stephanie larking about whilst putting the tape into my jacket pocket. I played the tape a little later and heard the following:

"Hello, is that the Travelodge Hotel in Eastham?"
"Hello I want to make a reservation for today please."
"Erm, in the name of Banks, John Banks. Can you tell me how much is the room please. Thirty five pounds. That's fine. What time is the room available from?"
"Yes please."
"No, it will be by cash."

It was Karen speaking to the receptionist, booking a room for her and John Banks. What a way to find out. She was still seeing him after

33

swearing to me she would never see him again. And it was my kids who unbeknownst to them brought it to my attention. I listened to the remainder of the tape and silence (along with my sadness) reigned to the end of the tape. I got the kids' clothes ready and said we were going away to Grandad and Grandma's house for the weekend. The in-laws were in Spain and we had their key, as sometimes we would go down for the weekend. They were excited and I felt bereaved. I got the children in the car about 4.30-5pm, and popped back in the house and made a call to the Travelodge. I said "Hello, can you put me through to John Banks' room please, I believe he's staying there today?"

The receptionist said, "Just a minute sir," and put me through.

At the other end of the phone and sheepishly, Banks answered slowly, "Hello?"

I said, "Put Karen on the phone." Which he did and I remember her pathetic tone and I said, "I am taking the kids away for the weekend. You are a fucking evil monster, and I hate you for what you are doing to the children and this family. I hope he's worth it."

I heard her crying, "I'm sorry, I'm coming home right now, where are you going with the kids? Don't hurt them. Please, please wait for me, I'm coming right back."

I remember repeating this back to her in normal tones. "Don't hurt them? These children are my life, you fucking evil lying monster of a bitch. You will rot in hell one day."

I then put the phone down and got in the car with the kids and went to Abergavenny. Karen must have phoned the neighbours in Abergavenny as she arrived late on Friday night, all tearstained and drained. She was like a lost soul who appeared to have got on the wrong bus in life and gone in completely the wrong direction. She was out of control but was a master of saving face to people that mattered to her – her mother for instance. I remember her asking me, "Are you going to tell my parents about this?" Unbelievable, but true. She had lethal self-preservation for actions self-caused. The whole thing was becoming a continual living nightmare that no one else on the planet knew about. If they had they wouldn't have really given two fucks about it. It was between Karen and me, and it was becoming god-awful boring. Boring, boring, boring.

The same old clap-trap would fall from her mouth every time, only each time more desperate. "It'll never happen again, I swear, it's only you I want, I never married anyone but you, you are who I want to spend the rest of my life with," and so on. "Please find it in your heart to forgive me." (Again, I thought)

The university course finished and Karen was the proud owner of a Master's Honours Degree. She got her first job as an Educational Psychologist, working out of an office in North Wales.

At this stage, I know categorically she had dropped John Banks, ('...till you dropped them like a hot potato, they know they've been had...' – lyrics from the song *'What You Doin' To Me'*.) and she said to him, "Don't leave your wife on my account." He was devastated and within 12 months of this news I believe he was to die of a massive brain haemorrhage.

I thought that when she'd finished with John that'd be it. I thought we'd pick up the pieces and start again.

The only people I told over this affair were her parents Jean and Ashley, in the desperate hope that they could make her see sense. I didn't want it to finish between us and believed I could turn her around. We were meant to be together for life, and I wasn't going to roll over and die at the first, second, third or fourth hurdle!

If I hadn't believed I could turn it all around, I wouldn't have gone on so long trying hopelessly to hold our marriage together and torturing myself in the process. Needless to say, when I told them Karen was having an affair, the mother-in-law didn't believe my story initially saying, "How d'you know Mike? How do you know?" in a rather dismissive and incredulous manner.

Ashley calmed her down and quietly and in a matter of fact way said to me, "Mike, please tell us, how do you know categorically that she is having an affair?"

In this instance I told them I was doing the housework one day in the bedroom and was putting some of Karen's things in her top drawer of her dressing table. I found a packet of 12 condoms, the type we used to use. The box was open, and there were only eight left in the box.

"Yes, and?" said Jean.

Well, we never opened this last box, because I'd had the snip, a vasectomy, and there was no need to use condoms anymore.

They looked at each other with a grim realisation, and suddenly, Jean countered with, "You must have done something wrong for her to do this. You must have."

I looked to Ashley and said, "Ash, I can't win."

Karen went on to have two further affairs, both with psychologists, thereby completing her hat-trick of psychos! ('Three foolish men, psychologists, 3 little bastards all in a row...' – lyrics from *What You Doin' To Me'*.)

One was from Harrogate and the other one was the Head of the Department where she worked. Again, without going into detail, she was considering moving to Germany and taking the children with her. She hadn't once consulted me about this or the impossibility of taking the children away from me. She would go with this boring, predictable, steady Eddie character, who guaranteed that they would both get jobs through his contacts in the forces. She then knocked him back and went instead for the 'main event' where she worked, namely the Head of Department.

This Head of Department lived on his boat, moored in a nearby marina. So, shit or bust, I thought, I'll confront him. This I did by saying, "You're having an affair with my wife." Which he categorically denied.

"I don't even know her, no I'm not having an affair with your wife."

I said, "At least the other guy (J Banks) had the balls and the backbone to admit it." I looked at this lying, deceitful, decrepit, tired old man and said, "If I thought it would be any good, I would break your back, clean in two. But I realise that you're just a sad old fucker, abusing your position in charge of the Psychology Unit. God help us all if a lying toerag like you is in charge of our children's welfare." I then left without harming a hair (if he'd had any) on his head.

I sat in the car, some distance away, and it finally dawned on me.

You can't fight City Hall. You can't stop the inevitable. Mike, I thought, brave try, you did your best. It hasn't worked. This was to be the straw that broke the camel's back.

I got back to the house only to find this time that the spineless one had already phoned Karen and was she in a right state. She said, "What are you doing seeing xxxx?"

I think she expected me to explode. But instead I calmly said, "Don't worry, you've won, that's it. I will see my solicitor tomorrow and get a divorce. That's it. You've won. End of story."

Suddenly, she didn't want to win. She didn't want the story to end. She cried wolf for the very last time and, for me, it was a howl.

How stupid had I been? And yes, I finally saw the light.

I think that when you are faced with a trauma such as I was faced with, you try your damnedest to resolve it whichever way you can, anyhow, anyway. It wasn't to be. But at least for the first time in ages there was a relief that the suffering would soon be over. Well, this suffering, at least.

Now, the following day I spoke to my friend and lawyer in Chester. I had kept him informed every inch of the way regarding our relationship, and it was him who kept saying try again, and again – which I kept doing. So I explained about how this time this was the last straw and I wanted to see him today and start proceedings. He agreed and said to me that he'd never seen or ever heard of such commitment to keep a marriage together, as he had done with me. I took it as small consolation that yes, I bet he's right. He looked at his diary and said it would have to be tomorrow, as he was fully booked up with appointments today.

I went home, played with my children and felt sick to the stomach, put them to bed, and then went earlier than usual myself.

The following morning came and Karen brought me a cup of tea and an envelope at about 7.30am. Now in all the years I had known her, she never ever brought me a cup of tea. It was always me bringing the tea.

I expressed surprise and asked what was in the envelope. She said, "Just open it." It was a greetings card with musical instruments on. Inside, she had written – *From now on let us not argue anymore and stay special friends*. I still have the card.

When I asked why she had got me this card, she kept on replying, "You know, you know, you know."

I said, "Will you stop playing games and tell me what you are going on about?"

She said, and I quote, "I think you are going to get a letter today from my solicitor."

"About what?" I said.

She said, boringly again, "You know." Eventually, she said she has applied for a divorce. I was speechless. To save face she had beaten me to it. She had gone and got a divorce before I could. So for the entire world, her mother in particular, she was able to give some half-arsed, pathetic horseshit reasons as to just why she was divorcing me. Just to save face. Talk about being stabbed in the back, as well as the front, and sides, and the heart for good measure!

4

My Mantra, My Focus
(My Three Months Mantra.
My Three Months Focus)

During this terrible period in my life, something extraordinary was to happen to me.

But that was to be a full six months later and not before the following sequence of events occurred.

I suppose I was shell-shocked with all the 'carryings on' from Karen. It was slowly registering on me by the day that I'd lost her. Always in my thoughts were our children. I felt like I had let them down, and I didn't know why. Our little angels never did deserve to lose both their parents. It was meant to be that children are nourished, protected, loved and brought up by a man and a woman, together. God knows I tried to keep it all together.

It started one morning, as soon as I woke up; I looked at the clock by the side of the bed. It read 7.30am and the news suddenly came on.

My Mantra

The date was15th May, 1992.

To this day, I don't know why it happened, but my thoughts were only of Karen, Karen.

I listened to the news and at the same time this was going on, which felt even stranger.

And from that moment on, for three months solid, it never stopped. My every waking second consisted of quietly chanting this 'Karen' mantra, ad nauseam, without beginning or end. It was involuntary, I didn't want to do it, and I couldn't stop it. When I describe it as 'chanting', it was in my thoughts. I wasn't speaking her name; I was thinking her name. Had that been the case (and I went around speaking her name, ad nauseam), I am sure I would have been locked up and seen as an absolute maniac.

It was just strange. But true.

I would feed the kids, conduct business, eat my food, run, go to the toilet, bathe, shower, drive and everything I did, in the background, this involuntary mantra just kept repeating. It became exhaustive because no one knew. I couldn't tell anyone. You just couldn't tell what was going on in my head because I was acting normal; I answered people's questions, spoke in my usual manner, and generally dialogued as I had always done before this occurrence.

I would wake up with Karen, Karen, Karen, Karen… playing like a monotonous dirge. Right the way through the day. I would go to sleep and drift off to Karen, Karen, Karen, Karen, Karen. I would wake up in the morning to exactly the same, and it continued for all those months. Throughout all this time I conducted myself as if nothing was happening. But deep down I was very concerned about this personal phenomenon that was happening to me. It was physically and mentally draining. The physical probably because it kept me awake at night and I would wake earlier than before.

It just wouldn't go away. I grew very tired and my days were growing longer and longer. I wanted a release, but I couldn't get one. Three months solid.

My Focus

It's like driving from Liverpool to London, there and back in a day, 500 miles, every day. Day in, day out. Come hail, rain or shine. That's how exhausting this mantra made me feel. Something had to give.

And it did: in the middle of August 1992 when I least expected it. I call it

The coffee cup and the three month release

I called to see a friend who lived in the next village to ours. I was sitting in his conservatory and it was 10.30am. He asked me if I wanted a cup of tea, which is what I always drink, especially as I've tasted his coffee and it was never that good. In fact, 'yuck' comes to mind!

However, that morning, I decided to have a coffee. He was in the kitchen talking to me quite loudly and I was responding, quite loudly, as

I was looking out of the conservatory across the beautiful meadow and onwards towards the spectacular surrounding hills. As usual, all this time, the Karen mantra was still going on around and around, ad nauseam, in my brain.

Then he came into the room and put a cup of coffee in front of me. It gave me quite a start, as the table was glass and there was a loud-ish bang.

That was it... the mantra stopped dead! No more Karen. From that day forward, it ceased to be. Peace at long last. It was heaven.

But, and isn't there always a 'but' folks?

I 'locked onto' this coffee cup, whilst still talking, as if nothing had happened. During the next 45 minutes, or however long I was there, we had a normal conversation, but, and here it comes, I had focussed totally on the coffee cup. During the 45minutes or so we were chatting I was asking myself a myriad of questions about it, the coffee cup, whilst at the same time trying to answer those same questions.

Actually, it was a mug. It was a bright red mug with the word Nescafe, in white, on the side of it.

I asked myself hundreds of questions about that coffee cup whilst having a normal conversation with my friend.

Questions that came to mind, from nowhere, such as - where was it manufactured, who made it, how old were they, man or woman, where did they live, did their relatives make mugs, are the colours natural pigments, what clay was used, how much did it cost, who had decided on the design and why, is it made of clay or ceramic, what was the furnace temperature at its hottest, how long to cool down, overall time to make the cup, how many colours do they make? And so on, and so forth, on and on.

I left my friend's house in fantastic spirits. The Karen curse had somehow been lifted.

I remember getting into my car in blissful silence. But although the thoughts of the coffee cup had vanished the moment I left his house, I questioned just what that 'coffee cup' incident had all been about.

I began appreciating the wonderful surroundings around me, and that sunny day I was re-awakened. I got about half a mile when I noticed my big, enormous mobile phone alongside me. I always kept it by my side. Just like the farmer with an old faithful sheepdog at his side. We were both inseparable from the tools of our trade.

I found I was focussed totally on the mobile phone. And I began asking a myriad of questions about it, just as I had done with the coffee cup. These questions were not the same as before. If anything they were more technical, and I'm not remotely technical, but I was still trying to find an answer to the questions.

By the time I got to my appointment, 15 minutes away, I had asked myself what seemed like hundreds of questions about that phone. When I got out of the car the questions stopped. I would speak to people, as I had always done, in fine form. They didn't notice me focussing on something in their office that would keep the never ending questions going on around in my brain. The questions always lasted for the duration I was there or with someone and, as always, didn't interfere, but ran in tandem with whatever business or topic it was we were discussing.

This went on for three months solid, from mid-August to mid-November 1992. This was such a relief and release from what I had been used to the previous three months, especially as at bedtime I would just go to sleep without any interferences or disturbances. It was great. Still not normal, but it was 1000% better.

Throughout this 'coffee cup' period, I wondered, as a normal, intelligent human being, why I was focussing on things, wherever I was. What was the reason for this? Was it just to blot Karen out of my mind? No, definitely not. She went that first day the coffee cup was put on the glass table and I couldn't have got that mantra back if I'd tried. I just know it. The light hadn't only been switched off but the bulb had blown, that's how I'd describe how I knew the mantra would never come back. A simple, clear analogy.

There are many, many 'focussing' incidents I could go on to talk about, questions and all, but I'm sure by now you've got the picture.

I was cocooned in my own little world. I was cushioned from the nightmare of our pending separation and the probable loss of time I would have with my children. I went into myself and depended on the strength I found from within. All of this, I reasoned, was just to keep me going, just to keep me alive and dare I say, sane! All done using this tremendous God-given tenacity that I appear to possess. To go on, go forward, without harming myself or anyone. Don't tell anyone anything.

Rely on no one. You have to look after yourself without outside interference from anyone. Like some impenetrable castle you will get through this, and you will not be harmed again.

How many people have experienced matrimonial break ups, or have had friends tell them of theirs? It's not nice. In fact, like people tell you about how lovely their kids are and you get bored quickly, it's the same in the marriage split department. So, essentially, you are on your own anyway. There is only so much sympathy you can give a person before you tire and bore of the subject.

I never told anyone about our break up for that reason, and primarily I believed I could make Karen see sense and turn the whole thing around. I wasn't able to but, hindsight and all, I would do the same again. I never went off the rails. I didn't drink and get pissed and make a 'show' of myself. I didn't become aggressive. I didn't take drugs. I didn't seek solace in some other ladies' thoughts or drawers. I didn't break the rules that so many other poor bastards do, and when it's over they've been shafted, and they lose the plot. They can't cope with the emotional explosions of injustice and cruelty laid on their front door by their 'loved one', now their hated one. A rather large generalisation, but I've seen and heard all sorts about exactly just what people are capable of when rhyme and reason goes out of the window and are replaced with a dark, evil, black, foreboding chasm of nothing. A nightmarish force to be reckoned with. Complete emptiness all around, and frustration and logic awry.

And so it came to pass.

And weighing everything up in my marriage and subsequent break up, looking at the way it was, throughout our relationship and marriage, I reached this conclusion:

There are givers, and there are takers.

I am a giver. Karen was a taker.

I would have given my life for her and she would have taken it.

It was Karen who wanted me, and she got me. She wanted to get engaged and married, so right away we did. She wanted a Catholic wedding. We had one. She wanted a baby on a particular month, and repeated the request, two years later. We did both, with duly impeccable timing. She wanted them to be confirmed into the Catholic faith, not my faith. They were. She wanted me to have a vasectomy, not my suggestion for her to be sterilised, so I did. She wanted to get a bigger house, twice. We did. She wanted to get a bigger car. We did. She wanted to make the biggest house bigger, and have a big extension. We did. She wanted time solely to study for 14 months and go to university. She did. It meant me looking full time after the kids, which I did and adored. She wanted to have an affair. So she did. I looked after the kids, while she looked after the man. She wanted to have another affair. She did. She wanted to have yet another affair. She did.

I wanted Karen. She didn't want me anymore.

I told her of my intention to divorce her.

She went out that day, and in a pre-emptive strike she divorced me.

So you see, I gave Karen everything.

And she took everything she ever wanted.

5

The Seven Days That Shook My World

Picture the scene.

It's November 8th 1992. It is a cold, wet, miserable day, and I venture through the Mersey Tunnel from the North Wales side. I call to the printers in Liverpool to pick up some print as pre-arranged, if not a little early. Bill McNab, my co. director, said, "You are a bit too early Mike, call back in an hour or so or go into the canteen and read the paper and have a coffee."

I decided the first choice was far better than listening to the four colour presses clattering around, whilst retching at the smell of ink, thinners, ink cleaner, and other poisonous substances that abounded at the time in a typical jobbing printers establishment.

I did used to give the impression of being aloof, but I wasn't. It was just that all the aforementioned was going on and like my thoughts, I kept myself to myself.

What to do? Where to go? I was particularly down that day; emptiness abounded as per usual.

The 'focussing' was still kicking in, but like having a broken limb you learn to cope and live with it.

I found myself driving the one and a half miles to Anfield. I wanted to see our old street, Lyell St, where we, 'the Powells', grew up. It was no more. I knew this already because it had been bulldozed to the ground in 1980. In fact I took the cast iron street sign that was pitched on the floor like a forgotten script, that day when the bulldozers levelled our street in 1980. The only terraced row demolished from all the surrounding streets. Lyell Street was no longer there where our homes used to be. In its place was a small grassy area that was filled with dog shite and rubbish such as chip papers, fags, chewing gum, etc. I walked down our street and stood outside where our house used to be. I filled up with sentimental nostalgia and thought of the one person I loved more than anyone, and missed more than anything on this Earth. It was mum.

I thought of her constant battle to live through ill health. Her breathlessness, her gaunt stare, the oxygen bottle permanently at the side of her bed and oh God, her bed sores. All over her back and bottom. She was in so much pain one day, holding her back, I had to look. When I saw them I cried inside and outside and clung onto mum so she couldn't see me crying. I was powerless to help her. But I always took her out in the company repmobile and when I was doing my calls she would sit in the car and read the paper. Sometimes I took her into the countryside, like Ormskirk or Southport, and we'd have lunch. She loved it. She used to like me driving fast, but really had no idea just how fast I really was driving. To say I used to drive like a scalded cat is an understatement. Mum liked the excitement and so did I.

Standing there where our old step used to be, I also thought of when me and my mates used to kick a ball, all day on this tiny area. I remembered the good times. I remembered my darling, irreplaceable mother. I would have given my life for her to live one more day.

I remembered what used to be; all the terraced houses in the neighbourhood stretching from Breckfield Road beyond. Now waste parkland. This had happened early in the 1980s when a deputy left wing militant councillor by the name of Derek Hatton was running the whole of Liverpool council with a fist of iron. He lived the high life and what he said, went. In fact across the top road, looking all the way down Hamilton Road and to the right, virtually down to Scottie Road, Hatton had cleared all the fine, solid but neglected imposing Victorian houses. Whole families were moved to where they didn't want to go – Kirkby, Speke, Knowsley and so on, all out of the district. Away from the friends and neighbours that had really been home and a great community. I thought to myself, it's all gone now, mum, dad, house – all gone.

I then looked at my watch and still had 40 minutes to kill, so I drove to Stanley Park Cemetery. It was still wet, cold, miserable and lonely, which suited my frame of mind. I got out of the car and walked through the imposing cast iron gates to one of the oldest cemeteries in Liverpool and walked directly to an area where my mum and dad's ashes were scattered, plot 16.

There was nothing special about it. As with all the plots, or areas, this area was alongside the tarmacked pathway that snaked past old gravestones. The chained off areas separated them from the graves. It was an area where rose bushes blossomed.

I stood in the rain, soaked to the skin in a suit and tie and thought of Mummy and Daddy.

I said, "Mum and Dad, if you can hear me, please help me. I've lost everything and it's as if I've got everything to give. Please help me."

I left this place and drove straight to the imposing and spectacular Liverpool Anglican Cathedral. I don't know why to this day; I just don't know why. I know it was only five minutes drive from the printers, but I hadn't gone to a place like that just to waste some time.

Once inside I walked straight on along its quarter of a mile central core and straight up to the cordoned off area, directly in front of the magnificent gold altar. This rich red sandstone temple, rising to the heavens with intricacies of angels, saints, and Jesus Christ's statue, all sparkling in bright gold was so imposing that it gave me a real humbling feeling.

It's true that many men started as mere boys, as apprentices, working on this building, and worked all their lives here, right through to retirement. The craftsmanship is world class.

I sat in the nearest pew to the altar that I could and waited for some Chinese tourists to take their photographs and leave. They did so and I closed my eyes and said a prayer. I opened my eyes and looked up at Jesus' statue and said, "Dear God, you can see the way I am, please help me. I've lost everything, and it's as if I've got everything to give. Please help me."

And that was it. Nothing happened. No more thoughts, nothing more to be said.

I then went on to the printers. I picked the jobs up, delivered them and then went home to my house, to my children and to my wife. The following seven days passed and were uneventful. But come the 15th November 1992, my life was to change forever.

6

The First, Second and Third Sightings.

1st Sighting

Song No.1: IT WAS YOU

Between 1.30am and 2.30am on 15th November 1992, I awoke and saw what I believe was the image of John Lennon standing at the end of my bed. I thought I must have been dreaming so I sat bolt upright and rubbed my eyes in order to make this image/dream disappear. When I stopped rubbing my eyes and looked again to the end of the bed where I thought I had just seen him, he was still there in exactly the same position and with exactly the same expression on his face. The image was black and white, and he was just looking straight at me. There was no movement but his eyes never left mine. I would say he appeared to have a forlorn look about him. He had round glasses on and a denim shirt and jeans.

I was petrified and turned over, pushing my face into the pillow to try and get away from this terrifying moment, in the hope that he would go away. (I suppose like the child who covers his eyes and believes he can't be seen.)

Curiously, like a child, I had to have another look. By this time my arms were over my head to protect me. So I looked under my right arm and hoped he had gone away, and if he hadn't, I hoped he wouldn't see me doing this. I was terrified.

The image I saw then was one of hundreds of the backs of peoples' heads, all walking away from my direction. It appeared that they were all of a similar size, but they were smaller than Europeans. I saw John Lennon's face in the middle of the crowd, looking straight back at me, the only face I could see. He appeared to be on his tip toes, as he gave the impression his neck was stretching and his eyebrows were slightly raised. He was being taken with the flow of the people, as you might well imagine, where there are too many people trying to get through a small exit, and not unlike when the final whistle was blown on match days in Liverpool FC. Everyone was being squashed together and John was being taken with the crowd and, for all the world, against his will.

When I saw this happening I was no longer afraid. I knew he didn't want to harm me. But I was powerless to help him. As he was being taken away, both our eyes were fixed on each other, and moments before this crowd left John Lennon transmitted, through thought to me, the song *'It Was You'*. He was being taken away against his will. He was still in the middle and still facing my direction.

The chorus was first and then the first line. 'Saw your face in a crowd the other day.'

I lay awake until 5am trying to understand what I had just seen and experienced. I wanted to get up immediately but I thought Karen wouldn't be too pleased, being disturbed at 2.30 in the morning. That's why I left it until 5am, a more acceptable hour. Obviously, we were still sleeping in the same bed but that was all we were doing. I then got up and went downstairs and into the lounge, where I picked up a guitar that I had bought earlier in the year but had never played.

And at this point, you must be thinking, isn't *that* convenient, he's got a guitar.

And what was the reason for me buying it? Well, let me tell you.

The previous New Year's Eve we had gone to our best friend's family New Year's Eve party in Northop. John and Patsy Golledge and their kids, Sarah, Matthew, and Andrew, and their gorgeous thick set lovable old Labrador. They were an absolute diamond of a family. Generous of spirit, successful, down to earth, no side to them, and lovely level-headed kids too. We'd been several years running to the Golledges' New Year's Eve parties, and truly, it was a joyous occasion that we always looked forward to going to. There would be lots of kids running about playing tick, dancing, playing with their Christmas toys and games and always excitedly running riot in the nicest ways that kids express joy and happiness at just being themselves, playing with their best friends. They would have jam on their faces, gateau on their clothes and rosy red cheeks. They would fan themselves out in this quaint but large house – bedrooms, sitting rooms, kitchen, dining room, study, garage, garden – all over. We, the parents, all knew they were safe and we all had a relaxing and lovely time.

All the parents and friends at these New Year's Eve parties used to have a good old drink, chatting, playing 'catch up' from the previous year (although we used to see the Golledges quite regularly). They always had a beautiful spread of food on the table. We all contributed and used to take something exotic and special. I think that year we took a fabulous gateau that Karen had made. A few of the men used to play guitars and bash out stuff like Bob Dylan's *'All Along the Watchtower'*, Clapton's *'Wonderful Tonight'* and other oldish pop stuff such as Buddy Holly's *'Peggy Sue'*. John Golledge's claim to fame was that when he was at university in Leeds in the 60s, he saw Buddy Holly playing at his uni club. Apparently, it was the last time Buddy Holly came to England, or anywhere for that matter. A week or so later he was on an internal US flight with the Big Bopper when his plane crashed and killed all of the passengers and crew. Alan Sherwood and John Golledge used to play their guitars, and everyone in the party would dance, sing along, and generally join in the fun.

It was a great party, and as per usual our family were given a bedroom and stopped overnight.

When we got back to our house it was peaceful, and we somewhat went back into our own 'different from public domain sphere'. Karen had said, "Why don't you get a guitar as a hobby? It would be good to play along with Alan and John, maybe at the next New Year's Eve party?"

I said, "I haven't got a clue how to play, wouldn't know where to start."

She had said, "Get some lessons; I'm sure you'd be able to play a few tunes with them. You've got 12 months to learn." So Karen persuaded me to buy a guitar so I could learn to play along with our other friends. Just to stop me moping around, I guess. Don't forget at this time, none of our friends knew what was happening regarding our relationship.

So I decided to seek out some guitar lessons.

The following week, I was doing a call in Deeside and in a shop window I noticed a sign, which read – 'Mike Clark, Guitar Lessons, £8 per hour, all aspects of Guitar and Bass Tuition. FIRST LESSON FREE!' I went for my free lesson and the first thing Mike did was hand me a guitar, but I took it the wrong way, and proceeded to hold it in readiness to strum it with my left hand. He said, "Turn it around and play it the other way." We tried this for the hour and in the end he said to me, "It's no use, you'll have to get a left hand guitar if you want to continue." He told me he had experienced 'left-handers' being able to play right handed. Alas, not me. I bought an acoustic guitar from Mike's friend's music shop in Wrexham and I got a 10% discount for being recommended by Mike Clark.

So I had some lessons from Mike but couldn't hack it, or more to the point couldn't be bothered to learn. He would set me some homework to do for the following week's lesson and I wouldn't even lift the guitar out of its bag until I got to his. Fair play to Mike, he said to me, "Mike you're just wasting your time and money. What's the point?"

I took his advice and kicked the lessons and any hopes of playing the guitar into touch

I had picked up this guitar that had lain dormant in our big lounge, for close to 12 months.

And that's how the guitar came to be there.

The song, *'It Was You'* took 10 minutes from start to finish writing down words and music.

I used basic bar chords and found some 'open chords' instinctively. There were so many verses to the song I left a few of them out, and 10 minutes later this three minute song was completed.

Then I sat down for half an hour and tried to understand what I had just seen and who had just given me this song. It was a completely humbling and earth-shattering experience. I felt totally special and privileged. I was drained, but somehow exalted, like I'd never been before. You know, like you know something that no one else on this Earth knows. That's exactly how it was. All I kept asking myself, when this song was falling out of me, was a simple question over and over again. Why me? Why has John Lennon come to little old me, why?

At 7am I took my wife a cup of tea. Something I had always done since I had known her. I had the guitar strapped over my back and I put the tea on her bedside cupboard. And I asked this question: "Have you ever heard this before?" and I proceeded to play *'It Was You'*.

She replied, "No, I haven't heard it, but it sounds like a Beatles' song." It was to be three or four weeks before I told her what I had seen. I did tell her I had just written it and she dismissed it totally, saying, "You couldn't have done, it's a Beatles' song, I'm sure it's a Beatles' song."

This first sighting was seven days after I had visited the cemetery and the Liverpool Anglican Cathedral. Seven days previously I had pleaded for Mum and Dad and God to help me.

The Second Sighting

2nd Sighting
Songs No.2 & No.3: YOKO, I LOVE YOU & LOVE'S TWILIGHT HOUR

I had no idea if John Lennon would ever visit me again.
I hadn't hoped either way that he would or would not. All I know is how privileged I felt. The three month mantra and the three month 'focussing' had disappeared. I was back to normality, which was like being reborn afresh, a clean sheet of paper.
Maybe that was why he came to me, to rid me of the mantra and the focussing fiasco.

Or maybe, exactly the opposite?

Maybe that happened, or was instigated by some higher power, just to prepare me, to ready me to see John Lennon.

I pondered and reasoned after the sighting on November 15th that maybe I had to go through the three month 'mantra' period specifically just to focus on that moment John was to come to me.
I also thought about the following three month 'coffee cup release' period, and the thousands upon thousands of questions I had been constantly asking from the myriad of situations I was then living through. These questions over this period I always tried my best to answer.
Maybe this six month period prepared me to be able to focus and be able to answer the questions that John was laying at my door, through thought transferral. Like - can you see me, can you feel my pain, I didn't want to leave life, I didn't want to die, can you feel my feelings?
Are you the one that will see me, will help me? Are you that special person?
Who knows?

I kept an open mind and my mind open.

I also kept a pen and something to write on close to my side of the bed, on the floor, so that Karen couldn't see. I did this in case John Lennon should decide to 'visit' me again. I wanted to note everything down in case I might forget something I had seen. The reason for this was that when he came to me the week before I had spent several hours, after he had gone, just lying wide awake, not daring to move and disturb Karen. I lay there remembering, over and over and over again, what I had seen. I didn't want to forget it. If I'd had pen and paper, I'd have written it down and been more relaxed in the knowledge that I wouldn't have forgotten something he was sharing with me. This moment was so special, I stayed focussed on it totally, until I got up at a more acceptable time. Don't get me wrong, it wasn't that if I'd got up that early I'd have been 'told off' for disturbing her. It was more than that. I was now privy to exclusive information from someone who had died and had visited me. In a perverse way I felt guilty, a bit like a schoolboy who had nicked something and didn't want to tell his mum. So as a consequence I didn't want to move and this 'guilt' be revealed. Strange logic, but logically strange, I think.

If something like this had happened to you, you'd have probably wanted to be able to note it down. Much the same way you would wish that you had pen and paper in the glove box of your car, after an accident. That way, you can take all the necessary details down before you forget them. A number plate, the make and model of the car, number of passengers, witnesses, etc. To me it was the same, just pure common sense.

Seven days on. It was 23rd November 1992.

It was 2.30am, early in the morning. Our room was pitch black.

I woke up and saw in the same position as before, at the end of my bed, the back of a woman with straight, long black hair. She was looking out of a window where huge snowflakes the size of snowballs were gently falling. A calm stillness was all around. She had a white sort of crocheted loose fitting trouser suit on. I was convinced it was my mother. At this time I didn't sit bolt upright, but craned my neck off the pillow, almost 90º to see. I whispered, "Mum, is that you?"

I couldn't see whether it was her or not.

Then I had the strangest feeling ever. It was definitely to have the most profound effect on me, of all the sightings. It was to be the very first out of body experience I had ever had in my life. It just happened. It happened to me.

I was lying on my bed with my neck craned up, looking at this, when I felt myself sitting up and going towards this image. I believe my body actually stayed on the bed, but nonetheless I went across and found myself standing three quarters on to see if I could see the woman's face. It wasn't mum, it was Yoko Ono. I was disappointed that it wasn't my mum.

But it was Yoko Ono, for sure.

She never saw me but I know at that moment she felt an incredible closeness to John. I know she felt his presence. And you know what? I bet if someone were to ask her had John ever come to her, she would probably describe that moment I have just told you about.

I was overcome by the most powerful feelings of warmth, closeness and love that John obviously had for Yoko. I then looked behind me for some reason, as if to get my bearings in this warm, nice-feeling room. I saw a fireplace with a table in front of it, which had two brandy glasses on it one-third full of brandy. The light of the fire behind was catching the crystal glasses and sparkling. The fireplace was off the ground with a shiny brass or chrome frame.

I then looked towards Yoko, who was gazing downwards out of the window. I followed her line of vision to what appeared to be a park, shaped like a baseball pitch. It was still snowing and silence reigned. Transfixed by this feeling of love between John and Yoko, words and music filled my head. Three songs were going around in my head.

Words that John definitely wanted to convey to Yoko.

There were hundreds of words and beautiful melodies. Could I hold onto these words and melodies, could I remember everything? Everything? Could I? You bet your life I could!

I found myself going backwards, from the way I came, back onto the bed, and back into my body, at which point I felt an excruciating severe pain in my neck. It was as if the body was frozen in the cranked up neck position during all the time I was with Yoko. Be it that it felt like one minute or so, my neck suffered real pain.

Thank God I had put a pen and paper down by the side of my bed.

I looked at the neon alarm clock on my side of the bed. It read 2.30am

Slowly, and very quietly, I lowered my hand to pick up the pen and paper without disturbing Karen.

I began writing words in the pitch black. I couldn't stop. I was racing the words, all over the paper, that I couldn't see but I could feel. I was writing hundreds of words, as if I was possessed. Words being written all over the place, on top of one another, all dancing on the page as the melody dictated. I was writing like a lunatic in the pitch black. I was in absolute full flow.

I must have made a noise, because Karen heard the feverish goings on and shrieked at me, "What *are* you doing?"

I put the pen and paper down by the side of my bed and realised she must have heard my scribbling, so I said, "Oh, I'm just making a note about a customer's bill I have to invoice. I didn't put the light on because I didn't want to wake you."

Although a weird and strange explanation, she seemed pacified by it and soon I heard her breathing deepen into her regular sleep pattern.

I lay awake until 5.30am.

I got up and went downstairs into the lounge and transferred the squiggly writings into readable words. I was in awe at the words and the music given to me by John. There were so many words and beautiful melodies.

I split up the words that came to me in the strongest order. I rationalised them and within half an hour I had written two of the three songs called, *'Yoko I Love You'* and *'Love's Twilight Hour'*. I played them and cried my eyes out. They were the most beautiful songs I had ever heard in my life. And I cried again. My humbleness had just consumed me. I didn't deserve this privilege, this view into the next world or some parallel universe, that the likes of Einstein, Newton, Da Vinci or the greatest people on this earth may have seen that made them who they are.

I am just an honest, ordinary, normal man. I am no one special. God knows.

The Third Sighting

3rd Sighting
Song No.4: MOMMA I'M HOME

The heavily lined curtains that Karen had made for our bedroom a year earlier certainly did the trick at keeping the light out and the heat in. We had large 8'x4' windows and we were glad we'd made the decision to buy the best and heaviest material for the job. The sun used to come up in that window, but until you opened the curtains you couldn't tell whether it was night or day, whether it was 'cracking the flags' or it was raining.

The third sighting was to be the strangest of all experiences I have ever had in my life.

It was about 3am on 29th November 1992 when I was awakened from my sleep. It was pitch black and the room was in stillness, a perfect ambience; the perfect place for the perfect night's sleep.
I awoke with my head on the pillow looking up towards the ceiling. But I felt so relaxed and was just slowly waking up when I saw a chink of light at the end of my bed. It was a bit like a torch beam, shone for a second or so. I awakened instantly and sat up. Was it a burglar? I knew categorically it definitely wasn't coming from outside. It wasn't a car headlight or anything like that. That was impossible because of the curtains. No, someone was in the room. Momentarily, I began slowly to reach over for my bedside light, so as not to lose the surprise advantage I had over this intruder. I got my hand to the base of the small table light, moved it upwards towards the lampshade, and began to delicately fumble for the switch. The following sequence of events was to unfold which made me stop in my tracks and stop attempting to turn the light on.
Imagine being in a film projectionist's room. (I've never been in one, but I would think it would have the capacity to be almost black, so no light is spilled onto the film that is being shown to the audience through the opening where the lens would go.) A dark room, not unlike that very

bedroom.

That instant I moved my hand away from the light; this was no burglar. This was something to do with John Lennon. I saw what looked like a projectionist's opening and I saw in rapid but definite succession, five film stills.

It is the strangest of all experiences I have ever had, and I don't apologise for reiterating this to you again.

Five stills that I reacted to and became a part of. I lived the dream and I was wide awake whilst I was doing it.

I saw, at the end of my bed in that same position where I'd seen the previous sightings, film stills that appeared to be no more than 12 inches wide and six inches deep. That's why I describe to you this 'projectionist's' type room. I could see the serrated holes, top and bottom, like on camera film. I focussed intently.

These five 'stills' lasted no more than one second each, but took me into John Lennon's mind.

I was to be privy to what he saw and what went through his mind the second he was shot.

THE STILLS WERE AS FOLLOWS:

No.1 Still. I saw an image of a snub-nosed gun, smoking, that had just been fired. I didn't feel any pain but felt myself fall and my head hit the ground.

No.2 Still. I saw a picture of the Queen, at an angle, as if the picture was lop-sided on the wall, but had already seen this picture as I felt myself falling to the ground.

No.3 Still. Overhead it was black, but there were millions of stars in the sky.

I was looking up from the ground at this point.

No.4 Still. I then saw the entrance to the Mersey tunnel at which point I felt myself hurtling through it – over what appeared to be stationary cars. (I put the 'stationary' aspect down to the fact I felt I was travelling so fast overhead of these cars.)

No.5 Still. I saw people waiting outside the tunnel entrance (Liverpool side) apparently waiting for me – not me. I mean John, waiting for John Lennon.

I didn't recognise any of them but I remember a feeling of elation. And the elation? 'MOMMA I'M HOME AGAIN, MUM I'VE COME BACK HOME AGAIN, AND MUM I'VE COME BACK HOME AGAIN TO YOU.' But no one appeared to be surprised to see me. I would say there were two grown-ups (a man and a woman), and three children. I didn't recognise anyone.

Also behind these people I saw an arched stone doorway with a doorman standing, blocking the way. He had a dicky bow and a black suit on – just like a bouncer. For some reason I ran through the alphabet as 'doorman standing in the door, man' didn't make sense. I got to the letter V and thought, Voorman fits. I didn't know who, if anyone, this person was.

This was to be the third sighting where I know John Lennon went back home to his roots in Liverpool. You don't, but I do.

He and I, with what I'd felt and witnessed, were elated.

The song was already there: *'Momma I'm Home'*. I didn't try. The words and music were all there, just waiting for me to write down as fast as I could, which I did at the side of the bed, in the pitch black as per usual.

7 days after asking for help from Mum, Dad, and God (8.11.92), I see John Lennon (15.11.92).
8 days later, I have an out of body experience, and I visit Yoko (23.11.92).
7 days later, I'm shown 5 images, and 'feel' what John Lennon felt when he was shot (29.11.92).

By this time I just accepted without question that it was John Lennon who was coming to me. John was 'channelling' his thoughts, feelings and songs through to me.

I still didn't know why me, but I just accepted it, and would do my best one day to share what had happened to me with the world.

There have been cynics and people who think I am a fake. This story is *so* unusual; I can understand that some people find it hard to believe. I was a printer but I had also become this musical blank sheet of paper that John would use to continue producing his music. Perhaps I was the one who had picked up his 'frequency', or he mine. Did he already know that I had the capacity to focus and interpret? What was happening to me was unique. I was being allowed to have privileged viewings of this 'other' world by a person called John Lennon who didn't mean anything to me.

Did he know that? Was that the very reason he chose me? Did he know I was just an ordinary man?

I don't know why this has happened to me.

But I can't let what has happened to me be ignored. It is unique, amazing and unfathomable.

I had the option to make money from a world famous man in 1994. I had a contract offered to me by Uri Gellar, and a record deal with a huge record label called Polydor.

IT just didn't feel right. It was and still is about me getting John's music out into the ether, once again, where it belongs. The place were real people listen to real music. The music that still continues to flow.

The music that is coming from John Lennon, to me, and from me to you.

I was asked a question on a TV show once in 1994. It was Lorraine Kelly, from a breakfast programme. She asked me, "Were you not afraid that you would become a laughing stock when you went public with this story?"

I replied, "No, not at all. I am just a very ordinary person. I've not changed at all, I'm married, got two beautiful children. So to answer your question, I don't care if everyone looking in is saying this guy is completely crazy. Because, I'm not. I'm just a very ordinary person. And where did these 120 songs (and that's just to date) come from?"

After everything I have gone through, not a lot has changed. I don't care if people think I'm crazy. I'm just me.

Something has changed though. If I was asked the same question today, I wouldn't follow on to say, 'and where did these 120 songs, and that's just to date, come from?'
I'd be saying, 'and where did these 300 songs, and that's just to date, come from?'

Very early on, in 1994, I had been advised by someone, a giant of the music industry, to get sworn affidavits from just about everyone who knew or had known me and been close to me. I questioned why that was important, to which he replied, "It's not important now, but it will be in the future." I didn't understand then why it was to be so important. But I do now.

Those affidavits confirm from 15 people that they had known me for however many years and that I had never played music, written songs or had any interest whatsoever in music in all the time they had known me. These affidavits are from closest friends, relatives, work colleagues and even my wife.
Every affidavit was sworn in front of a solicitor, by ordinary people, for an ordinary person, asking them to tell the truth.
Even Karen swore an affidavit, and this was at the most acrimonious period of our bitter divorce, when she wouldn't have given me the steam from her piss.

7

The Musical Mystery Tour
The Next 32 Sightings

The sightings would always take me to a pinnacle of emotion. I would feel as if I had reached a creative high and my soul was filled with hitherto unexperienced feelings of elation and massive self-worth. I was still being allowed to see on the other side, and at times felt almost like Christopher Columbus discovering new worlds. It was like being on a journey that you know one day will come to an end. But when you arrive back from 'whence you came' you will want to tell the whole world, and they will want to listen. I had a great feeling of pride, an unsurpassed knowledge of uncharted waters and new found land. Like walking on the moon. Out of this world, into the next and back again. All orchestrated and guided by the late, great, John Lennon. He was taking me into his new world. A world he wasn't ready to enter on December 8th 1980. A world that kept this genius doggedly and tenaciously trying to find somehow, someway, someone to channel the songs, still very much inside and a part of him, back to the land of the living, the land from 'whence he came'.

I was to have the honour of many, many more sightings of John Lennon as the years passed, and another 32 sightings whilst I was still in Greenside in Mold.

All this time John was entrusting me to relay back to a cynical, musically voided and starved world his message, his message of hope, his message of LOVE and PEACE.

All was to be revealed to me on this **MUSICAL MYSTERY TOUR**.

Around the time of late November 1992 the days seemed to merge into one another. I would be receiving so much music and information I just wrote as fast as I could for all my worth. Sometimes it was crazy. I'd be getting not one but three songs to take down simultaneously. Sometimes I didn't even give a thought to the song it needed to be taken down that quickly. I'd think oh that's good, write it down, put it away in my box of writings, and forget about it.

This is my analogy of why I seemed to be able to harness all this information from John and have the capacity and song writing ability.

Imagine a kid in a chocolate factory being allowed to pick as many chocolates off the shelf as he wanted. What would happen is that greed would set in, his eyes would be bigger than his belly and he would end up dropping half of what he had picked up. The same way as if you gave a monkey a biscuit jar with a narrow opening to get its hand into the jar full of biscuits. The monkey, recognising lots of biscuits, would open his hand and grab the biggest handful it can get hold of. Trouble is, the monkey can't get its hand out of the jar no matter how hard it tries. Its greed is all consuming. It won't let go. It wants the biscuits for itself and nobody else.

However, with me, it was a different story.

Remember when originally I asked for help, I said, "Please help me, I've lost everything and it's as if I've got everything to give." An unusual saying in any event, don't you agree?

I said that because I felt that I was a totally empty being, but had everything to give. I am a giver, not a taker. I believe I was empty to the core. So when these songs, music and other information came to me I had the space, the capacity on my computer – my brain which was empty but had massive unused capacity – to download it.

I would always scribble down the songs that came to me and I'd put them away in my box and forget about them.

Then when I had some time to pick the piece out, I'd try to get from the paper to the finished song. And I always did it. It was so easy because the words and music came at the same time. Once heard, never forgotten. I didn't know music and used to write dots, highs and lows, you know when the music goes higher, I'd put dots above the words, higher or lower.

One such sighting was the fourth sighting. I had put this piece of paper away and retrieved it from the box, days later.

4th Sighting
Song No.6: GOD IS LOVE

I awoke about 2.30am early December 1992 and saw at the end of the bed, in the usual place, John. This time he had white robes on and appeared to be sitting on a cloud, just floating and gazing down towards the ground. He then looked straight at me. I was lying down on my bed and he continued to stare at me. He looked at peace, but as always focussed on me totally. John was, as always, deadly serious about getting his message across. There was definitely a 'thought transference' happening again, though this one seemed longer than others I had seen to date.

All the words and music were there in an instant. The song took 15 minutes to finish. The first thought that went through my head was – John's in heaven and he wants me to tell everyone that that's where everyone is going. No matter who they are. This song seemed bizarre to me as I am not religious and have in fact never been a church goer since leaving Sunday school in Liverpool when I was ten. I have not been baptised, although the priest who married me to Karen in 1984 had set three months aside before our wedding with a view to teaching me, then baptising me into the Catholic faith. This I was prepared to do for the love of Karen.

Strangely enough, two weeks before the wedding I asked the question, "Are you going to baptise me, Father, before the wedding?"

His reply was even stranger. "I don't think you are ready to enter the Catholic faith. You will need more instruction." At 29 years old I was being told I wasn't ready to enter the faith. I knew when I left his house that day that I was never going to get baptised if it wasn't by him, and before I married the girl I loved.

I was married two weeks later on 26th May 1984, in St. Columbus Roman Catholic Church, Newton, Chester. Now this wasn't strange at the time, but considering what has transpired, it now seems worth recording that the priest's name was FATHER JOHN LENNON.

5th Sighting
Song No.7: BETCHA BOTTOM DOLLAR

It was mid December 1992. I saw John with three other lads in tight fitting suits and thin ties. I am sure the other lads were not the Beatles. I didn't recognise any of them. They were in a street with gas lamps walking into town. (Liverpool, I felt.) They were all in high spirits, everyone one was laughing as if they had already had a drink. They were swinging around the gas lamps as they passed them. Words and music came simultaneously. It was clearly a rocker. I did change some of the words a day or two later, particularly following on from 'I drank a lake the night before'. They were a bit obscene, and they described a one night stand John had had this particular night and made reference to the 'girl having a period, and discarding the 'rag' on the floor'.
I believe this song *'Betcha Bottom Dollar'* is the follow on to *'I Saw Her Standing There'*, an early Beatles' song.

What was tending to happen to me was a naturally occurring 'heightening of awareness' in general. Similar to a graph where it would peak after a sighting and for several days later – songs, words and music seemed to flourish for no real reason. Then they would eventually tail off until the next sighting, *'World Beatles Song'*. The *'World Beatles Song'* has had some real life coincidences added to it over the years all of which will be revealed at a later date.

Song No.8: WORLD BEATLES SONG (Incomplete at this time, stored in my files)
(Part of a previous sighting, and as such, not listed as a separate sighting)

A special letter was written from me on 2nd December 1992, which included this song title.
The above song was to come out of a sighting, or should I say in the background, or backdrop of previous sighting, where information was there for me to pick up, which I did. I describe in it how I was offered this music, and how this music will be heard in this and the next life, for 'Every nation, every station, yeah, and the man in the moon.' Strange and phenomenal. But I just couldn't complete the song. No matter how

many times I went to my box and took it out, I couldn't finish this song.

6th Sighting
Song No.9: CHIMNEY POTS

January 1993. A new year just beginning! I awoke from my sleep and felt I was in another place. I felt as if I was on a train, just like you used to see in Liverpool. I was on this train seeing 'lots and lots of chimney pots'. My destination was never clear, but the thing was the sound of the train - dedede, dedede. Dedededededede. The tune was that train running. Nothing special, I thought, but one week later I was travelling into Chester with my family when Tim, my boy said, "Look at all those chimney pots over there!" (British Aerospace Factory, Broughton.) That was it. Everything fitted into place. The song took 15 minutes to complete.

7th Sighting
Song No.10: TOMORROW NEVER COMES

It was 6th January 1993 about 3am and in the usual place, at the end of the bed, I saw John sitting on a chair, just looking at me. His thought transferral to me was of yesterday, and how tomorrow never comes. Still don't know to this day whether he meant his tomorrow or was generalising about 'our', or 'one's' tomorrow. I wrote down the words and music to this haunting cello-sounding ballad very quickly. Whether they were his thoughts of life in general, I don't know. This song is unusual in as much as I just wrote word for word to the tune, right until the end. It is a sad, reflective song that affected me deeply at the time.

By this time we, John and I, were both totally familiar and comfortable with each other's company through the sightings. It was John who decided when, I guess, it was the best time for us to communicate. And if not John, then a power greater than the both of us put together. These sightings were now becoming easier, for some reason, to understand. Never once did I try and call to him, or seek him out. It just happened. There was no need for explanations; no more, 'why me', or from him 'can he do it'? We both knew and forgot about everything but my being able to capture, and in his case being able to relay, the song or the piece concerned.

John just sitting there looking rather forlornly at me. That's how he looked when he transferred his thoughts to my head. And that's how the song *'Tomorrow Never Comes'* came to be.

8th Sighting
Song No.11: CRAZY LADY (Wrong Side Of The Tracks)

It was 12th January 1993. It was 2am and I was awakened with a start.
I had been in a very deep sleep. I had done a day's work and been for a run up the local mountain, Moel Famau, North Wales. Whenever I had the opportunity, just like when I was a child, I'd run on my own in my own little world. Running always gave me a release. A time to think, a freedom, a pleasure. An enjoyment I cherished.
I used to take Tim and Steph up there. We would drive to the top car park and although Steph never wanted to start the walk, once going she loved it and the games would start. All three of us laughing, playing and enjoying the good clean air and the fabulous views. Moel Famau was the highest point around. It had 360 degrees of panoramic views. At its pinnacle it had an obelisk. This place was one of the ancient sites in the United Kingdom that had a beacon. This was an early 'telephone system' to warn of impending attack or planned tribal meetings. It was used to celebrate the Queen's Jubilee. The first beacon was lit in London and the nearest beacons around waited until they saw the fire from the first beacon, then they lit theirs. This was done all around the country and the mushroom effect was incredibly quick. Soon, every beacon was ablaze, not by some countdown from a clock or watch but all lit and blazing based on the human eye, watching, waiting to see the flames from far away. One can only imagine in years gone by how focussed the tribes would have been. No interruptions from mobiles, no depressing thoughts of bills, council tax, mortgages, cars, breakdowns, etc, etc. All they needed to do was kill a wild animal to eat and clothe themselves. Find water from a spring or river to nourish them. Keep their eyes peeled all around for potential enemies. Tend their animals, find a place to sleep. Procreate. And just keep doing that. Progress? I

digress. Suffice to say, I loved this place and went up 'Moelly' whenever I could.

So I was awakened with a start.

I saw John clearly and slowly handing a piece of paper to another man. This other man was in the shadows, and initially I was a bit concerned not knowing who this person was. And in fact I thought was this other person good or was he bad? This person moved forward to take the paper from John. Although still in the shadows, I could make out this man had long hair, was quite skinny, but had full lips. I am sure it was Mick Jagger.

As soon as I saw the piece of paper being handed over, I knew it was a song.

But what was written on that piece of paper? I didn't know. But as had been the case in so many of the sightings, I knew sooner or later the song would come when it was ready.

It did the night I re-read 'Tomorrow Never Comes'. It was late and all the family were in bed. It was about 12.30am and I was very tired. But just before I went to bed I saw a basket of dried flowers by the piano, which my wife must have moved that day from just inside the front doorway, in the hall, to this new position. That was the catalyst. That was it. The song. That's the song on that piece of paper John handed to Mick Jagger!! The song was written in 10 minutes flat, words and music. This was caused all because I'd seen those flowers minutes earlier. The song, 'Crazy Lady', was done and dusted. And I knew my conscious, honest, focussed, dogged tenacity wouldn't let me down. I'd figured out what John wanted me to figure out. A song for Mick Jagger from John Lennon.

'Are you serious Mike?' I hear you asking.

I am deadly serious. 'Now that's all well and good, but prove it.'

I can't.

But bear with me. Incredible as this may sound.

Mick Jagger brought out a solo album. It was called 'GODDESS IN THE DOORWAY'. It was slated, I never did hear the album, but it only sold a couple of thousand copies. For Mick, it was a reality check and a disaster. I suppose his ego led him to believe it would be as successful as any Rolling Stones' album. Wrong Mick. Don't you know by now, you never change a winning team? Now just supposing Mick would have shared, collaborated with THE man in the Stones, namely his long time music writing partner and genius – Keith Richards. Supposing he would have shared the songs instead of keeping them for himself, how very different the outcome would have been. At the time of the launch of Mick's album, Keith Richards was quoted as saying about the album – 'Goddess in the Doorway? More like dog shit in the doorway'. Keith is a giant, worth a fortune and knows his worth, and basically didn't give a shit what Mick thought of his outburst anyway. But he was the only one with the bottle to tell him what he thought.

The song I wrote for John to Mick was done and copyrighted the day I did it. That was 12 TH JANUARY 1993. The song was *Crazy Lady'* and the opening line is 'a basket full of dried out flowers in her hallway, a million shades of oatmeal, ochre and red, a friendly welcome from this goddess, looking, a million dollars in her Dior dress'. I actually talk about this 'GODDESS IN THE DOORWAY'.

Mick's album 'Goddess in the Doorway' came out and was released almost NINE YEARS LATER, 19TH NOVEMBER 2001.

At the time of Mick's album, like so many coincidences that were to unfold, it was being confirmed to me, somehow, that I was still on the right track. Time after time, just keep going. It's difficult to convey but these 'coincidences' always brought me back into focus. Not once in all these years have I ever wavered. But if say for a period of time maybe John was at the back of my mind, these coincidences would bring him right to the forefront. Was it John creating these coincidences, in order for me to complete this 'long-haul flight'? Remember that the first sighting was in 1992. I'm in this for the duration. And along the way it's nice to know 'someone' keeps helping me, like the fable with the white pebbles shining in the moonlight to guide me on my way. Dog shit in the doorway, funny eh?

Song No.12: LOVELY DAY

The inspiration and the happiness I got from finding the identity of the song on the paper led me directly to the song *'Lovely Day'*. It typifies how easy it is, when the senses are heightened, to continue at a dramatic pace. I wrote this song immediately after writing *'Crazy Lady'*. This song was a five minute ditty, but it's beautiful.

And this occurrence started to happen more frequently. I would have a sighting, and it would be like scaling Everest, the peak, or the core of the sighting. I would write down the information John was relaying to me, with my/his/our creative juices at full flow, but on the way down from a sighting I was able to 'write' songs, like this one.

9th Sighting
Song No.13: CAN'T YOU SAY YOU LOVE ME

This song was to be a one-off. Up until this point I had never conceived the possibility of this ever happening to me in any shape or form.

It was 20th January 1993. I had seen John, all be it very briefly. He stirred me from my sleep, I saw him and he vanished. It was about 4am. I lay there and smiled to myself. It was my very own early morning 'get up' call from John. There was no music; in fact there was nothing in my head. I just smiled. I felt this was John's sort of 'come on, get out of bed, you've got things to do'. I got out of bed at 5am. I went to the lounge and picked up my guitar. All the songs written to date were developed from basic bar chords on the guitar.

My thoughts were, start this song with a different chord. I picked my way into a melody and proceeded to write the lyrics as I went along. My mind was clear, no thoughts of anything whatsoever, and no preconceptions. The song seemed to follow a natural course and flowed. I was positive I had heard it before, somewhere, because I hadn't consciously thought of a single word to go into it. The melody wasn't in my head when I picked the guitar up. It flowed before my very eyes and ears. I needed an hour to sit down and try to understand this unusual occurrence. I had a strange feeling because, even at the end of the song, I wasn't even thinking about it. The song took three minutes to write. Did I believe I had just done that song? No. I believe it was already there through John.

10th Sighting
Song No.14: I WISH I COULD FLY

I had previously noted a 'bald-headed man, wearing round glasses, smiling, doesn't like me I can tell' on 29th November 1992, during the *'Momma I'm Home'* sighting. But the information I received didn't fit into that song, and again it was too many words for a reasonable track. So I put it in the box with other songs that I was still to work on. I knew that one day those words/information would be used on another song. This proved to be the case.

It was 8th February 1993. About 3.45-4am I was awakened and I saw John, not standing at the end of the bed as usual, but in the far right hand corner, where the bedroom door was.

I saw him 'standing on a corner watching a man, digging a hole to hell'. Between John and me was a navvy holding what appeared to be an industrial-sized brace and bit. The handle was about 3' wide and the navvy was turning this bit, which had a huge drill/bore of about 18 inches wide. As he turned it, the earth he was boring was spewing up out of the ground and had already formed a five foot mound. He wore a leather sleeveless worker's jerkin. He was standing side-on to me.

John was leaning against a street wall. A brick wall, by a street lamp. I could see his face in profile; he was deep in thought, he was 'wondering why all the fuss, when Isaac Newton said – this is the apple that fell'. It was very lightly spitting rain, there was a yellow 'orb' created by the street light on this dark evening. John was looking straight into that street light. Suddenly, he turned his head and looked straight across at me and just stared. The hairs went up on the back of my neck as I looked intently at what was before me. The length of time this all took might have been about one minute. He was dressed in denim, wore a cap and sunglasses, which I thought at the time was strange on this rainy, dark evening. I was awake. I heard a lorry from the local quarry in Gwernafield near Mold make a huge noise outside, over the field, on the Ruthin Road. The empty lorries returning to the quarry about 4am always used to make that noise. That noise was caused by the lorry going over a low drain cover on the Ruthin Road, and as usual, this morning, the lorry had jerked its large plate steel empty shell over the manhole cover. There seemed too obvious a logic for that lorry not to be included in the sighting/song. My brain connected the mound of earth with quarrying, getting stone out of the ground, and of course taking it away from the quarry. John's thoughts were of someone 'dropping a pile on me'. I believe John heard that lorry noise as well as me. I wander if he knew, at that precise time, that the noise was going to occur. It makes you think. It was a very late sighting, which happened at about 4am.

Song No.15: PARTY SONG

As with the song *'Lovely Day'*, this was another example of the creative flow. This was written immediately after *'I Wish I Could Fly'*. It is light-hearted and jolly and mentions my best friends, etc. It was sung happily as opposed to *'I Wish I Could Fly'*, which is meant to be sung in a sort of screaming fashion –'watchin' a man digging a hole to hell'. The *'Party Song'* I just wrote down in 10 minutes, straight after the other one. And it relieved me of the 'tension' of the previously written song.

In one 1993 painting he depicted a man drilling into the earth. Years later Lennon's first wife Cynthia revealed in a book that a workman using a pneumatic drill outside drowned out their wedding vows. There were no photographs taken of the ceremony - but a cartoon Cynthia drew bears a striking resemblance to the man Mike painted.

Spooky... picture painted by Mike of his 1993 visit and, inset, Cynthia Lennon's cartoon of their wedding with driller outside
Other clues in 'visits' from John have led Mike to predict the title of Mick Jagger's 2001 album Goddess In The Doorway eight years early - and even the launch of the new Volkswagen Beetle car.

He said: "In a 1997 newspaper article Paul McCartney said that The Beatles made a pact that if any of them died young, they would try contact the others fromt he afterlife. This is what I think is happening."

72

11th Sighting
Song No.16: LISTEN WHILE I TALK TO YOU

It was early February 1993. I awoke and saw John amongst the clouds, looking towards the ground. He was earnestly looking for his son. I don't know which one, but he had travelled great distances and it seemed that he couldn't find him. He was thinking as he was looking for his son, 'listen while I talk to you, listen's all I ask of you'. His position was similar to how one would imagine Superman flying, but with his arms by his side. He was flying high above the Earth and his eyes appeared to have like a rainbow 'x-ray vision' coming from them. He flew around the Earth at great speed, in earnest. He couldn't find his son to convey his sentiments, now he was 'on the other side'. He wanted to tell the child how he felt, how humble he now felt, and how proud he was of his son – things he had perhaps always wanted to say to his son, but never did.

This is the only song I created on the piano. We'd got the piano so that the kids would learn to play as their mother had done when she was a child. Anyhow, the only reason I created this song on the piano was that friends of ours on a weekend family visit, the week or two before, had shown me three basic chords.

Believe me, when I heard this song for the first time, the moment of the sighting, I knew why that friend had shown me those simple chords. At the end of 'converting' this number to this new medium it was too tempting not to put my daughter's name on it. 'Listen while I talk to you, little darlin' Stephie Lou-Lou.'

I was surprised at the depth of feeling simple chords and a piano can give a song, unlike the guitar. Over the following months there were six or seven songs meant for the piano (these are still in my box file). I'd never pursued it because I'm left-handed and the piano felt awkward. I had smashed my wrist when I was 14 years old. It was broken in five places, painful and had been almost ripped out of its joint. It really hurt, nasty to say the least.

The song took no time at all to do. I knew that John wouldn't mind me changing some of the words and I was not doing this for any reason other than, with hindsight, it is how I and I guess many other parents would like to be remembered by our own son or daughter. I felt a bit cheeky doing this, but I'm sure the crux of the message John wanted to convey to his son is still there. In any event, I turned it back again to its original lyric, and recorded 'Listen'.

And anyway, give me a break, if I do sing 'little darling Stephie Lou-Lou' it's OK.

I don't get many perks on this job!

I have since played the piano many times when writing songs from my boxfiles and can't remember the last time I played the guitar.

12th Sighting
Song No.17: BRECK ROAD

It was 12th February 1993 when this song came to me, in a similar fashion to *'Betcha Bottom Dollar'*. On that occasion I was being told through thought transferral from John that this was in fact the follow on from *'I Saw Her Standing There'*, an early Beatles' number.

Breck Road was where I grew up. I went to my senior school (from the age of 11) called Anfield Comprehensive School for Boys, which was about a mile and a half away from our house. I always ran or walked to school to save the bus fare; the odd tuppence each way meant four pence for sweets. From Lyell Street I'd run to the bottom and into Thirlemere Road, turn left and carry on down 'Thirly'. I'd turn down one of the side streets on the right, Coniston St, or maybe Grassmere Street. If it was raining, I'd choose the first road on the right, a sort of 'short cut' to school, which it wasn't, but somehow always felt like it was. I'd get to the end of the street which would bring me onto Breck Road, a main artery that ferried all the buses, lorries and traffic directly into Liverpool centre a mile and a half away, or the other way from town towards Clubmoor, Queens Drive and onto the then main roadway joining Manchester to Liverpool, the East Lancashire Road. I would turn left and run the half mile or so down 'Brecky', turning right at the massive, now under-used, sadly rundown, grandiose façade that was called The Cabbage Hall Public House. It was once a place where fields of cabbages lay, now row upon row of little terraced houses stood and surrounded Cabbage Hall. It was a ginormous old public house, and when it was constructed no expense was spared for the working man to enjoy his pint. Like the sumptuous and lavishly decorated cinemas of the 30s and 40s, this building was the master brewer's effort to bring real quality and luxury to the lower classes, to the working man. It was so big and had so many rooms, like ocean liners, different levels, all opulent, that could house many, many people, all spending an extra copper or two to be transported up a class or two. It was meant, for a few hours, to take them out of their miserable lives, where for a while they would feel better about themselves sitting down in the then opulent surroundings of the deepest, most luxurious carpets and beautiful carved hardwoods that came from all over the world, and the glorious granite and stone, which in the main was reserved normally for buildings that passengers from all over the world would see every time they docked at the Pierhead, like the great Royal Liver Buildings.

I'd turn right at the 'Cabbage' and run the remaining three quarters of a mile along Breckside Park and on into school. I also ran home every dinner time for 'dinner' to see Mum. She knew I had a voracious appetite and oh the joy, particularly on a Monday or Thursday when I'd rush in about 12.15pm and last night's roast remains would be piping hot, with a big chunk of bread, just as I sat down at the table. Mmm! Mum was always there for us. We would talk about what we had done that morning and half an hour later I'd run back again to school. Mum was never really well; all the time I can remember just how poorly she was, trying to catch her breath when I had all the breath in the world. The harder I ran the more breath I had, not the other way around. It's a great pity she couldn't have had some of mine.

So Breck Road was a major part of my life and for six years I'd be running 30 miles a week back and forth from 'Lyelly' to school and back, twice a day.

The morning of 12th February 1993, I sensed John's presence. I didn't see him clearly, but saw a flash of him for an instant. It was no more than half a second. It was like seeing someone standing at the side of a road and hurtling past them very fast in a car. You have just seen the person, but does your brain 'compute', and do you remember any detail? That was it. I saw nothing else but wondered which road he was standing by. As soon as I saw John, in that half second he sent to me and I received his thoughts.

He was thinking Penny Lane, Penny Lane – meanwhile back in Breck

Road.

It was as simple as that.

As soon as I heard those five words the tune came automatically, and didn't I know all about Breck Road? This is the follow-on to 'Penny Lane'. Everything I wrote seemed rich and right. This number took half an hour to write. (Note sounds I heard, foghorn, cannon, traffic, bus, etc.)

My question is why should John produce follow-ons to the two Beatles' songs I mentioned: *'I Saw Her Standing There'* and *'Penny Lane'*?

Did he write the original songs?

Did Paul McCartney??

Or did someone else??? I just don't know.

Or an even more bizarre thought: Did someone else write them, for someone in the band????

I wonder if this is why John relayed the two songs mentioned to 'prove' to someone that undoubtedly this was his work. I don't know. Did John want to 'push the envelope' further, thinking, 'anything you can do...'? I wish I knew.

Where John is now, I believe, is a place where no more harm can come to him, or anyone there. It is a place that is all knowing, no secrets, where, like on Earth, people have the same mentalities they were born with. The same thought processes but a nice, peaceful feeling like they are 'permanently on holiday'. They just see more with that same mentality they had on Earth. It's a place, I believe, where our former loved ones are now. Observing, perceiving, knowing all, and where possible, helping as they can the people still on Earth. Of all people to embrace this with open arms, it would be John.

John is inquisitive and his intriguing mind always looks at things, at situations, dare I say it, from 'outside the box', differently from the way most people see things. How do I know? Oh, just from what I have seen and witnessed from the very first sighting.

A story comes to mind as an instance of this 'help' I describe, from my brother, in 1982.

My younger brother Jayson had joined the police in Liverpool and had become somewhat tainted by my dad. Jay was a very immature thirteen-year-old when my dad took him to 'meet the love of his life', Pat. She was a school teacher on the Wirral. Poor Jay just couldn't handle it and was devastated. Perhaps he joined the police to get his own back. To be able to throw his weight around without question, just like my old feller. No one in the family could ever argue with Geo. His word was law. I remember even at the age of 21 moving out of his chair when he came in. Once when I was at the caravan clubhouse in Anglesey with Rocky and Stan (about 17) Geo bowled into the clubhouse with this same woman and tried to introduce her to me. Needless to say, he got short, sharp shrift from me. She was plastic. She was false and my dad thought he was Mr Big Bollocks, invincible, and thought he could do, or did, no wrong. Parading this 'floozy' among members of his family and all our caravan friends, who all knew and thought the world of our mum, Gwen. How could he?

No wonder Jay went off the rails.

Anyway, this particular night Jay had been out on the town, on the 'piss' with his mates. He was 24 and was used to throwing his 'police' weight around. As a consequence, he used to drink and drive everywhere. He was a policeman and could do what he liked. He got in his car, pissed out of his head and proceeded to drive through the old Mersey Tunnel, back to his new patch, which was Wallasey. He told me the following day what had happened; he was driving through the tunnel, which snakes and is full of bends, about 2am in the morning. All he can remember is crashing into, or driving into one of those bends. He realised the crash was imminent and he closed his eyes tightly and cried out the word 'MUM!' and waited for the smash to occur. His eyes were closed for what he thought was an eternity. The 'slow motion' override of the brain was closing down in anticipation and had kicked in. And he waited, eyes still tightly closed. And he waited. Thoughts now only of one thing – Mum. But there was no crash. He opened his eyes to find he was 50 yards past the bend and in the centre of the tunnel. This old tunnel had four lanes, two each way. It had no central reservation, so the two way traffic was always perilously close to the oncoming traffic. Now he swears on that night that our mum came to him and saved his life.

He has no other explanation, because all he remembers was shouting out for mum to help.

Who knows, perhaps when I asked my mum and dad for help, she/he/or they brought John to me. God knows, and of course it was probably God who did come to help in my darkest hour of need.

One thing's for sure. I would have definitely known if I had only asked one person, or one being, instead of my mum, my dad, and God!

13th Sighting and 14th Sighting
Song No.17: HERE I STAND BEFORE YOU (On a Train to See You)

It was very early in the morning of 15th February 1993, around 2.15am.
I awoke and remember seeing John's face in the reflection of a train window. It was sunny and warm and I was almost squinting to see his face. John was anticipating meeting someone to tell them what he thought of them, how much joy and love they had brought to him. I could feel an excitement. The feeling was that it had been a quite a while since John had seen this 'loved one'. I could actually taste wine as I saw in the window the reflection of the lips therein. But those lips, on closer inspection, weren't the lips of John but of Yoko. Yoko Ono. John was 'on a train to see you, looking forward to greet you, driftin' off in a world of my own, I dream of you'.
As usual, the whole song was there and it was all I could do to write it down as fast as I could.
Near the end of the song there is a line that says, 'You think of me in the corner of your mind, I see you in the corner of my eye'. This line was taken from a previous sighting that made no sense to me at the time but technically it was a sighting, so I have included the two sightings in one.
This is what happened on that previous sighting.
John was standing at the end of the bed, as usual, but then came towards me and stood right beside me. He leant forward, and his eye peered right into mine from a distance of no more than one inch away. He wasn't looking at my eye but right through it, into my head. It was a bit scary at the time, as this was the closest he had ever been to me. He was looking deep into my left eye, right out of the corner of his right eye. It was strange and almost had a weird 'medical' feel about it. As I say, my mind was blank, no thoughts of any song at all. But I knew there had to be a reason. Somewhere, this sighting was to be included in a song, along the way. That was to be the case on that day, 15th February 1993.

Song No.18: BLACKBIRDS

It was 16th February 1993. I was still creatively 'high', but coming down from the previous sighting. No sighting, just going about my life, routinely.

I had just dropped my daughter off to the childminder, Sue, in Queensferry. The major road carriageway was down to two lanes from four. One side of the road was up for resurfacing. It was 8.30am, wet and drizzling and I was thinking about the song *'Little Darling Stephie Lou-Lou'*. Temporary traffic lights had been placed on the dual carriageway and my lane had to wait two to three minutes. Workmen had just erected a tall carriage light, when I saw two blackbirds land on this light and they appeared to be kissing each other. I got a piece of paper and wrote all the words and the tune (by a series of dots) and before the lights had changed for my lane to go, the song was complete. I believe I was able to do that by being at or near one of these creative peaks from the last sighting.

15th Sighting
Song No.19: BABY JAMES BULGER

I was stirred from my sleep to see John. It was 2am. It was 19th February 1993.

I think at the time the James Bulger tragedy had just happened. A poor little innocent two-year-old child had been taken from his mother by two evil, wicked children. They had killed him on a train line, near Bootle, Liverpool. I heard the news properly on 'News at Ten' the day it was released.

It was about 2am and I woke to see John holding out a duffle coat toggle towards me, to show me. He then put it slowly in his pocket. He then got a Liverpool Echo (like a broadsheet), rolled it up and looked through it. He used it like a telescope, looking towards the sky. He then placed the rolled up Echo into an epaulette on his unusual denim jacket, just like army people do with a beret. John then looked up, to about 2 o'clock, when the Liver Buildings came into view. It had become quite windy, then I saw between the two Liver Birds, which are perched at the top of this building, a blue and white flag. It had a blue background with diagonal white stripes from corner to corner. This flag was fully outstretched and appeared to be hovering, but still, in this wind. Then, like a flash, it flew off in a northerly direction. At this time the River Mersey was on my left as I was looking at the building.

I later found out that this was the flag of Scotland, although at the time I thought it was a maritime flag of some sort.

This was also the second piece I did on the piano, and like the song 'Stephie Lou-Lou', you will see no chords or musical notes because I couldn't write them down. What you will see are my drawings of piano keys and the notes to press, having a cross put on them. This tune is simple with complicated bits around the chorus. Through Chris Wharton I was to play this for a certain Billy Kinsley (lead singer and songwriter with Merseybeats and also Liverpool Express), who said, "It is a very good song, but you'd get lynched if you put that out." Feelings were running very high over the tragedy at the time.

16th Sighting
Song No.20: THE DREAM FACTORY

It was 1st March 1993. I awoke and found John sitting at the foot of my bed. He was sitting on a 'canteen-type' chair. He was looking right at me and was positioned sideways-on to me. His head was turned towards me. Behind him was a pool table and what I actually saw (for the first time) were the other Beatles: Ringo, Paul, and George. They were busy potting balls. Ringo and George had the cues; Paul was on the right-hand back edge of the table, resting his hands on the corner. At no time did John take his eyes off me. Meanwhile, between John's chair and the pool table, walked an extremely tall beautiful woman with the longest legs I've ever seen in my life. She had jet black hair all lifted up like a beehive, which made her look even taller. The other three lads' jaws dropped; they stopped playing and followed her with their eyes to a sort of bar, which she leaned on. John was still looking at me. He had just given me another rocker, called 'The Dream Factory', or as I care to remember it, 'Long Long Legs'. Phew!

I wrote this the next day, 2nd March 1993. It only took 10 minutes from the outset, words and music simultaneously. Later that year, I had called to a printer in Heswall, Nicholls Print, waiting to pick a job up. As this was part of Merseyside, they used to be in the catchment area of the Liverpool Echo. Now whilst waiting for the job, I started to read this Liverpool Echo special publication called '30th Anniversary of Beatlemania'. In it, it virtually mentions everything I had seen in the sighting for the song 'The Dream Factory'. It was the day the Beatles met Elvis Presley. It describes the lady with the beehive jet black hair. Obviously in the early days before she dyed her hair blonde, and not as a lot of younger people at the time would know, including me.

I had copyrighted the song on 2nd March 1993.

The publication was produced on 24th August 1993, almost seven months after my, or should I say John's, publication was produced. Another coincidence, or just another white pebble confirming I was on the right track?

17th Sighting
Song No.21: VIRGIN BOY

2am on the morning of 10th March 1993. I saw John looking into a shaving mirror, as he was having a wet shave. Something I never used to do as it used to make my skin blotchy. I always used an electric shaver. Phillishave I believe.

He was looking into this mirror thinking about how a boy becomes a man. The words and music came together, simultaneously. I heard a beautiful instrumental piece that seemed to divide the song clearly in two, which made me relish hearing the second half.

(I think he was perhaps thinking of one or two of his children, and if and how they would make the transition. It was a sort of sad, reflective time of misunderstanding.)

In the song, he gives hope and strength through his words. The first line being, 'Virgin Boy, you're growing up, soon you'll be a man. A man inside a boy's frame, hard to understand...'

Song No 22: THIS FLAME IN MY HEART

It was 20th May 1993. I didn't see anything. I remember at the time I had been running through a few of the previous songs and soaking up – taking in – this whole happening. The quality of some of these songs

81

often left me feeling extremely humble. However, I believe that the emotions sometimes carried on from the sighting which was the case with this song. Words and music together as usual, in no time at all, in fact, 15 minutes flat.

18th Sighting
The New 'BEATLE', or BEETLE Sighting

This sighting occurred in May 1993. There was no song to come out of this sighting, but a strange 'sighting' nonetheless that is worth noting for posterity. I woke up and looked to the foot of my bed. I saw an old Volkswagen Beetle with its rear window removed. I was looking into the back of the car and I could clearly see John sitting in the back right hand seat. Next to him was Paul McCartney, on the left. In the front on the left hand side, driving, was Ringo Starr. George Harrison was the front seat passenger. It was raining and dark. A car passed in the opposite direction, on the wrong side of the road, i.e. the left hand side. The mood in the car was upbeat, and they were having a laugh between themselves. As the car passed, John visibly leaned forward and put his hand right across Ringo, towards the oncoming car and said, "There's the new Beetle." Then everyone howled with laughter.

I was so totally convinced that there was going to be a new Beetle produced that I phoned Milton Keynes and asked to speak to the UK Marketing Director. He was away until the following day. So I called again and spoke to him. His name was Paul Buckett and he flatly denied there was going to be a new Volkswagen Beetle produced. He asked me, why my interest? I told him what I had just seen and how music was coming from John Lennon to me, within the various other sightings, and his reaction was incredible. He said, "I'm the biggest John Lennon fan on the planet, I'd love to hear your songs and if they really do stack up I will put it to the Board, and maybe we can use one of your songs on one of our adverts."

I sent a cassette tape with some of the songs to him and he promised me that he would play it to the Board. One week later I awoke to the alarm clock and found a Radio Four programme was on and the subject they were discussing? There was talk of a new Volkswagen being produced, similar to VW's most famous car, the people's car, the Beetle. Again, on the programme, the spokesman for VW denied that there was to be a new car. Some weeks later, I chased up the Marketing Director, who told me that the Board did not wish to use any of the songs, but asked me to keep in touch with him.

The new Volkswagen Beetle was produced in the following year.

84

Déjà vu. No sighting, but real déjà vu

Song No.23: ETRATAT (In Normandy)
Song No.23a: IT'S YOU FRANCAIS

ETRATAT

I copyrighted this song on 21st May 1993. On what was to be our last family holiday together we took our touring caravan and had 10 days travelling around Normandy. Three days before heading home, we parked the caravan and drove 40 miles to a place Karen wanted to see called Etratat. We arrived about lunchtime and immediately went onto the beach. The bambinos – the kids – were as excited as ever. Something strange happened to me as I heard the pebbles on the beach 'crunch' as I walked to the water's edge.

I felt I had been there before.

I glanced to my extreme left following the water's horizon. As soon as I saw the rocky outcrop this whole song was there. I made an excuse and nipped back to the car and wrote down the words and 'sketched' in the tune. I have since had this song translated into French, although why I have no idea. The song was called *'Etratat'*.

The 'crunching' had been when we were walking on the pebbles, but mainly because every time a wave came in, the steep carved out gully would send pebbles crashing back out with the waves, causing an 'applause' effect.

IT'S YOU, FRANCAIS

We visited another charming village called Honfleur. Another place I was sure I had been before. It was another intense feeling of déjà vu. It was a gloriously sunny afternoon when we arrived in Honfleur. We parked the caravan up and walked into the village, which was about 50 yards from the campsite. We lazed around the harbour and soaked up this nice atmosphere. Tim was drawing the boats in the harbour, Steph was sitting right next to him on the quayside, and I remember thinking 'Parlez vous Francais, but only for today, who knows what tomorrow will bring, a harbour studio, a ballet dancing girl? The young man drawing in the sun...' I wrote the song down immediately, called *'It's You Francais'*. I started the first line by describing French things like 'French brandy you're so warming to me now, French champagne, you'll see the sparkle in my eyes, only you and I we both realise, it's you, yeah you, Francais'. Then I wrote about what I first saw when we walked into the village, which was 'the market place, and the harbour side, no wonder Monet came here...' Although there was no piano player, the line I wrote was this, 'the market place, piano player in Honfleur, the harbour side, no wonder Monet came here...'

A possible answer to the déjà vu I felt could be that my father's grandfather fled France, God knows when, and came to the United Kingdom. His name at the time was 'La Vash' – the cow. But he changed it by deed pole to an 'off the shelf' name and the name I bear today: Powell.

He had been a shoe maker in France but not your normal common or garden shoemaker. I always felt that he made shoes for the upper echelons of high French society, until the fall of the aristocracy.

The reason I used to think that was because for years, in Lyell Street, in the old cupboard where the gas meter was, there had been lain for donkey's years the finest, most delicate and intricate pair of baby's soft leather booties. These my great grandfather had made and had brought over from France. These 'works of art' were probably a keepsake to remind him that he too was a true artist. It was a gift my father was to inherit. A natural gift I was to inherit and who knows, maybe our Tim is to inherit too. They say 'it's in the genes'. My great grandfather went on to marry a Romany Gypsy so there is definitely a mixture of French and Irish in this Scouse, potent cocktail called Mike Powell formally nicknamed 'Mickey Drippin' and 'Mickey Plum'.

Often I'd hear the likes of Mrs Skinley shout to me as I was kicking a ball, "Hey! Mickey Drippin', get up your end of the street."

Song No.24: NICE TIME

It was the 29th May 1993. My friend Steve 'Ashy' took me to see another friend of his, a Blues singer, for her opinion of my songs. She was like a big momma, friendly but aloof. She liked the stuff and after hearing two or three bars of *'Love's Twilight Hour'* she turned to me and said, "Yes... Yes, you sound like McCartney." Now at the time neither she nor Steve knew what I was going through. I hadn't told anyone about the sightings. So any Beatles 'connection or resemblance' was purely coincidental. I left her place and took 15 minutes, words and music, to write *'Nice Time'*. (It was written by the time I drove home to Mold from Chester.)

19th Sighting
Song No.25: ABBEY ROAD

It was towards the middle of June in 1993. I woke up at around 2am.

I saw John standing by a street sign called ABBEY ROAD. It was unusual in as much as the sign was only three feet off the ground. It was supported by two poles, and John was leaning on the top of the sign, with one hand. He was slouching against it, you could say. I wondered what it meant, as no song was apparent, although I knew there was a Beatles LP called 'Abbey Road'. I scribbled down what I had seen and put it in my box of writings. Always, if something didn't come instantly, I knew not to force it, and sooner or later something would come of it. In fact I thought, well if it's to be a song, John will tell me when he's ready.

One week later it was Stephanie's bedtime and she wanted me to read her a story. We were in the 'snug', our cosy room just off the kitchen. So I got a book from the bookshelf on the other side of the room. The book she wanted me to read was near the end of the shelf. She came over with me and picked it out. Now these bookshelves had no ends to them. The right hand side of the bookcase was against the wall, but the left hand sides were open ended. She picked a book out from the open-ended side. As she picked the book out, four or five books began to fall off the shelf and onto the floor, one by one, causing a domino effect. I was puzzled at the last thing that fell, after I put my hand in to stop the rest of the books falling. It all happened very quickly. But it happened and Steph led me to it.

The last thing that fell onto the floor was my dad's old 1960s' Liverpool street map. An old fold-out white and red A-Z street map. The price on it was two shillings. Now I am no reader, and I had never seen this map, or most of the books, since we had moved into the house in Mold years earlier. I had probably packed all our books into boxes from the previous house and just put them onto the shelves I'd assembled when we first moved in.

I opened it and all the street signs were listed in alphabetical order. Low and behold, to my astonishment, the very first name at the top of the list was ABBEY ROAD.

I thought, ABBEY ROAD? ABBEY ROAD! OH, ABBEY ROAD!!! And that is exactly the chorus.

I waited until I had read to Steph and put her to bed, then promptly re-opened the old map. You will see all the street names next to Abbey Road are mentioned in the song. (I even heard a cello in the chorus part.) I wanted to find out where Abbey Road was. I'd never heard of it. It transpires it is off Breck Road just past the junction of Priory Road and First Street on the left, going out from town towards Clubmoor – right where I grew up, right under my very nose, and I didn't realise it. In fact when I was about 17 I was seeing a girl from Claude Street called Pat. Looking at the map, Claude Street was only two streets down from Abbey Road, but on the right hand side. Also, the Cabbage Hall Public House, which I previously mentioned, is at the next junction up from Abbey Road, towards town, and no more than 100 yards from street to street. The song took no more than 15 minutes to complete. As soon as I did the song I couldn't wait to get over to Liverpool and see Abbey Road, to see all those street names mentioned. I would also see and drive right down the length of Breck Road. I was going back to my roots, I was going on a musical mystery tour, to the area I was born and bred in, and as it unfolded, it was magical.

The next day I went to Liverpool and found Abbey Road. So shocked was I at seeing this street, which was really only half a street. I spent some 15 minutes walking and looking around. I remember it was unusually warm and sunny. As I basked in the warmth I was drawn to an old battered maroon door. The windows were dirty and the net curtains needed a good boil. It looked run down and empty. It was number five. I simply had to knock on the door, to which a cheery old woman answered. I asked her how long she had lived here and she said, "Most of my life." After a while she gave me some information about another Abbey Road in Bootle, another suburb of Liverpool. I had looked at the street map before walking down the street and there was definitely only one Abbey Road, the one I was standing in. I was talking to this 'old dear' who was adamant that there was another Abbey Road in Liverpool and I would say she was compos mentis.

Since this conversation with the lady, I have also written a play called

No.5 ABBEY ROAD. It's set in the 60s in a kitchen/living room, and all based around a typical family growing up in Anfield. In essence, the typical banter and the trials and tribulations, hopes and aspirations of people of the time, as seen through the eyes of an unaffected nine-year-old. In the background, on an old Grundig radiogram can be heard belting out the songs, not of the era, well, they could be, but in fact are the sounds and the music coming to me from John, to you. The play took three hours to write, and that was only because I couldn't write any faster!

Prior to this, the last time I had ever been in this part of Anfield was in 1983 when I took my then fiancée, Karen, to meet Jayson, my younger brother, in a pub on Breck Road called The Priory. Ironically, it transpired that the very next street down from this pub is Abbey Road. I was keen for Jayson to meet Karen and to show her the area I was brought up in, and even prouder for her to see and realise firsthand how well this boy from 'nowhere' had done.

(See strange coincidence, Mike McCartney.)

20th Sighting

Song No.26: EVERYTHING IN REVERSE
Song No.27: SUFFER NOT LITTLE CHILDREN (Oasis of Innocence)

It was around the 13th July 1993, two weeks before I copyrighted the song *'Everything in Reverse'* on 27th July 1993.

This is possibly the most complicated yet extraordinary song ever to come from these sightings.

It entails part of my own life, going back to when I was a 15-year-old. It seems to speak with a maturity and knowledge of life far exceeding the majority of people's comprehension.

It was in the usual place at the end of the bed, about 2.30am, and I was awakened to see a big round disc object, with colours of yellow, green and blue. I rubbed my eyes and clearly focussed on what was in front of me. I saw a band of between 12 to 15 people appear to walk around a flat, circular globe. They all wore robes, not normal 'western' clothing.

It was the world. And they were walking right around the edge. In fact, they were nearing the top of the globe as I watched. The leader had gold mirrored sunglasses on and turned towards me. It was John. He was leading a band of travellers, helping people – mainly small children – to deal with sorrow, or dare I say it, death. I watched and heard John say to the others, "Quick, this child is near the end, get your instruments out." To which they all gathered around, sat themselves down in the sand, and they, and me, watched as John Lennon held a poor, starving young boy, who looked old but was probably about five years old, in his arms. The child had a huge bulbous head and was clearly lapsing in and out of consciousness. His poor face was pained but past the suffering stage and ready to pass away, ready to die. Ready to go to the other side in the sky.

That moment I could have cried. I watched how John gently stroked the child's head, looked around to the musicians, and nodded to them. They slowly and quietly began playing their instruments. He turned back and looked intently at the child. John sang in the most beautiful whispering way I had ever heard. This was unique. John had never once sung, in any of the previous sightings; it had only ever been through thought transferral to me. This, without exception, was always the case. Always.

This had to mean that this moment was very special indeed. He sang, in an almost whispering tone which was crystal clear, the song 'Suffer Not Little Children.' And the opening line was this – 'Hush now, hush now, suffer not little children, wherever you may be. If you're feeling weak and tired with no one to help you, I will comfort thee, - if you go, I'll hold your spirit, and you'll live again through me...'

I watched this man, John Lennon, show untold kindness in such a gentle and moving way.

As he proceeded to sing this reassuring lullaby, I watched intently as I saw the child's poor pathetic contorted face seem to 'smooth out'. He slightly opened his eyes and raised a smile, and he passed away, gently, without fear or pain, comforted in the arms of John Lennon.

I was drained but that song was complete and unforgettable. It took me five minutes to write the song down - words and music – that John had just sung. It was so easy to 'copy' down. The song wasn't to be copyrighted until 13th January 1994. It was complete but went into my file.

This song was just part of the sighting.

Remember, I have said to you, the reader, a few times that sometimes, like in the song *'Abbey Road'*, the song didn't materialise there and then. But I sensed it would come, if it was meant to, at some stage. So if there was no song 'present' I would put all my writings away I'd got from this sighting and carry on as per usual.

The week that followed was strange because things would happen; I got a tremendous amount of déjà vu. I give only one example, but there are more intriguing examples.

I was in Prestatyn, North Wales, which is a coastal holiday town, about 20 miles from my home. I found myself sitting in the car outside a house near a campsite. And as if suddenly I'd woken from a dream, I wondered why I was at this particular location, and bizarrely, why I had come to be in Prestatyn of all places. After about 10 minutes I started the car to head for home. I'd stopped trying to think why I was there and how I hadn't even remembered driving to that location. Then it hit me. Bang, straight between the eyes.

When I was 15 years old I went with three friends camping in Prestatyn. Now as we were running out of money I had gone across to this particular house to nick two pints of milk from the doorstep. At that moment, the lady of the house came out and said, "What are you doing?"

To which I replied, "I'm taking your milk as I've got no money to buy any."

She said, "Put them down, I'm going to phone the police." I put the milk down and bolted like greased lightning.

The whole point of this and other incidents that happened to me seemed to be as if I was witnessing a 'righting of wrongs' that I had done in my life. As if I was being forgiven and was being made to realise I was being forgiven.

The question was why? Was I being prepared for greater things?

Is this showing me, that beyond everything you see, there is so much more? Or was I being given a glimpse of the future, which actually returns to the past? Either way, several wrongs I had done in my life were righted, and although nothing terrible really, these wrongs were lifted from my conscience and I was starting to feel as if I was undergoing a purification exercise, some kind of cleansing process.

At this stage nothing musical entered my head, just an almost numbing, incredibly humbling experience. Then one week on from the sighting of people walking around the world, and a couple of days after the Prestatyn incident, I called to get some petrol from a petrol station in Heswall, on the Wirral, on route to pick some print up from Nicholls Print.

I filled up the car and went to pay. As I got my Access card out of my wallet, I looked up and turned towards the assistant to hand the card over. I was almost blinded by these gold mirrored sunglasses reflecting the sun onto me, which were on a counter carousel. Instinctively, I said, "Oh, and those sunglasses please." When I got in the car I put the sunglasses on. Round, gold mirrored, just like I had seen in the sighting, and not the sort of sunglasses a smart rep would wear. I looked down to put the key into the ignition; I started the engine, engaged first gear, and let the clutch out.

Being a rep all these years, what with the thousands upon thousands of miles covered on one's territory, I used the common signals of most reps. Not mirror, signal, manoeuvre, but manoeuvre, signal, mirror. So I had let the clutch out, I'd put my indicator on, and lastly, I looked in my mirror.

What do you think I saw? I was dumbfounded. Instead of seeing in the mirror what was behind me, I saw what was in front of me! Certainly, not what I'd expected.

What I saw in front of me was in fact a car pulling in towards the front of my now moving car. I jammed on the brakes so hard I thought I'd almost buckled the footwell where the brake had pressed against the floor. I made my apologies to the other driver and stopped the car.

That was it. I had the song from the sighting. Complete. I wrote the words and music down before I set off from that garage. The song is called 'Everything's In Reverse'.

There is a line in the song that says 'gold coloured specs in the mirror, rear view, and I see the way forward too, Everything's in reverse, just like the universe, it's like we must rehearse, for when we come again.'

This was a major happening. Everything was beginning to make sense.

This was also to be the song that within 12 months from then, Uri Gellar would want to use for the film about his life. Previously, he had asked for Yoko Ono's permission to use John's 'Imagine' for the film, but Yoko refused and he then wanted to use mine, or should I say, John's.

21st Sighting
Song Nos 28: VILLE D'AVRAY, 29, 30, 31, 32, 33, 34

I had been in a deep sleep that morning of 27th July 1993 when I was awakened by John. He seemed very impatient and almost edgy. He looked not dissimilar to the very first sighting, in as much as he appeared to be asking for my help with this facial expression, which had urgency about it. I was stirred and he made me feel edgy as well. John was to transfer his thoughts to me, which were 'you can start this very unusual album this morning, by doing 10-12 songs this morning.' How ridiculous, you probably think. Well actually, so did I!

Can you believe it? Write 10-12 songs in a day? Well, it was not even a day, but in five hours.

Believe it! I did it, with John's help.

I got up, went down stairs and sat down at 6am. By 11am I had written 14 titles, completed seven songs AND copyrighted the song *'Everything's in Reverse'* as well.

Strangely enough of those seven songs, there are a few lyrics that to date I still haven't written. This album is extremely unusual. I have much to tell about it, but that's for another time. Suffice to say, as well as this very unusual album, there is something that's linked to it involving micro-electronics.

Above, I name only one song of the seven completed that morning. I do this for two reasons.

1st reason: I had gone to bed the previous night (26th July 1993) and I remember sitting, feeling really tired, on the end of the bed where John used to appear. I was admiring my favourite painting by Corot, called Ville D'Avray, which was hanging on our bedroom wall. In my tired state I thought to myself I would love to write a song, something as lovely as that painting.

This was the first song of the seven, completed the next morning.

2nd reason: The other six songs are complete but not yet recorded in the manner that they need to be, and I don't want to disclose them at this moment in time. I hope you understand.

Song Nos - 34, 35, 36, 37, 38, 39, 40
Likewise, with the remaining seven of the 14 song titles that morning, they are to be part of this 'special' album I have still yet to reveal.

Song No.41: TONIGHT

Whilst still 'coming down' from this emotional state of creative awareness brought on by the sighting, I wanted to unwind and relax and thought – now play a rocker. I played one chord - B – and the rest flowed. The song was complete within 10 to 15 minutes.

Song No.42: MARIO FROM ITALY

I had been invited up to dinner at a friend's house in Mold. It was 2nd August 1993.
At this time, still only Karen and one other person knew about my sightings. I kept back from the world this great secret. I reasoned that one day Karen might, just might, see sense. But there was also another reason that played a crucial part in maintaining my silence. I should have known better.
At the beginning of the sightings I told you how I played the first song to Karen. As I played the first one to her at 7.30am on the morning of 15th Nov 1992, 'It Was You', her response had been, "No you couldn't have written it, it sounds like a Beatles' song, I'm sure it was a Beatles' song.' There and then her thoughts of the remotest possibility that I could have written a song were duly dismissed.
The following week, after the second sighting, I also played the second song, 'Yoko, I Love You'. That was on 23rd November 1992. Her reaction to the song was to take me by surprise. She enthused, saying, "That song is beautiful, who sings that? That is the most beautiful song I think I've ever heard in my life. I wonder who sings it?"
Praise indeed!
My response was to tell her, "I've just done it, I've just written it, this morning."
After the usual taunts to me as before, saying, "No, you couldn't have written it, it's just beautiful, but I don't think I've heard it before", I again said, "I've just written it, I have."

She became angry at my insistence that I had just written this beautiful song, and said, and I quote, "HOW CAN SOMEONE WHO CAN'T READ AND WRITE, WRITE A SONG?." God's truth, that's what she said to me. It hurt me, but with what I'd seen, with whom I'd seen, my resolve was unshakeable, and I knew one day I was to tell Karen and the world.

A further two weeks went by and I had, in the meantime, the 3rd sighting, *'Momma, I'm Home'*.

Now I wasn't to play this to Karen, I believe it had John Lennon's fingerprints all over it. It was so obviously a John Lennon song. I didn't know what response I'd get and I never sang it to her.

But this day, she came into the large lounge I was sitting in, a lounge we usually kept for visitors and special occasions. (With hindsight what a load of bollocks!)

Anyway, I was playing the *'Yoko, I Love You'* song, and she sat down and listened. This was about four weeks from the first sighting. And again, she said, "That's the most beautiful song I've ever heard, I'm going to try and find out who sings it."

I replied, "You won't find it anywhere in the shops, because I've written it."

She looked at me in a more sympathetic light, perhaps slowly coming around to the possibility that, yes, Mike has written it. She seemed more understanding and thoughtful about this possibility. She asked me to explain how I was able to write such a beautiful song. I didn't have an answer. I didn't know what to say.

"How did you come up with the first line then?" she asked. Again, I didn't know what to say and remained silent, like a scolded child.

Seeing my reaction, she said in a gentle tone, "Mike, you've probably just heard it on the radio in the car, and remembered it. Something like that."

There and then I decided that enough was enough. I wanted to tell her exactly what had happened. Whatever the outcome, I took a deep breath and said, "You're right. I didn't write them. I didn't write these two songs. John Lennon wrote them. Are you satisfied?"

She said, "I knew it wasn't you!" feeling absolved of any possible guilt she may have had in disbelieving her husband.

I said, "You still can't buy them in the shops though."

She said, "Why ever not? John Lennon's been dead for years."

I said, "John Lennon came to me in this house, in our bedroom, at the end of the bed."

I explained how I'd asked my mum, my dad and God for help and how one week later this happened. Well, you'd have thought she'd just seen a ghost! She turned white, as if the blood was drained from her face.

Immediately, instantly, without a thought for what I had just told her, she said, and I quote, "Don't tell my mum and dad. Don't tell the children. Don't tell any of our friends and don't play any of 'that music' in this house." And she walked out of the room without any discussion, or help or advice, or comfort. She put it out of her head as if it hadn't happened.

If I was sick in the mind, if I was having a nervous breakdown, if I really needed help, at that moment she would have let me go insane; she would have let me die.

Thank God I wasn't sick, thank God I never went off the rails, thank God I didn't 'lose it' and thank God I went deep within myself. I went deep to the core of my existence. There, I found an unshakeable, steadfast belief in myself, a resolve to carry on against all the odds, whatever people might think or say. I found the truth. Deep within, I found a bombproof impenetrable place that I was safe. A place that no one could ever get to and a place where no one ever again could ever hurt me.

Back to the 2nd August 1993.

I had been invited to dinner by some friends of ours called Mario and Julie.

Karen and the kids were holidaying in Spain with her parents, at the outlaws' flat. The flat was near Duquesa, some 30 minutes drive from Gibraltar, the airport they flew into. Her father ran GIBAIR, a subsidiary of BA, and was offered the job as soon as he'd taken retirement from British Airways. We, the family, had been and stayed quite a few times when things were rosy, but this was not the case this time.

Mario was a good friend of mine who I believe was psychic. Mario used to have a party piece whereby he would ask you for an item, something personal from you: a watch, ring, or jewellery. He would then hold it and in normal conversation tell you about things pertaining to the item he was holding. Now he'd never done this with me personally, but at

John and Patsy's house parties we saw him do it loads of times. Always the person he was dialoguing with would say, "Yes that's true, but how did you know that? Someone must have told you." etc. People's reactions were always something in a similar vein. He was always spot on, that is of course if you believed the person whose personal item it was he was holding.

Before we ate, or had a drink, he asked me to come into his little office at the back of the house. Julie had offered me a drink and I said, "I'll have a lager in a minute, thanks." When we got to his office, he asked me if everything was alright, to which I replied, "Yes, fine."

He said, "Are you sure?"

And I said again, "Yes I'm fine, why do you ask?"

He looked puzzled and said, "No real reason." Then he said, "Have you got something on you, that's personal to you, a watch maybe?"

I have never been one to wear rings or necklaces, but, yes, I did have a watch and I handed it to him whereby he told me strange things. He began talking to me, just matter-of-factly through normal conversation, and in a normal way he mentioned the following:

He told me he could see an 'Asian lady', saying, "It's a very, very strong feeling I have, there is an Asian lady, somewhere, and a Ford Zodiac, and a white-haired lady with a nice smile sitting by the right hand side of a very old fireplace." He could also see a tall woman with long black hair. He could see a motorbike which "is causing a huge row".

I didn't utter one word, and in fact he told me whatever he said for me not to agree or disagree with what it was he was saying and wait until the end, so as not to 'sway' what he was telling me. I didn't. Then, with Julie, we sat down and had our food.

Now what I did tell them was my dad used to have a Ford Zodiac.

I told them that in her latter years of living, my mum had white hair and always wore a lovely smile. She always sat on the right hand side of the fireplace in Lyell Street. The fireplace itself was the oldest in Anfield; it was the original cast iron grate, with side ovens, that all the houses had in them when they were first built, some 150 years before. That period, through the 60s and 70s, these black-leaded fire grates were being discarded and replaced in favour of the new, modern, concrete and tiled shite. Mum always resisted the temptation to change that old fireplace. It truly did make our house a real, warm home. I still have the very same old cast iron kettle that used to sit on that grate that used to boil the water for the old tin bath.

I told them that my mum was very tall at 5'10", and she used to have jet black hair, and she used to always wear it long, well past her shoulders. She never got her hair cut even when it became white.

I told them, Mario and Julie, that when I was 15 years old I had a moped, which I used to hide in the entry (that's the area between the back to back terraced houses) where usually only bin men went to pull the bins out of the walls. I hid it there so my dad couldn't see it. It had no tax or MOT or anything. I'd paid 30 bob for it off a mate. It was an old Raleigh moped. Uncool, but it was a little bit of speed and I enjoyed razzing it down Brecky and Stanley Park. I started riding it to school, Anfield Comprehensive.

One day I was riding it back home and I came into the bottom bend of Lyell Street, like Stirling Moss or Mike Hailwood. The machine was virtually on its side – how I stayed on I just don't know. It felt fantastic. Just at that moment I'd cleared the 90º bend, straightened it up and twisted the grip accelerator right back and began to 'gun it'. This was real excitement. It was just then I saw dad's car slowly but majestically turn the corner and turn into Lyell Street in his big shiny bottle green Ford Zodiac. I was 20 yards up the street, he was 10 yards down the street and as I'd seen him, he'd seen me. At the time there were hardly any cars so I couldn't hide. I panicked and banked the bike to get off it and do a runner up the nearest entry, just down from Jimmy Cassidy's house, whereby it slid to a halt and I was off. It happened very quickly and as I was belting down the entry I heard my old feller's voice bellowing like a demented bull, "Mickey, get back to this house right now!!" He was screaming it, and he repeated it, and although he never raised his hand to me in his life, I was sure I was going to get battered. I had no choice. Sooner or later, I'd have to face him. So I stopped in my tracks, turned around and walked back to No. 14. We had the biggest row I had ever had in my life. Dad was screaming on about what if you killed someone, or killed yourself etc. etc. He got the bike and got rid of it.

I never found out where it went, but no question in my mind what Mario had 'seen' was that huge row. He questioned me, did I know an Asian lady, and reiterated the strong feeling he got from my watch. I never told him at the time, denying any connection, but there is only one person, I thought at the time, who that 'Asian lady' could possibly be. It had to be YOKO ONO.

Now, since I let my sister Diana look at the original draft of this book, she informed me that my father had a mistress, at the time my mum was pregnant and carrying me. This mistress was Chinese, and mum knew all about this young beautiful lady. She was in mum's thoughts, most times throughout the pregnancy. Apparently when I was born I had eyes very much like a Chinese baby, and in fact when I was growing up, my friends used to call me 'Chinese owl'.

I left Mario and Julie's house at 12.15am. It took 10 minutes to walk home to my house and once there, another 10 minutes to complete the song *Mario From Italy'*. When I was at their house I had been struck with a painting Mario's eleven-year-old son had done. It was a masterpiece. It was a left hand guitar, painted in vibrant colours and was exciting to look at, it had unbelievable energy. This is also mentioned in the song.

Song No.43: BIZZIE LIZZIE

It was 5th August 1993. The week before I had called to see a friend, Dave, who had previously phoned me, enthusing over something. He said he couldn't talk about it on the phone. So I called to see him. Now when I used to call and see Dave, his mum always went on about her seeing a psychic, Rose Lea, in Liverpool, and suggested many times to me that I go and see her. His mum always used to say how accurate this psychic was. I never did go and Dave and I both thought she was off the wall, believing all that twaddle. To say Dave was a cynic is a gross understatement. So I saw Dave this particular day, we sat and had a cuppa and he said, "You know that Mum sees this psychic regularly and how she was always asking me and you to go and see her?"
I said, "Yes?"
He said, "Well I went last week with Mum and Dad. I told them both that I would be first in, so no one could prime Rose Lea. Mum swore to me that she had never told Rose Lea anything about me."
He went on to say that as soon as he sat down in front of Rose, she leant forward and put her hand on his knee. She said, "You have injured

yourself," just as she placed the hand on his knee. He felt a burning sensation on his knee, then felt nothing. Rose said to him, "The pain has now gone, and you can go about your normal business." She went on to tell him a host of 'truths' that no one else could have possibly known.

Now what Rose didn't know, but I did, was that Dave, like me, was a runner. He used to regularly run around the Carr Mill dam, some six miles, several times a week. But the last six or seven weeks he couldn't because he had injured his knee. It was very painful just to walk on it. It was the same knee that Rose had put her hand on. The knee Rose cured. Dave went running around the dam the day after seeing Rose and it gave him no problem whatsoever after that. Now what Dave and his folks didn't know at the time was what I was going through, seeing John Lennon, and how I believed in psychic phenomena, just from Mario's showing.

So I took the bull by the horns and phoned Rose Lea. She asked could I come to see her the next day, which I agreed to. At this time I never told Dave and his parents that my marriage was in tatters, I always put on a 'brave face', but Dave's mum had a soft spot for me and used to tell Dave, "How nice Mike is, but sometimes seems so down."

It was 10.30 in the morning the next day when I rang the bell at Rose Lea's house, near Edge Lane. It was drizzling and Rose spoke to me on the intercom. She said, "I'll be down in a minute." She lived above a shop between Wavertree and Old Swan.

She opened the door, said hello and shook my hand.

We went upstairs and she proceeded to tell me that I, - me, Mike – was a healer. I laughed and said, "I don't think so."

Categorically she said, "Oh you are, I know, I can tell. As soon as I touched your hand I felt your healing power. You have an incredible gift to heal people, just like I have. And I found out, just as you have done today, from a man who called to see me and told me the same. I was 40 at the time." He had told Rose she was a healer and Rose had laughed in the same manner as I had just done. Rose went on to tell me how well known she was and that to date she had cured thousands of people. She said, "I will give you a special form to send to the Healing Society. I am going to personally recommend you. You must use this gift."

She then went on to tell me outrageous things, things that had happened and things that hadn't happened. This was over a period of about 15 minutes, as we had taken time up discussing 'healing powers'. All the time I didn't confirm whether they were right or wrong, I didn't give her a clue. She said, "You are going to move house, the number 14 is very special to you. You have children, a boy and a girl. The boy, I think is called Timothy, and the girl is called Sophie or Stephanie. One is very artistic, and one is academic. One will go on to university and be very successful. They will both be very happy. You are going to live a very long life. You are going to have a red car."

At that moment I laughed, probably nervous laughter, and said, "I don't think so, I have just bought a new car, but it's blue!"

All she said again was, "You are going to have a red car." She went on to say, "There is something that you should be doing, but are not. Maybe it's your job. You need to be doing something, telling people about something, change your job." She asked me, "What job do you do?" I told her I was a printer. She replied, "No, that's not the job you should be doing, you should be talking to lots of people about something, but I don't know what." She then said, "Now what about your wife?"

I said, "What about her?"

She said, "I know all is not well with her. I'm afraid I don't get a good feeling about it. Are you still with her?" I said, "Yes," and she muttered something and mentioned again that I was going to move house. She also said, "There is a girl you know and have strong links with, called Lizzie or Maggie." She spoke with conviction, but I thought she was only half right, which, I thought was still amazing.

From that moment, I was to remain firm friends with Rose.

I then told her about my Timothy and Stephanie, and how artistic Steph was. I told her that the No. 14 was where I grew up in Anfield. I told her that I was going through problems with my wife. But that was all I could tell her. Because that's all I knew, at the time she told me these things. This was in August 1993.

But what I can tell you, the reader, now in chronological order, is that:

Later that week I wrote a song for a client who, by some quirk of fate, from that day forward became great friends with me, called Liz. She opened up to me one day for the first time in three years, saying how she hated being a buyer and how she longed to be a musician. She poured her soul out to me, which took me by surprise. She asked me to call her 'Lizzie' and I said, "If you want to do music just do it, what have you got to lose?" I left her offices and on the motorway wrote the song all about Lizzie called *'Bizzie Lizzie'*, a slow rocker, in 15 minutes flat. I phoned Lizzie on my mobile within half an hour and told her. She was excited and two days later I sent her a copy of the song. She rang me and said, "It's brilliant!" It was to be later in Jan 94 that Lizzie translated the song *'Etratat'* into French for me. Not long after that she left the company and was to pursue a career in music.

The number 14 was where I grew up but since the first sighting the number five has been special to me, and is my number. I believe John's number was 9. Add the two together, and you get the number 14.
In November 1993, I bought a red Vauxhall Calibra.

In March 1994, I talked to lots of people about something I should be doing, which was going on GMTV and Radio 1 and telling the world I had seen John Lennon.
In September 1995, I was to move house.

In November 1995 Karen and I divorced.

In December 1995, I bought and moved to my own house.

In September 2005, after a 'gap' year, Tim went onto London University, studying product design. A creative degree where he showed outstanding flair and thrived.

Food for thought!

A few weeks after our first meeting I phoned Rose Lea and asked could I meet her as a friend (as opposed to a paying customer). She agreed. I felt I had to find out more about this 'healing' she had mentioned, and that I had to tell her John Lennon was coming to me.

We met at Rose's home and she gave me some basic instruction in how to go about healing people. I won't divulge what she told me. But I took it all in and put it to the back of my mind.

I then mentioned John Lennon was coming to me. She wasn't fazed in the least, and asked what he wanted. I told her I was receiving songs from him, lots and lots of songs from him. I explained the first three sightings and she said to me, "Oh, that's what you should be doing, you should be telling the world. Isn't that marvellous?"

She then went on to tell me that she had been called by the manager of the Cavern in Liverpool (this is where the Beatles started playing). I have forgotten the date she told me.

Rose was special and had built up a huge reputation, unbeknownst to me, in Liverpool. She had a column in the Liverpool Echo and had been on Billy Butler's show. Billy was a client of Rose's. As I've said to you, she was a healer, and only one of 12 registered in the UK who was paid by the National Health. She was always called to 'help' patients when all traditional methods had failed (medicine, treatment etc.) and her track record was second to none.

She said the manager of the Cavern (she told me his name, but I've forgotten) had phoned her and said, "I've heard all about you Rose. Can you please come to the Cavern and help me out?" He mentioned that two of his staff had left petrified one night. They were tidying up, after 2pm, when they had separately seen John Lennon on the last step of the cellar stairs, just standing there. He, the manager, said, "I don't want to lose the staff, is there anything you can do?" Rose went to the Cavern, walked down the steps and, sure enough, saw John just leaning against the wall, on the bottom step. She told me this in a very matter-of-fact way. She said to John Lennon, "Look John, everyone loves you and your music, but you are scaring these poor girls. They work here and they are frightened of you. They need their jobs, but won't come back, they're terrified. I know you don't mean to frighten them." She told me John just disappeared and to date has never returned to that spot or indeed the Cavern at all.

After seeing Rose on this occasion I was sitting with Karen in the lounge one evening, when she doubled up on the floor in absolute agony. It is a complaint she has had since a child. She never knew, or if she did she didn't tell me, what it was, but I had witnessed it at least once a year since I had known her. It appeared to be a 'strangling' of the stomach. Excruciating pain, followed by Karen lying on the floor and adopting a 'frozen still' position. I wanted to call the doctor but she said, "No, I'll be alright." This pain would subside over the following few days and eventually die down. I lifted her onto the sofa after about half an hour and held her hand and her head. I did what Rose had told me to do to heal someone. I did this, and Karen remarked how hot my hands were. She said she was feeling much better but still sore. I carried her up to bed, we lay down and I repeated what I had just done to her downstairs. But this time I felt more focussed.

In the morning she was up with the larks like a spring chicken. She went to work and there was no mention, as there usually was, of any pain.

A few days passed and as we were talking, she said to me, "It's really strange."

I said, "What is?"

She said, "Of all the years I've had this complaint this is the first time that it's gone away completely. Normally it takes days to go."

I said to her, "You won't have that pain ever again."

She said, "What are you talking about, how do you know I'll never have this pain again?"

I told her the story of Rose Lea and how she told me I was a healer, and how I had healed Karen of this complaint.

Sadly, she was fazed by this and made some snide remark to me as usual, totally disbelieving the remotest possibility of what I'd said, that I could have cured her of this complaint. Truth be told, I think she was just frightened by such a possibility, again!!

Song No.44: I'M HIGH
Mid October 1993

Two months later, I went for dinner again to Mario and Julie's house. We had a drink and Mario said, "I want to show you something." Mario handed me a gold ring and asked me, "Can you see anything?" I began just talking, matter-of-factly to him. I saw a man with a wide brimmed hat and a huge feather in it. I saw a red and white colourful market barrow that had big cart wheels on and the barrow was crammed full of fruit. I described the man in the hat. I went on to say other things. All the time, Mario never said a word. He just seemed to be busying himself in his drawers. Didn't even think he was really listening.

I stopped and he had gotten out of his drawers some old photographs.

He showed me a man in a uniform, a military man. He had a wide brimmed hat on that had a huge plume of feathers on it. The man I had described to him was the man on the photograph. It was his grandfather. The barrow 'busting full of fruit' was his grandfather's business. He had the largest fruit growing business in Italy. He had been fabulously wealthy beyond one's wildest dreams. Mario would have one day inherited all this from his father, had his father not divorced Mario's mother. He was a serial womaniser, so Mario's mum brought him and his sister away, right away from her husband, and moved to Glasgow. It was tough going, they had no support and she was a proud, hard working mother who wanted the best for her children. It was also a time that they started going to the Scottish Spiritualist's Church. It was here, Mario told me, for whatever reason, that he was to get this 'special gift'. He had this psychic ability.

I then came out with it and told him straight, exactly what had happened to me. His reply was simple and to the point. He said, "Mike I believe you 100%, you don't have to explain any more." He hesitated for a while and then said, "So I was right about that Asian lady wasn't I?" I said "yes", and we had a good meal and a real good chinwag all about my sightings. In view of what my sister had told me, whether it was Yoko or the mistress, either way Mario was right.

I wrote another song on the way home from Mario's called *'I'm High'*. Mario was only the third person I had told about what happened to me.

22nd Sighting
Song No.45: HOLD THE ANSWER

It was Christmas week 1993 and my best friend, Steve Asplet, was home from sea. He was a merchant ship's officer and worked eight weeks on and eight weeks off. As a consequence, when he did come home, he always liked to live the high life. No expense spared, the best clothes, food, wine, and usually he ended up with a woman as well. No surprise really. We always used to have a ball. Steve was as outrageous as I was, and by comparison, our friends acted like choir boys. He lived like a king for half of his life and the other half he sweated blood in the hold of some huge ocean going merchant ship, making sure the engine kept spinning for his lords and paymasters. They have included the likes of Shell Oil, cable laying ships in Egypt, oil exploration sorties etc. I suppose you could sum up Steve by saying he works hard and he plays hard. I think it was the day before Christmas Eve, in 1993. It was the one day a year, historically, since I'd been married that I would go on the piss. I would get the bus in from Mold to Chester and go on the lash with Steve and all the other lads. We'd pub it, club it, and then we'd end up having an Indian. So I'd doss at Steve's in the top of the house. He lived in a small terraced house, right in the heart of Chester. Originally it was a two up, two down. He'd extended into where his yard was and made a nice kitchen area. The upstairs, that once had two bedrooms, he had broken through and created a third bedroom, which was basically the loft. It was small and he had fitted a small Velux window. In one of the two bedrooms on the floor below he had fitted a luxury bathroom, so the house was quite some pied-a-terre.

We'd got to Steve's house this particular morning about 2.30am, now pissed as farts. We'd had a great time. It was great catching up with all the gossip. There were a few difficult moments when someone would ask how Karen was, as most of my friends had been present at our wedding. Apart from that, it was a champion night. We got back and polished off a bottle of red wine. I said goodnight to Steve, saying, "See you in the morning."

Steve said, "Yes, have a good night's sleep Mike, thoroughly enjoyed the evening, AGAIN!!" (We never ever had a bad one!) "See you in the morning and we'll go and have a full hit, breakfast on the river." I climbed up to the top bedroom and promptly passed out. When I awoke, it was dawn. I looked up and towards the small Velux window. I didn't know where I was but I saw John and he appeared to be talking to Paul McCartney. This was something else new. This wasn't at the house in Mold, this was outside of where I was used to seeing John, at the end of my bed in familiar surroundings. John was standing next to Paul and as he began talking to Paul he was transferring this dialogue in thought transferral to me, in a rather abrupt and frustrated manner.

The whole song was there in an instant - 'Hold the answer, till you hear the question, then you'll know where I'm coming from.' When I got up in the morning I told Steve all about the song. In fact, I sang it to him. I showed him the paper I had just written the song on. He was flabbergasted.

Song No.8: WORLD BEATLES SONG (now completed)
MIKE McCARTNEY, the tape, and the WORLD BEATLES SONG

5th January 1994. This is the song I was told that, after letting him hear some of the original songs from John, Paul McCartney would complete with me. This is the only song I COULD NOT COMPLETE. Look at the date on the copy – 5.1.94. I had the title and the first verse in 1992. Every time I went to try and complete it, all I could see was a blank piece of paper. It wasn't about to come out.

Months and months passed by and I must have taken that piece of paper out of the box a dozen times. I couldn't believe this blank feeling I was getting.

Needless to say, Paul McCartney never got back to me. I believed that it would all happen organically, in this case via Mike McCartney, Paul's brother.

However, due to my TV appearance on 'The Time, The Place', in November 1993, a John Lennon soundalike calling himself 'Billy Shears', Ray Yoxhall was watching the program and phoned me. Cutting the story short, he sang four of my songs and they were almost as I had heard them, or as I had 'translated' them.

This seemed to release an inbuilt tension in me and as a result, maybe for a few weeks or so in the early morning, I would go into the lounge, play the tracks and savour the future. On one such morning I felt the 'lock' being undone on this song, *'The World Beatles Song'*. It is a belter. I looked at the first few words I had previously done, ignored them but kept the same tune, and rapidly wrote the song. You will see reference in the song to –

'Look out baby, what d'you hear, keep yer day job said that man McGear'. This is a direct quote from Mike McCartney, who didn't know at the time what was happening to me. And this is another series of strange coincidences.

It all happened one morning I called to the printers in Heswall on the Wirral. I was waiting for a print job that was needed urgently. I remember sitting alongside the artist, Richard, and having a chinwag. Now pasted up on the spare artist's board was a Special Invitation ticket, ready for proofing. It was the grand opening of the new Maternity Wing of Clatterbridge Hospital, to be opened by none other than Mike McCartney and his wife, Rowena, giving times, dates etc.

I asked the owner, Lawrence, if he thought I would be able to meet Mike McCartney, or should I say, McGear, which was what he used to be called. Lawrence said, "I'll give you his address, but don't tell him I gave you the address." I agreed, picked up the print, and bade everyone a good weekend. It was a Friday.

Monday morning at 9.30am I called to Mike McGear's house. He answered the door and I said, "Sorry to invade your privacy Mike, but I've just written some songs, and I would really value your opinion on them." He asked me how long had I been writing songs, and I replied, "About two months."

He smirked, contained his laughter and said, "You probably won't like what I am going to say, but OK, I'll have a listen. Have you got the songs with you?" I gave him the tape with seven songs on. He then said, "Leave it with me and call back, a week today, that's next Monday morning, same time, 9.30, but you're not going to like what I say." I thanked him and left.

One week later I called to Mike's at 9.30am, and he answered the door. Directly he said, "Hi Mike, sorry, I've had no time to listen to your tape, can you give me another week, and call, say, same time next Monday at 9.30?" I agreed, but I have to say I found it a little strange, the fact he asked for another week to hear seven songs from me, a nobody.

Monday morning arrived and I was knocking on Mike's door again at 9.30.

This time, a maid/cleaner came to the door. I'd never seen her in my life. I asked, "Is Mike about?"

She didn't ask who I was but went into the hallway and I heard her say, "Mike Powell's here."

I also heard Mike whisper, "OK."

He then came to the door and abruptly, almost defensively, said, "Hi Mike, I can't give you an opinion on these songs, I'm not qualified." He hardly made any eye contact with me, and I'm sure he felt awkward.

I was shocked at his apparent rebuttal, given that he'd told me twice before, "You're not going to like what I say."

I pushed him for some feedback saying, "Can't you just give me an idea Mike?"

His reply was spontaneous and he said, "You know Mike, it's all rap in the charts now."

To which I replied, "Yes, but sooner or later everyone is going to want to play music with nice melodies and clear lyrics."

Which again he spontaneously replied to, in knee-jerk fashion without any thought of what was going to come out of his mouth. He said, "I know, our kid's done stuff just like that, and is waiting for the right time to put it out." I think he'd wished the ground would have swallowed him up. He wasn't meant or didn't mean to say that, I'm sure.

I asked if he could pass the tape on to Paul (who he refers to as 'our kid'). He said no. I said, "OK Mike, I'm sorry if I disturbed you, can I have the tape back please?" He went back in the house, and seemed to take a while looking for it, asking at one stage if the cleaner had seen it!

He came out to the door a couple of minutes later and handed me the tape. He then volunteered the following information to me, saying, "If you want to write to Paul, his address is.." and told me where to contact Paul. He then uttered these immortal words to me, "Mike, I wouldn't give up the day job if I were you."

I said, "Thanks Mike," and began to walk down his path to the road.

I got about seven paces when I heard him say, "Mike, our kid only writes and produces his own songs." He winked at me and said, "You know what I mean?"

All in all it had been an eye opener, and begs the following questions.

1. Why did it take two weeks and three visits from me before he 'couldn't give me an opinion on these songs'?
2. How did the lady, who'd never met me, know my full name, as unimportant to Mike as I am?
3. Had he prompted her I was going to call, and why did he whisper 'OK' when she told him I was at the door? Was something secretive going on?
4. He referred to Paul, his brother, saying, 'our kid's done stuff just

like that, and is waiting for the right time to put it out'. How did Mike know unless Paul had divulged 'his stuff' to Mike, and in fact Mike had divulged my stuff to Paul in order to compare?

5. Why hadn't he volunteered to give me my tape back, instead of me having to ask for it?

6. I was encouraged by him 'not to give up the day job', yet he couldn't give an opinion on the songs. Why not? I'm sure, judging from his first comments to me, he would have relished telling me how rubbish they were.

7. Why did he give me Paul's London address to send the songs to?

8. Why did he wink at me after saying, 'our kid only writes and produces his own songs' and, critically, went on to say, 'you know what I mean?'

9. Of the seven songs he and/or Paul listened to, one song was 'Abbey Road'. Within the two weeks of him hearing the song, and keeping me waiting for a response, the old cast iron street sign Abbey Road had been removed and disappeared from where it had been for well over a 150 years, high above the pavement. Not, I am sure, the act of some foolhardy person, because it required a 15' ladder to take it! And why now? The timing in Beatles terms was nothing special. The sign I went to see immediately after my sighting was very old and original, just like the Lyell Street sign I picked up off the floor during demolition in 1980 and still have to this day. The Abbey Road sign that I had seen days before giving Mike the tape had vanished just two weeks later. The only possible 'why now' answer I could come up with was that my song contains controversial words, pertaining to - 'someone else writing the signs, writing the songs, here it belongs, Abbey Road in Liverpool where nobody's fooled...' Strange that Mike McGear winked at me after saying 'Our kid only writes and produces his own songs. Know what I mean?'

In Scouse language it's like a plumber loosening a pipe to a boiler and telling his apprentice to, 'Go and tell the owner that they need a new boiler,' winking at the apprentice, 'you know what I mean?' In Scouse language it's dodgy, it ain't kosher, it's not right but it's how some things are done. And that is what I was being told, and how I assimilated the information given to me by Mike McGear.

There are other strange coincidences, appertaining to the other songs, as given to Mike McGear, but they will wait for another day.

After these meetings the penny seemed to drop and I was able to complete *'The World Beatles Song'* without help as I'd thought I'd needed from Paul, through John's sighting and thoughts originally.

23 rd Sighting
Song No.46: FIVE YEAR BLUES

It was about 3am, 3rd January 1994 and I woke up to see John lost, wandering through the streets. I am not sure where he was. He appeared to be drunk or drugged. He was crying out for what was inside him to come out. He was confused; he saw shadows of people in doorways and corners. The buildings were brick. I don't think it was a terraced street. It was bigger than that, like old office buildings, or some sort of warehousing. He was lost and had wet himself, all down the front of his trousers. There was an anger bubbling beneath John's exterior.

Remember, I have said that the number five has been very special to me from the outset of these sightings. One week before this sighting, a magician was performing around the tables in the lounge bar in Theatre Clwyd. He invited me to help him with a trick; it was a very casual affair. I turned over the cards from the deck he was dealing to me and it was unbelievable. He dealt me five number 5 cards, every one interspersed with the joker cards. I knew it was going to be in a song in the future, but I didn't realise it was going to be so, so quickly. The song *'Five Year Blues'* makes reference to John's 'state', or feelings he had at the time. This song, as with *'Wish I Could Fly'*, is meant to be 'screamed'. The first line reads, 'fingernail, thumbprint worn upside down, seems it's gonna be all the rage, secret service envoys pretending to be rent boys, why follow me I'm off the world stage...'

The last verse makes reference to 'the joker in the theatre bar, screamin' was I dead or alive...'

24th Sighting
Song No.47: ALL THAT I HAD

The marriage was well and truly over, but I had to stay put on the advice of my solicitor. These past several months I had no money left in 'our' account. I couldn't afford to keep pace with all the 'reply to correspondence' via my solicitor that her best friend's husband, the solicitor, kept sending. So I arranged to pay some of the accruing costs by standing order, £80 per month to my solicitor, and I was successful in being granted Legal Aid. All it means is at least you can now afford to continue lining the pockets of the legals, but you can't afford to live. And then, when it's all over, the Legal Aid Board requests their money back. What a great little legalised cabal we have going here. Nothing I could do. Just keep building a file of useless paperwork and copies of copies of bullshit, lies and continuing innuendo, all adding up to thousands of pounds, and the dream – shattered.

It had been months and months since I had shared my bed with Karen. So acrimonious were her constant demands, threats, actual violence and lying innuendos in front of our children, all designed for me to crack. Perhaps she wanted me to retaliate and knee her where she had kneed me, in the privates. Perhaps she just wanted me to go, then lay down and die somewhere. Perhaps she was blotting out the truth with Prozac and Stella Artois, and perhaps the barrage of solicitors' mail was sent regularly like dripping water to wear away the stone.

I forget the precise date it happened, but by now I'm sure you have twigged that I am getting certain visitations from a certain John Lennon. Always, whatever the situation, I have never felt threatened, only on the very first sighting but not for long, and the initial couple of seconds of the third sighting.

Well this particular night I woke up about 2.30am. And I felt that someone was standing right over me. Inches away I thought. I thought it must be John. But John didn't show himself and I suddenly got a 'bad vibe' feeling. I can't describe it, but I know someone was there, and it was not John. Slowly, as before, I stayed focussed on where this 'thing' was, and reached across to the light switch. I slowly found the switch without daring to move or blink my eyes.

I switched on the light to find Karen standing in the pitch black with her arms behind her, leaning right over my body. I always slept on the left hand side of the bed, and she was leaning right over from the right hand side of the bed. Her face was no more than three inches away from mine. When I saw the big black dilated circles of her pupils I screamed at the top of my voice, as if I was going to have a fight, "Get out! Get out!!!"

It took her by surprise and she rebounded backwards, enough for me to spring out of bed and protect myself, in case she wanted to do me harm. As she left the room quickly, I couldn't see if she had anything in her hands. But, still screaming, self-preservation kicked in and I promptly ran after her. We confronted each other in the kitchen and I asked her what the hell she was playing at. She seemed almost as if she were drugged as she nonchalantly smirked, "I just wanted to see if you were in bed." I asked why she didn't just put the light on. She didn't have an answer, but I did.

I told her never, under any circumstances, while I'm in this house, ever to go in my bedroom again.

The following morning, after no sleep and after barricading myself into my bedroom, I fitted a bolt on the inside of the bedroom door. That very horrible and nasty incident would never happen again. This incident, I stress, happened ages before this sighting.

So, it was 18th March 1994, 1.30am and John appeared before me for a brief few moments.

No music entered my head and to be honest, this sighting, this time, I didn't understand what he wanted. There was nothing categoric, I just lay there and got up just before 5am. I thought about why John had come to me that early morning, as I made myself a cup of tea and sat at the piano. After about three hours of playing the piano I hit three chords and in a flash the words 'All that I had, I gave to you, gir-rl...' came to me. I then wrote the whole song, word for word in less than 15 minutes.

Times they were a-changing.

At this time my world was upside down. We, Karen and I, were living totally separate lives. We tended to the children and never argued in front of them. We would alternate taking them to school and picking them up. Always, when I picked them up, I would have this impending feeling of dread about the future. I would think about all our futures. I'd think about my future, not with the children and not with Karen. I would think about the children's future, with their mother but not with their father. I thought about how the children would react to me having to leave the house. Would they think that I was abandoning them? Should I tell them the truth? No, I couldn't. They were too young. I couldn't tell them what their mother had done. I kept it to myself.

It was awful. Karen would goad me, almost as if she wanted a reaction that she could capitalise on through her solicitor. She wanted me to just go, leave the home, get out of her life forever, as if I had never existed. She wanted me just to go, just to leave, so she could put me out of her mind and dismiss me as an embarrassment that she could well do without. The fact that she had destroyed our marriage never seemed to enter her head, that she had been the cause and the blame for it during this period. We would go to school events and services together, and to the outside world everything between us was hunky dory. My mail was being opened and resealed. I found detailed documentation about my limited company, its workings and my pension plan broken down in incredible detail. This was all in Karen's handwriting. Where did she get this information from? Who authorised it? Certainly I didn't. I also knew that my pension company had informed me that my wife had been trying to access details about my account, to which she was told they were not authorised to give her. There was information over four foolscap pages. Some of the information and figures that were written down I didn't even know! She was obviously planning in detail exactly what she would be entitled to. I had always been an open book regarding our finances and I kept nothing from Karen. But it just shows how someone so close to you can deceive so wholeheartedly.

25th Sighting

Song No.48: NO TITLE, retitled LOVING AWARENESS.

Six months earlier, in October 1993, I had seen John standing at the end of the bed, just looking at me. He looked blankly at me. And I wrote what I believe he was thinking. It was clearly a song, but it was incomplete.

His thoughts (and of course the song) were – 'there's only one way to go, only one way I know, there's nobody you can phone, you gotta do it on your own – there's only one way for sure, you'll get out so much more...'

So I put it into my box and forgot about it. But I remember the incident clearly, the song was complete but the title wasn't, and I gave the song an unusual title, called *'No Title'*. The chorus, although complete, didn't have a 'hook'. I guess it was just a bit 'blank' and what I'd written I didn't know whether it was because John was looking at me blankly, but I did know that No Title wasn't meant to be the title in the scheme of things.

Another coincidence was to happen on 27th April 1994. I was coming out of the Mersey Tunnel and my mobile was ringing. I eventually pulled over and spoke to Ronan O'Rahilly. This was the Irish entrepreneur who in the early 60s had started the pirate radio station Radio Caroline. He contacted me after seeing me on GMTV and was one of John Lennon's closest friends. (John asked Ronan to manage the Beatles after Brian Epstein's death, saying, 'Ronan, you are the only one I can trust.') Ronan was advising me and as he had all the credentials I never questioned him at all. We talked about what I had been doing, and, during the conversation, he said two words to me – LOVING AWARENESS. Immediately, I said to him, "I've got the song that those words belong to. At the moment it's called *'No Title'*, but now it's called *'Loving Awareness'*." And I promptly sang the whole song to him.

He was taken aback and said, "If I wasn't hearing this first hand, I'd find it so hard to believe. It's incredible. It's weird. There's definitely something going on. Perhaps John is orchestrating everything?"

That night I got the song *'No Title'* out of the box and finished it. Firstly, I renamed it and copyrighted it with its new title *'Loving Awareness'*. The whole original chorus went, purely because it was replaced with – '...Loving awareness, a warming and a nearness, loving awareness, showing some people kindness, anything else is meaningless..'

At this point in time I had been on GMTV and had received many offers for management, a record deal, many, many interested parties inviting me to speak at various lectures. I appeared and was interviewed on a few BBC radio stations around the UK. Amongst them I list BBC

115

Coventry, BBC Merseyside. BBC Radio 1 with Emma Freud. Through the BBC and on the strength of the Radio 1 interview I was contacted by Dominic Savage. He was a producer for BBC's Forty Minutes. He spoke enthusiastically to me about doing a whole programme about me and my experiences. Eventually I contacted GMTV and told them not to give my phone number to anyone else. In fact it was two days after my request that I got the last phone call, which was from Ronan O'Rahilly. It was Ronan who advised me to go underground, say nothing, accept nothing, speak to no-one, and it was Ronan who said if I worked hard he would get me the right deals for record and TV. He advised against going down the route of the BBC Forty Minutes programme, as well as the Uri Geller contract. He said to me 'If anyone asks you Mike about John Lennon, tell them you went a bit 'doo-lally' and you don't want to discuss it anymore.' He also told me not to mention his involvement with anyone. I have to say I believed him totally. Alas, nothing was forthcoming.

On board Radio Caroline with Ronan O'Rahilly

Year after year went by. Then 10 years went by (10 YEARS!!) and always, when I expressed my frustration at jumping through his hoops and no nearer to a deal or 'the launch' he used to talk about, he would always say to me, and I quote, "You don't think for one minute you are ready do you?" Then he would go on to say, "I am not prepared to jeopardise my reputation, which is solid." He would always throw serious names into these conversations, such as, "I had coffee with Cynthia Lennon today. When we're ready, she will be on the programme..." or "I was with Yoko and Michael Phillips at the Chelsea Arts Club, I am organising something for her... when we're ready you will meet her."

He met Paul McCartney in a nightclub, and McCartney came up to Ronan and they had a great chat, with Ronan saying, "He was all over me." A far cry from when they had met on the set of Give My Regards to Broad Street (but that's another story). Same dialogue about Sir David Frost, Melvin Bragg, Clapton, the list went on and on. This happened year after year. It was always 'when we're ready', always. During many frustrated conversations I had with Ronan, I'd ask him outright, can you arrange for me to meet, say Yoko or Cynthia or McCartney. He would simply say, "Mike, you're not ready, and I am not going to jeopardise my cred." When I would say to him 'you said you would arrange for me to meet Yoko', his response was – 'I said I could, I didn't say I would'.

Why did I put up with this over all those years? Firstly, I am loyal. Secondly, Ronan was a master at dangling the carrot. Thirdly, I believed him. He was always heavily into conspiracy theories. It made me think. Eventually, I started to question the reasons why he was holding me back. He'd always say to me, "You only get one shot at this." I asked him for that shot, but he wasn't prepared to take it. The more I went on, not questioning his judgement, the more uneasy I became.

One day, when the penny was dropping for me that he wasn't going to get the deal he'd promised me, it brought back memories of the very first meeting I had with him in the Oriel Brasserie, Sloane Square. After the three hour meeting, my old friend Steve Asplet came in and I introduced Steve to Ronan, Katherine and Michael Joseph. Katherine was beautiful and French and was married to Ronan and had been a model for Vogue. Michael Joseph also went by the name Michael Dean and was Ronan's old friend and confidante. Ronan told me he and Michael had set up the London Actors Studio, a place where method acting was taught. Steve is a realist and also a bit psychic, and after that first meeting he would ask how it was going with Ronan. After a year with nothing happening, apart from me relaying to Steve the stories Ronan had been relaying to me of the heavy duty people he knew and was meeting, Steve looked inquisitively at me. He said, "Mike, Ronan O'Rahilly has sent you underground because the Beatles, or Yoko, or Apple don't want you upsetting the applecart. I bet he is being paid to keep you down. What other reason can there be? The music is brilliant, you have been on GMTV and Radio 1, and BBC wanted to do a 40 minute documentary about you. It's a fantastic story. Someone is paying him, and he is doing a fantastic job keeping you down. Do you realise the power and money behind the Beatles? They don't want a no-mark from Liverpool ruining everything."

I thought of the conspiracy theories Ronan had talked about in fine detail. He was making a film about Bob and John Kennedy and Martin Luther King, and how their assassinations were not the work of lone gunmen, but some government agency or other. He told me how John Lennon's assassination was exactly the same. The more I thought about the possibility of him keeping me down, the more concerned I became.

By the way, at this time in 1994 the as yet and secretive unknown Beatles Anthology was still one year away. The irony was that when it came they had taken two John Lennon songs (*'Free As A Bird'* and *'Real Love'*) and added to them in a studio. For Christ's sake, even Paul was quoted that John Lennon was around, saying, "I can feel him in the studio." Also, one of the speakers in the recording studio blew, and Paul quipped, "Oh it's only John." These statements I point out happened a couple of years after Paul had heard about me through his brother Mike, after we dropped a tape off to Paul's PA at his offices in London, and the GMTV interview, and no doubt his agent I sat with at the Brit Awards in 1994 (Geoff Baker). Geoff gave me his business card after I relayed the story to him. (My friend Steve Asplet was also witness to this.)

THINK ABOUT THE ANTHOLOGY AS A REASON FOR A POSSIBLE 'CONSPIRACY THEORY'!!

The last time I ever talked to Ronan was in summer 2006, I asked him if there was any news for me. His reaction, the way he talked to me, was dismissive, as he had been over the last several conversations I had with him. In fact, the last time I ever met him was outside the Oriel Brasserie in Sloane Square with my son Tim. It was in September '05. Tim was at London University and I had gone to visit him for the weekend. I stayed at Tim's hall of residence. Several days before I had tried to contact Ronan to let him know I was in London to see my son, and wanted him to meet Tim. I never got a reply, which was virtually unheard of. We literally bumped into him and I introduced Tim to Ronan, who was with an Asian woman. He looked embarrassed and although I invited him into the Oriel Brasserie in Sloane Square for a coffee, he declined and left very quickly. In 12 years of knowing Ronan, I would have sworn he would at the very least had a coffee with me and Tim, particularly knowing how dear Tim was to me. And he was supposed to be my manager.

The last phone conversation I had with him he was reluctant to talk to me, again. He told me he wouldn't put another pound coin behind me. I felt very sad and felt he was washing his hands of me. More hurtful than anything was that he never gave me a reason. Over the whole period, I had never been given his home address, I never knew where he lived, despite asking him for his address several times. He had stayed at my house and visited me there many times. When I periodically became disillusioned with Ronan, I would write letters to him and had to send them to his solicitors – c/o Schilling and Lom. He would get them and feel it an affront, an embarrassment if you like, that I wrote via the solicitors, and of course at the contents contained therein. I used to say, "Where else can I write to you, you haven't given me any option." He did have an address years ago on King's Road, where I could send mail to him, but he had since told me not to send anything there, two or three years before.

Ronan, as I have mentioned before, would often drop so many names to me in our conversations. One he mentioned as being a good mate was Neil Aspinall. This name meant nothing to me and for some reason, he mentioned this name again in our last telephone conversation in 2006, about him 'not being well... it's all ending.' This didn't make sense to me, but as we were parting company, I didn't ask him to explain what he meant, because I was still reeling at his decision to drop me.

In 2007, a year after we had parted company, I got a call from an old friend who wanted to discuss what the last 12 years had been about with Ronan O'Rahilly. He asked had I checked the internet or done any research regarding the Beatles and Ronan, to see if there was any connection that may have been written about them. I told him I hadn't, to which he implored me to look. This I did and to my astonishment, I was flabbergasted to find out that 'RONAN O'RAHILLY WAS SPECIAL ADVISOR TO APPLE CORPS, AND THIS WAS ORGANISED BY NEIL ASPINALL, CEO OF APPLE CORPS.'

I was still having visitations from John, and I was busy writing all the different songs. I was also singing in my car between calls, all the time, for hours on end. I would sing at the top of my voice, at full belt. I knew I was straining my voice, but I felt I had to keep doing it. I had a dictaphone and would listen back to the songs. I had a throat infection and went to the doctors. I then got a letter referring me to the ENT (ear, nose and throat hospital). I was concerned, as this came right out the blue. The doctor had told me, just to be on the safe side, to have something checked out. I went to the hospital and the next thing was a tube was being pushed up my nose and down into my throat. It was a camera. I remembered the doctor saying to me after the examination, "I don't want you to raise your voice over a whisper for the next six weeks." I laughed at him and said that I had two young children, and I talked for a living. He explained the geometry of my vocal chords and box. He drew a cross section of my voice box and told me, where most people have a large bass box, with a small triangular treble or 'tweeter', mine is exactly the opposite. He was very concerned that I may lose my voice altogether. He insisted that I only whisper for a six week period.
Of course I didn't, but was concerned of the possible ramifications of me abusing my voice.
Meanwhile, I would think about the visitations and question 'why me?' and I would strain my voice hour after hour, day after day, and I knew no harm would come to it. (In one of the sightings, this worry had been on my mind, and through thought transferral, John had told me to keep going, that one day I would sing to the world. I ignored the doctor's instructions and if anything sang louder, harder and longer than before. I broke through so many barriers at this time. One of them was the

ability to be able to sing hour after hour non-stop. Many times I would sing for five hours. A couple of times, I actually sang for over eight hours, non-stop. My throat healed, the doctor gave me the all clear, and my voice improved beyond recognition, so much so that Ronan told me, 'You are now a contender, what you have done is pulled off seven miracles. It is unbelievable.'

26th Sighting
Song No.49: BLOOD TIES

In early February 1993, around the 5th, this sighting happened. It was another one of those encounters where John had passed a song to me that I had chosen to put away in my files until a later date. The later date was to be in May 1994. I got the song out of my files and recorded it, whilst at the same time I also copyrighted it as I do with all my songs to prove I have done them.

It was 2am in the morning, of that I'm sure. It was only the second out of body experience that I had ever had in my life. The first experience being that profound second sighting, when I saw Yoko Ono.

I woke up and saw John appear to be sitting in a plastic 'bubble'. I can only describe it to you as I saw it. It looked like two fronts of a domed helicopter, joined together. The bottom dome and the top dome were hinged together, creating a plastic bubble. John appeared to be hovering in this 'thing' that I could see moving up and down, slowly but irregularly. Only inches of movement, but nonetheless it looked like it was hovering. John was sitting in it and was looking to my right, the way the craft was pointing.

After experiencing these sightings, the more sightings I saw, though they were always special, the more routine they became to describe. I had accepted what was happening to me very early on. It was matter of fact, and, dare I say, it's like some job you get used to and just get on with it. Similar to a heroic ambulance man or policeman would say after saving someone's life. Aren't those heroes always quoted as saying 'Oh, I didn't do anything special; it's what I've been trained to do.' That's how I would describe it also. It was always the same. I would awake, see the sighting, usually rub my eyes, look again at the image, only taking a few seconds to assimilate what was happening, seconds to focus and tenaciously concentrate only on what was in front of me, only on what I was experiencing at that second. So clear it all became, instantly.

John turned and looked straight at me, and straight into my brain. He was wearing a white robe, and clear round glasses. I could see the whites of his eyes, and feel the depth of his concentration, and his deadly serious manner, as he focussed right in on me, to the back of my brain, to the core of my electrical system, charging right down through every sinew of my body. I did exactly the same, back to him.

I felt myself going forward out of my body, towards John and this 'craft'. I saw this 'bubble' open. John's eyes never left mine. He was sitting on what looked like a plain wooden slat seat, no more than 12" wide, unsupported, but to the edges, across this craft, similar to a rowing boat seat. I climbed inside and sat alongside John. It felt very small, minuscule. It was cramped. I remember sitting down and thinking, this is a time capsule, plastic bubble, watching the world go by, like the water bubble you can never catch, floating around in the corner of your eye. And that is the opening line of *Blood Ties*.

The domed 'bubble' top closed and we travelled extremely fast. There were no controls, just a clear view all around the craft. You could see everything. We travelled about 100 feet off the ground; the grasses were a blur, like palette knife painting, as was the blue water and yellow sand. This happened all in a lightning quick blur. We were then 'locked' into some other trajectory, as if we'd been catapulted, and then felt a 'whoosh' as we travelled away from our planet and was able to complete a sort of huge oval in space. On rounding this huge curve, heading back towards Earth, I saw a mist trail from where we had just travelled – that's how fast we'd been travelling. I then saw a group of Native Americans sitting in front of a tepee, thinking about their futures' past and their 'blood ties' from their world to their forefathers'. We then arrived back to my bedroom, and I remember going backwards onto the bed and back into my body. I had been sitting up, so when I went back into my body my legs and the base of my back were a bit sore. But nothing like my neck was on the 2nd sighting. This song was completed in about 15 minutes.

Looking back, how I kept myself together beggars belief. I would go about my business and no one knew any different about how emotionally drained I was. I would tend to the kids and play and read to them, but on the inside my heart was crying constantly. The thoughts of not being with them every day, sometime in the future, and the feelings they might eventually have of me 'deserting them' was sometimes too much to bear. I still did circuit training, twice a week, and felt a slight respite from the pressures brought on by Karen. Meanwhile, she would see friends and talk to her parents and Phillip, her brother, giving them a running commentary on her husband and his antics. Not forgetting, of course, to martyr herself. The kids were brilliant, and although we never argued in front of them, they must have felt something. Tim would do his homework and Steph would draw or play with her toys. She idolised Tim and hung on his every word. It was lovely to see.

27th Sighting

Song No.50: JOHN AND ME, AN ADVENTURE IN MUSIC AND SOUND

'A parity that I see, look through him, and you'll see me' - taken from the sighting, the song, *'John and Me, An Adventure in Music and Sound'*. What was perfectly clear was that all those months of 'mantra' and 'coffee cup release' enabled me to focus and allowed me to do what I'd been trained to do. Pure concentration, pure unadulterated clear mind to receive, just like a transmitter, thoughts from John and thoughts from me to John, so clear. It's just like having a normal conversation like we do today, but without the need to speak.

Around 10th February I woke to find John standing at the end of the bed, just looking at me. He was being very soulful and had a yearning inside of him that I recognised. He seemed to release his innermost thoughts to me and I empathised. I began feeling an intense ache in my heart, as I had done several times before whenever I thought about Karen. But this ache wasn't about Karen. It was about John. It was a feeling of no hope. It was a feeling of intense sadness, an incredible and frustrating feeling of 'unfinished business'. He needed to keep writing songs. It was his life, and in death it was still his life. He ached and longed to be able to finish his unfinished business. It's a bit like a loved one that leaves you. You continue to grieve. It's worse than bereavement whereby at some stage the grieving stops. The analogy is that John's in this all-knowing world. He has all these songs, he can't come and release them on Earth as he was used to doing, but he can see everyone and he wants so much to come back and help people through his music. But, simply, he can't. And he knows it. All he can do is all he did. He searched this Earth to find someone that could 'help' him. He knows how his music would help people. Remember Imagine? His frustration is immense. I was doing my best, and as I said in my prayers, one week before John came to me, 'Dear God, you can see the way I am, please help me. I've lost everything, and it's as if I've got everything to give. Please help me'.

John Lennon has got so much of himself to give. The more I go on, the more I am finding out he was also a giver. Now, only people close to him when he was alive would be able to confirm or deny this, but I am positive he was a giver. I believe this because people never change.
He knew I could do it. He knew I could receive and deliver these songs to people, here on Earth.
I think the song *John and Me* was done on a moment when he came to me, but I somewhat caught him off-guard, wide open and laid bare. It was like when you come across someone crying. Immediately they put on a brave face but they can't stop their tears flowing, you know something is wrong and they can't hide it. It was like that on this occasion, but before he knew I was there, off-guard, as it were. I felt his innermost being brought forth from within. Poor John. His death was an incalculable waste of such magnificent, sheer raw talent. It was oozing out of his every pore. Day in, day out. Ad nauseam.

JOHN LENNON, still very much alive in the 'other world'

My days consisted of taking print orders and delivering the finished goods to various customers throughout the North West. I would sing the songs that John was giving me, singing full belt in the car. People must have thought I was accompanying the radio, as I tapped the dashboard and drove along. I would call to the likes of Vauxhall Motors, where I would see the buyer and take down the necessary information to quote him on. I would get in the car and set off to the next call, picking up where I had left off on whichever song it was that I was singing.

How crazy it all was when on one level, in the cold light of day, I was dealing with the reality of my job in print and in the next instant, in the darkness of night, with the reality of John Lennon coming to me and giving me all these songs.

28th Sighting

Song No.51: BLINDMAN

It was 18th February 1994.

It was a Friday evening and I was on my own again. Karen had decided to take the kids down to Abergavenny to spend the weekend with her parents. No doubt out of duty, and a means of 'escape' from the truth she was still hiding from the world and from her parents.

What's that saying, you can run, but you can't hide.

So I was in the house when I got a call from my friend Mario. He asked what I was doing that night. After a chinwag we decided to go for a bevvy. He called to the house about 8.30pm. We walked the couple of hundred yards into Mold town centre and found ourselves quaffing a pint of best bitter, and in Mario's case a pint of lager, in no time at all. The evening flew by and we decided to take a cab to a rough club in Deeside. It was attached to the leisure centre, a place where I had been circuit training twice a week these last five years. This club I had only ever been to once before, and its reputation was not good. I suppose a taxi home from here (the nearest club, with the latest drinking times) was about £5. If we had gone to Chester the taxi probably would have been nearer £30. So we opted for the nearest, latest opening doss-house. We entered the night club. Can you imagine? It was the pits. People were wearing trainers, jeans and had tattoos, and the lads weren't much better! There was an aggressive air about the place and we were ducks out of water, although as soon as we started drinking again we fitted in, and we were like ducks on the water: 'one of their own'.

Now all I can remember, when we entered the club, was Mario saying, "You won't find any Lamborghinis in this car park." We had a good giggle and afterwards, about 2am, we ended up going to a burger bar.

We had our burger and chips – mmm!!... yuk! And duly got a taxi back to Mold. Mario dropped me off and headed for his house. This was by now about 2.45am. We'd had a great night downing beers and spirits, and Mario really did cheer me up and lift up my spirit.

I have told you about the curtains in my bedroom totally blacking out the room. It was pitch black even in the daytime with the sun up. So I fell into bed this very early morning and promptly passed out. I was awakened with a start. I was hung-over. Something that was more unusual than not, despite our situation and domestic arrangements. But in all the fuzziness, I saw John for a split second, and then just as quickly he vanished, disappeared. Now in that split second I saw he was wearing dark round glasses and a single word came into my mind. That word was PICASSO.

Let me try to explain to you the speed of what happened. Imagine picking a volume of a book up, say it's one inch thick. Opening it, grabbing all the pages, and flicking through them in fast succession, taking only two seconds or so. Now imagine from the book that you have just flicked through, you were able to take in all of its contents, in that two seconds or so. You clearly assimilated what you had just seen. That's what happened to me.

John had given me this song 'Blindman' through thought transferral, instantly. To date I have never had such a song thrust on me by John. It was in its completed form. I have done nothing to it. I couldn't write it down quick enough. A complete entity, given to me by John Lennon. I had never been so excited in all my life, and I ran to the toilet where in all this excitement I promptly threw up; something I never do. There was a complete awareness of what the song was. I never sang through it, it was like the words in that book I asked you to imagine. They were stacked on top of one another, clear as day, all there, in a fraction of a second.

There are references in the song, that refer to John as, 'A blindman sings so sweetly'. Also at the end of the last chorus it says, 'Art's not dead, Picasso's dead, his memory lives on'. I spent from 9am on this Saturday morning until 4pm on Sunday evening trying to use a four track machine. On two tracks I sang and played the guitar. On the third track I harmonised and attempt to play some sort of lead guitar. The fourth track was broken, I didn't know how to use the machine. I couldn't play the guitar properly, but I managed to do it. Then I set a video up and recorded me singing this rocking song, *'Blindman'*. This song was copyrighted the following day, which was Monday 20th February, 1994.

Some two years later there were some articles in the local and national press. In the articles it stated that... 'an old coffee bar in Liverpool called the Jacaranda was having building works carried out when the builders came across an amazing find.' The building had lain empty for years. Rain had got in causing the walls to require being re-plastered. The building was wet through and needed extensive work. On pulling off the old plasterwork and wallpaper, they discovered paintings that John Lennon and Stuart Sutcliffe had done, years ago in the late fifties. It transpired that John had a skiffle group and they played in this coffee bar whenever they could. He also got paid some money to 'paint some designs' on the walls with Stuart. These paintings, and I quote, were in 'THE PICASSO STYLE', and should be preserved for the nation. And that's what's subsequently happened.

Next page:
A cutting from the Daily Mail, 24th January 1996 about the murals painted by John Lennon in the Jacaranda.

WITH A LITTLE HELP FROM PICASSO, JOHN LENNON'S EXTRAMURAL ACTIVITY

Hidden talent: Two of the newly-restored murals in the Jacaranda

Artists: Stuart Sutcliffe and John Lennon

Unveiled after 35 years, pictures from Liverpool's lowly arts club band

THE style is heavily influenced by Picasso — and liberal helpings of bacon butties and coffee.

Free snacks were the young John Lennon's fee for helping paint these spectacular murals on the walls of Liverpool's Jacaranda Club.

With fellow Beatle Stuart Sutcliffe — killed by a brain haemorrhage before the group found fame — he worked on the paintings during lunch breaks from art college in the late Fifties and early Sixties.

Now, more than 30 years on, the newly-restored murals are going on show again as the cellar club reopens tomorrow amid a new wave of nostalgia for the Fab Four.

The occasion will be marked with a performance by Pete Best, the first-ever Beatles drummer who missed out on fame at the last minute, before Ringo Starr replaced him.

first dig. Its fortunes waned over the years, leaving the three murals to crumble.

They were eventually covered first-portrait by Lennon. The second shows two figures on a black background is being interpreted as a couple making love.

Design Association and himself a former Liverpool College of Art student, was brought in to carry out the restoration.

'However, these murals are important not just from the point of view of art, but because of who painted them.'

eloped into a very special one.

To this day I still wonder how I managed to keep firmly on the tracks, never going off the rails as many a cuckolded husband has done in the past, and no doubt many more will do in the future. You just have to look at horror stories where men have been wronged and they can't cope. They don't know what to do. They don't ask for help. They take drastic action, alcohol, drugs, women, physical violence, abuse, anything to numb the pain of being let down by their so called 'loved one'. But it's all short lived. My experience says go within yourself and find strength. I did, and John Lennon came to me. Before he came to me I was a desperate case. But I prayed to God. I asked for help from God and my mum and dad. And I got it. I saw the light.

Now, years later, and after recalling these special events, no wonder I didn't go off the rails. The more this story unfolds, the more honoured and privileged I feel I am becoming. To have shared these fascinating moments with John Lennon, and for me to share these same moments with you is, for me, lovely.

Song No.51: CHRISTMAS ROSE IN A STAINED GLASS WINDOW

It was now 15th May, 1994. I pulled out of one of my box files the song *'Christmas Rose in a Stained Glass Window'* to record it.

How did I come by it?

One morning in early December 1992, over breakfast, the kids and I were chatting. I was also getting the kids' gear ready for school. I was making their sandwiches, I guess I was multitasking! Suddenly, Tim said, in his oh so cute voice, "Dad, we're making a calendar in school for 1993." I asked him what it was about and he said, "The teacher said we shouldn't tell our parents, it's a surprise, but, well, IT'S A CHRISTMAS ROSE IN A STAINED GLASS WINDOW."

I immediately said to him, "That's a song Tim!"

I already had all the words and music, and Tim just gave me the title. It is now done on a piano, not as originally done on the guitar. The chorus is sung by a children's choir. And more information was added, like the following - on 5th January 1994, I had been to Mike McCartney's house on the Wirral, to ask his opinion of some of my songs. I remember seeing a stepped candle in his quaint cottage; I think it was of Dutch origin. And I thought... 'Candles burning bright in a quaint old window.' I think that that was twelfth day following Christmas that you are supposed to take decorations down, or it will bring you bad luck. Anyway those words are in the song. I did the song and then Tim brought the calendar home. I still have it, it is how I saw it and it's beautiful. Colourful and you would swear that the Saints and Angels were joining hands. In fact, the opening line of the song is 'Christmas rose in a stained glass window, Saints and Angels come together.'

Song No.52: OLD TOM, IT'S A FUNNY OLD WORLD

This song was originally done sometime in the early spring of 1994. I was sitting in a pub in Abersoch, waiting for my wife to bring the kids up from South Wales for a weekend in the caravan.

We kept our caravan in Crugan Farm and I had travelled down from Mold, going on ahead to open it up for the season. I would set it up and then Karen would drop the kids off before she returned home, on her own, or wherever she went. It was then of little consequence. All I knew was that I was going to walk and talk and play, and swim with the kids, in a place they loved. I had this tune, and literally read off the restaurant specials board, downstairs in the bar called The Brig. I had the tune, and on 29th May 1994, I replaced the words. The new words were about a man called OLD TOM.

The song is called *'Old Tom'*. It is a song about a fighter pilot who was now a dosser in London by Victoria Station. It's a true story that I added my own thoughts to as to why he may have become a dosser. I imagined a dashing young pilot off to fight a war, but his love begging him not to go. As they hold on to one another for dear life for the last time, they 'swear we will meet on this spot, after the war'. Old Tom had been standing on this spot, literally, for 50 long years. The big question was, was it the right spot? Because his love never showed up. I could almost hear the engine of the Spitfire as I was writing the song down. The once proud and dashing young fighter pilot was reduced to opening taxi doors and lowering his forehead and doffing for a few lousy bob, always to stand on the same spot. He was old, dishevelled, and hadn't thought straight for years and years. He was confused. In the song he questions himself... 'Has she been, did he miss her, is he standing in the right place, he would die a happy man if could just see her face...'

Song No.53: MORAR SKE MOR

It was August 1993 and I was on holiday with the family in Scotland. With us were our best friends, Heather and Allan, and their kids, Fiona and Nick. All the children played so well together, Tim, Steph, Fio, and Nick, that it would have been a tragedy for me not to see these beautiful innocent children playing away to their hearts' content on the beach, in the caravan, silly games around the dinner table etc. This was to be our last family holiday together.

Karen and I were going through the motions of playing happy families, as no one knew what was bubbling away in the background, which, to me, felt like a witch's brew of poison, evil, and green pus, all mixed in and simmering away, in readiness for the expected explosion. The trouble was, only Karen and I knew and it was unbearable. The poor children, God help them.

We had hired a huge old caravan in a place so dear to my heart; it's now almost become my second home. A place called Arisaig, opposite the Isle of Skye, in Scotland.

Years before I had met Karen, I was seeing a girl called Jean. I had met her in a Spanish resort called Calella. I was with Rocky and Billy Warburton (Warbo) and Tommy Prior, who was from the Dock Road. We were getting ready to leave the hotel as Jean was arriving. She caught my eye. Although she had a shock of wavy, mousey-coloured hair, she had amazing breasts, and with the white low-cut string top, she looked for all the world like Marilyn Monroe. We were in the hotel reception area, with our bags packed, waiting to get the coach to transfer us to the airport and onwards back to Speke Airport, Liverpool. This has since been renamed JOHN LENNON LIVERPOOL AIRPORT. We were sitting around having a drink and fooling around with the waitresses and waiters, as well as the hotel manager. They had enjoyed our Scouse humour for two weeks. It was about 7pm, there was disco music being played and we were dancing with some of the girls. We were all 'good eggs', not a rotten one amongst us. We were outrageous, but behaved like absolute angels compared to today's totally open displays of drunken, naked, drug-induced debauchery that supposedly seems 'cool' and usually follows with the phrase, 'I was off my face, I think I had a good time.'

I went over to Jean and said something like, "You're late, I'm just going, why couldn't you have been here a week or two earlier?" Before she had time to answer, I asked, "Where are you from, are you from England?" She told me she was from a place called Elton, nr Helsby and Chester. I quickly wrote my number down and told her I lived in Liverpool, and asked her to give me a ring and we would go out for a drink. We did. We had a ball for seven years; it was great but not 'the real thing' for me. My mum used to say, 'Mickey, one day you will meet a girl who will knock you off your feet, and you won't know what's hit you. When you do, I hope she never lets you down.' Profound words I was to dismiss so profanely. I swore I'd never get married.

I was 21 and I was 'Jack the Lad'. I was still living in Lyell Street where I used to 'club it' and be out five or six nights a week. I was a territory manager, or rep, for a company called RHM Foods. The lads always went to a club in Seel Street called 'Uglys' on a Tuesday night. That was because all the Liverpool and Everton players would go, and consequently so would most of Liverpool's teenage girls, all dying to meet a famous footballer.

We were mates with Stevie Sargeant, who played leftback for Everton and England. He was a local lad made good. It was Stevie who used to train our football team, The Thirlmere, who were Sunday league champions for years. I played on the left wing for the 'Thirly'. We would also train with Stevie's mate, Dave Johnson, the prolific goal scorer for first Everton then Liverpool and of course, England. It was so funny, we'd be in Uglys talking about football, tactics and training, and the girls thought I was some new signing that they didn't yet know. Was I to be the 'next' famous footballer? That's why we went! We'd usually end up walking home about half two in the morning, get up the following day and repeat last night's performance, all over again, in a different pub or club. You could afford to do it then. A pint was half a dollar (two and six), not half a week's wage!

One Monday morning I was standing in a queue with the other reps in the M6 Cash & Carry, just off the East Lancs Road. It could sometimes be a boring life on the road, standing around in a corridor for sometimes three hours just to wait your turn, your glorious 5 minutes, to 'make your mark' in front of a cynical, old, or worse young, 'Hitlerian' buyer, who's seen it all, heard it all before. I used to tell jokes before I sold to them. And I became very good at it, till I knew I could do it in my sleep, then I got bored of it and left. The reps at the time had freedom, there was no sat-nav, no mobiles, and only the under-achieving reps were followed or checked up on. This was something that never happened to me. It was a great time to be a sales rep on the open road.

In the queue was a mate of mine from a company called Batchelors, we used to swap price lists in the queue and be placing our orders. This day, he was extolling the virtues of 'the most beautiful place he had ever seen'. He told me it was Arisaig, and was about 7 hours drive up to the Highlands of Scotland. I rated this guy, he was successful, not an 'also ran', so I respected his opinion and admired his joy for life.

The very next weekend it was a bank holiday and I took Jean up with me to see this place called Arisaig. We went in the repmobile, which was a plastic seated, basic Ford Cortina 1300 – wow! Do you know? I was the only person to date I have ever heard of that broke the huge drive shaft, running from the engine to the rear wheels. That car could do nought to 60 in about eight seconds. And when I was in a hurry to get somewhere, and the engine was going flat out (about 80 mph), I'd kick the clutch right in, just stab it once, and the engine would scream and then shoot forward, and went a bit faster than it ordinarily would have.

We travelled through the night and at 7.30 in the morning we rounded a corner to see this incredible view. We saw this most beautiful sight of the sun coming up, the fishermen's boats, the wondrous rainbow coloured rock outcrops, the far reaching views and the water – millpond still. The silence hit me. The silence was all around. A place, it seemed, where old mother time stood still. It is a sight that will stay with me to my grave. It was a place of peace, away from everything. I still go back to this place, even now, to this day.

We, Jean and I, hired a 'clapped out' old caravan from Jean McDonald on the road leading to Back of Keppoch. She was a canny old spinster of about 75, who lived with her older brother. This caravan was inhabitable-ish, spiders' webs everywhere, dirty, damp, but oh the views were, to coin my sister's phrase, 'to die for'. I didn't want to try anywhere else. Anyway, it would be fine after we'd come home from the local pub cum hotel cum shop, which was to be the case. However, we thought we'd probably get back into the caravan about 11.30pm after a night in this local boozer. Not so.

Thinking about it, it didn't help matters, because after a drive to Mallaig, a walk on the beach, bed for a groove, a shower and some tucker, we headed straight for the bar at 6pm. It was Saturday and we were the only ones in the bar. Slowly it started filling up with locals. We were the only 'foreigners' there, and we stuck out like sore thumbs. Chatting together, it was obvious I was a Scouser. I was wearing combat gear; I loved not having to wear a suit when I wasn't working, and was always more comfy in the army trousers with big side pockets, jumper and this camouflaged string scarf. So the evening was going along at a pace when a man from one of the two couples sitting next to us got up to go to the bar, and offered to buy us a drink. I had whiskey, Jean had vodka and tonic. We joined their table and got into conversation. Normal sort of thing – are you holidaying etc? I replied, "We are just up for a couple of days, I have to be back down south by Tuesday morning." One of the men asked me what I did for a living.

I answered him by saying, "As little as possible."

A short while afterwards I overheard him whisper to his friend, "He's in the SAS, I'm sure he's in the SAS." The couples, I guess, were in their late 50s. Just then, with everyone in the room suddenly turning as quiet as a grave, one of the guys leant forward and said to me, "Are you in the SAS Mike?" I was mortified, but flattered.

I replied in my gentle manner, "No, I'm not." But guess what? They didn't believe me! Everyone was buying us drinks, as the whole room was awash with talk of 'Mike, the SAS hero'! I was slowly getting sloshed on whiskey, chased down by the odd pint of bitter. I then went to the bar and ordered a bottle of whiskey. I thought fuck it, in for a penny, in for a pound. The barmaid said, "Go through to the shop Mike, and help yourself." I struggled to pay for it, such was their regard for this 'hero', and the difficult job he did for his Queen and country.

I was pouring the drinks and soon finished the bottle, whereby we were invited to their house for a snifter and some food. One of the men bought another bottle of whiskey, which we took to the house and duly drained.

On getting to the house I could hear a big dog growling. The owner opened the door as soon as he could; I suppose to stop the din. The door flew open and this huge mother fucker of an Alsatian leapt towards me. I was on the offensive and drew an aggressive fighting stance and screamed at the dog. No more than pure 'pissed' instinct. Then the owner shouted, "No Mike, please don't hurt it!" If he only knew how shit-scared I was, he would have laughed his socks off. The dog calmed down and later sat by my side as I patted it and watched me and the rest get leathered. It was so funny, as they thought I was this incredible fighting machine. I thought I was more like a shite-ing machine.

We left their house about 2.30 in the morning. On the way back to the caravan I fell in a steep water filled ditch by the side of the road, twice. It was about a four foot drop, either side of this narrow little B road. Twice I'd fallen in, and twice Jean had managed to pull me out. Needless to say, in the morning, this non-spirit drinking man's head was in shreds. My tongue was bone dry, my face was gurning in sympathy with my agony from the mother of all headaches. I lifted myself off the bed and fell onto the floor. I crawled up off the floor and fell down again. I remember thinking through all the pain, 'never again'. Even that thought hurt.

After that we were to go up to this place at least once or twice a year, every year.

We went up in 1981, the year after my mum died.

After the first trip up to Scotland we always used the same quiet caravan site, but made sure we always had a decent caravan. I became great friends with the site owners, the McDonalds, sometimes phoning them up for a chat from North Wales. The site was very quiet, not many people about. In fact it was rare to see more than two families on the site. I woke up this particular morning and decide to have a run. Jean didn't do running, so I set off on my own on this glorious sunny May morning, about 7.30am. I still can't describe the feeling I got on that morning, of running with the wind in my hair. More freedom than you could imagine.

I had run about 5 miles to the road overlooking the stunning white sands of Morar. Unusually I stopped because the view was so breathtaking. I sat on a stone wall that was no more than two foot off the ground. I looked out across the sands of Morar, towards the small islands of Rhum and Eigg. The sun was in my face and I had the most wonderful feeling of contentment. I closed my eyes and said a prayer for my mum. My endorphins or something made me feel like I was floating. I opened my eyes within two minutes to find a sparrow standing about one foot from me. This was unusual. It moved closer to me. It came within two inches of me, and I was a bit frightened. I shooed it off but it wouldn't leave. It came back and this time landed about six inches from me. Not only did it land so close but it turned its head, almost like a knowing gesture, something I used to see my mum doing. When mum used to do that same gesture, it seemed to cause a ripple effect to her long hair, down to the ends of her hair. This sparrow was staring right at me. I don't know what made me say it, but I said, "Is that you mum?" The sparrow jumped onto my leg and looked at me with that knowing gesture again. It stayed there, on my leg, for an age. My hairs were standing up as we were just looking at each other and, transfixed, I was beginning to realise that this sparrow was my mum. She had come back to see me, she was a bird in this beautiful place and she was happy. At long last, she was happy.

I began running along the road, crying with happiness. My heart was filled with great joy. And I ran like a two-year-old.

So, moving on several years, and back to August 1993. The last family holiday.

It was about 7am and with all the family still tucked up in their beds I got up and went for a run, to that same place, where the sparrow - my mum – came to me. The weather was glorious and mirrored the same sentiments of my soul on that day in 1981.

I opened my eyes and looked across this expanse of still, calm water and the words and music, just flowed – The song *'Morar Ske Mor'* was complete just as soon as I had sung it, in one go. Straight through, no stopping to think of any words at all.

'There's a place you should see, where the eagle flies,
up from Arisaig, but down from Mallaig, facing the Isle of Skye.
There's a place I lay my head, so many times, peace and tranquillity,
On this beach I lay with my lover, she only wanted me.
Morar, Ske Mor, Morar, Ske Mor...'

Another strange coincidence was to happen, three years after Karen and I were divorced. I had moved house and was living in Broadbottom. I was seeing a girl called Elaine. It was in the year of 1996. As we sped up to Arisaig in my superfast, gleaming red, hot Calibra, I started singing the song *'Morar Ske Mor'*. There is a line in it that says -

'...Captain's face ruddy and smiling, he's seen it all before,
there's someone getting married in the village today, come on we'll have a ball...'

So we walked into the lobby of the West Highland Hotel, with its commanding views overlooking Mallaig harbour and out to the far reaching spectacular views of the Cullin Sound. This hotel was a throwback to the 30s, when the well-healed London and landed gentry would rest from their overnight sleeper train journey from Liverpool St, London, en route to their game reserves on Skye. This hotel, still to this day, offers a polite, silver service and homely welcome long since forgotten in many of our hotels.

We walked up to the homely receptionist, checked in, and then she said, "Will you be wanting to eat in the hotel tonight?" We said yes, and she said, *"There's someone getting married in the village today, you're welcome to join in, after your dinner if you want."*

I asked, "Are you sure it would be OK?"

She said, "Oh, no bother, it'll be a good old knees up and we will all have a ball." (The staff were invited as well, as this is a small, tight-knit community.)

Elaine looked perplexed, gave me a strange look, and said, "That's a line from your song!

Strange eh?"

I believe John Lennon had a relative somewhere in this neck of the woods, in Scotland, and also visited from time to time.

Song No.54: A B C

It was 30th May 1994, four days after our 10th wedding anniversary (26.5.84), or as I say in the song *'What You Doin' To Me'* our 'joke anniversary'. More about that song later on.

It was late at night and I had been playing the piano for at least three hours. I was really tired, when I had a melody line that I appeared to keep going over and over. I didn't know why but it felt structured and rich. I looked over to the bookcase, that same bookcase where the

Liverpool Street Map had fallen from, which had caused me to write the song Abbey Road.

As I was playing, I started thinking and the thoughts became actions and the actions became words.

'Playing the piano in a room, I see a bookcase over there, reading me the riot act,

so many books in all my life that I have never seen, as over there, never took the time, never cared.

My attention is drawn to a red, blue and green book, lying there.

I see the Oxford Dictionary, almost calling out for me.

Glancing at the keys, I think to myself let's go take a look and see.

The meaning of A B C, the key to my destiny.

It said, A is the sixth note of C Major, B is the seventh, C is a natural, as natural as the one who comes to me that no one else can see,

Always looking out for me for me...'

29th Sighting
Song No.55: MANKIND

It was the 21st May 1994 and it was to be the second and the last plea for help I would ask for from Karen's parents. They were having a few months break at their Spanish flat. I had just found out about Karen's affair number 3. I just didn't know what to do. It was almost like self-inflicted pain I was torturing myself with, time and time again. Like the priest in the Da Vinci Code, only I was mentally flaying myself, I just wouldn't let it go. I believed she would see sense. I told Karen I was going away for a few days on business and I drove to Manchester airport. I took a British Airways flight into Gibraltar with the mass of airmiles I had accumulated over a few years of putting petrol into the car. I got over the border into Spain and took a bus to Sabanillias. The ticket was for a three day return.

All this time travelling and I didn't have a clue what I was going to say when I would call to their flat and speak to Ashley and Jean.

I found myself walking up the steps to the third floor, with my small rucksack on my back, and a feeling of impending dread in my gut. I got to the door and rang the buzzer. Instantly, I heard Jean say to Ashley, "I'll get that Ash," and she opened the door. Her look of surprise was soon interrupted with the words, "What are you doing here Mike?" I asked if I could come in and she walked into the lounge. As I followed she said to Ashley, "Mike's here."

When they were both seated, I explained how I still hadn't told anyone about Karen's affairs because I wanted for it to work, so much. They looked at each other and Jean said, "Karen's told me that the affair is over."

I said, "She did finish with John Banks, but she had another, and now, there is a third affair she has started. I've no one else to turn to, she won't listen to reason and seems out of control, hell bent on ruining our marriage. Worst of all, I have said to her, if that's what you want, OK, just go and leave me with the kids. She won't, she wouldn't dream of it. It seems she wants to have her cake and eat it. Doesn't she think anything about Tim and Steph, what would they think? It's criminal."

They asked me if Karen knew I was coming to which I said no. I had told her I was just going away for a few days on business. Jean said she had not long spoken to Karen and she had said everything was alright. To which I replied, "Well she would, wouldn't she?" With that Jean lifted the phone and called Karen. She was more annoyed with me sharing this problem with them, interrupting their cosy little world. Although, as grandparents, they must have abhorred this hideous situation. This time they never questioned its validity, like they did before. They knew, that's why.

Jean spoke on the phone, "Mike's here in Spain, he's told us that you are having another affair. Is that true?" She then repeated the same question. She handed the phone to Ashley and said, "You talk to her, she is saying that she doesn't want to discuss the matter, and that it is between Mike and her." Ashley calmly asked her the same question, but received the same answer. When asked if she had thought about the children in all of this, she repeated again she didn't want to discuss it with them.

We talked at some length and I was finding out first hand, from Jean, how the best form of defence is always attack. She turned everything around on its head and took Karen out of the firing line. She then lined me up as the accused. And with it Jean spoke of the ridicule of 'me seeing John Lennon', turning everything back on me, in fact saying, "Come on Mike, this John Lennon thing, you've just made it up. What do you want, are you seeking attention, what is it?"

I drew breath and replied, "I want me, my wife and Tim and Steph to grow up together. I want to sit my grandchildren on my knee, come the day. I want to live and die with the woman I love. I don't want a bigger house, or a bigger car, or a bigger anything. All I want is for us to be together. I love her, and she said in the church of God, when we married, she loved me too. Can you not understand that? OK, people fall in and out of love. If she doesn't love me, and she wants to conduct these affairs, why can't she just leave me with the children and go, and leave and do what she wants? I don't want to leave my kids, they are everything to me. I don't deserve this, and THEY don't either. I have given Karen everything she has ever wanted, when I wanted nothing in return. I came from nothing, and we have done well. Perhaps she has started to look down her nose at me, the way you always have, Jean. Perhaps she always has, but I was too blind to see. Or perhaps I have served my purpose. I know one thing, I have given too much. I never kept anything for myself. I gave Karen 100% of me. I should have kept something back. I realise that now."

I went on to explain how after praying to God and my mum and dad, all this 'John Lennon thing' happened. I never made it up, I didn't ask for it, and I don't know why he came to me. "But Jean, think on, over all these years of knowing me, of knowing how I've conducted myself, honestly, and trying to do the best for my family, if you don't believe what I say I honestly feel sorry for you. Because it means you've never believed me, or should I say believed in me. JOHN LENNON CAME TO ME, I SWEAR, ON THE LIFE OF MY CHILDREN."

Ashley sat pale faced, pondering. With that Jean eventually said, "It's between you two. There's nothing we can do." I stayed in Spain for a few days. I went to a deserted beach and lay on the warm sand. I thought about everything. I thought about the last ditch attempt seeing the in-laws, to see if they may have some influence on their daughter. Was it worth it? The one thing I was sure of was if I hadn't tried everything, I might end up always thinking what might have been, if only I had etc. I had to try.

I was lying on the beach for no more than half an hour. It was about 3pm and it was brilliantly sunny and baking hot. Suddenly, I sat bolt upright. Someone had just walked over my grave. It was John. Every hair on my body was standing up. On this brilliant hot day and at that second, I felt like I had just been lifted out of a deep freeze. I concentrated on what was in front of me. The water was like a mirrored pane of glass. There were no waves in the ocean, just the delicate 'swashing' of the small tidal current landing no more than six feet away from my feet. The reflection and subsequent heat from the sun on the water was searing, and temporarily blinded me for a couple of seconds. Then I squinted and looked out at the sea and thought, 'that vast ocean is teeming with life, and the sun's piercing rays above and below the sea, where is everyone going?' I wrote the words in my diary.

When I arrived home, I had a letter waiting for me from a woman, D.C. She had seen me on the television in March 1994 and had phoned GMTV for my mobile number. We spoke about the paranormal and John Lennon coming to me. She claimed that John had actually come to her in 1984, four years after his death. She claimed that she too had been given writings by John. She too had never written anything before. She had sent me some writings. One of which was *'Mankind'*. As soon as I saw it, I saw the words I had written on the beach two days before: 'vast oceans teeming with life, the sun's piercing ray.'

The song was complete in minutes, the words, the music – the song *'Mankind'*. I spoke to her and she was thrilled. But she made me promise I wouldn't tell a soul for fear of ridicule. She said she didn't want anyone who knew her to make fun of her. And she was only happy to pass to me what she said John had given to her. She also said to me that I was very brave and it must have taken an enormous amount of courage to 'tell the world' that John Lennon had come to me. I told her, with the same conviction as I have always maintained, "No, not really. All I've done is tell the truth, people either believe or don't believe, it's up to them. But it's the truth."

30th Sighting
Song No.56: LOVE AND PEACE

It was now 2nd June1994, and I was awakened by John going out of the bedroom at speed. It was the latest time of day I had ever seen him in this room; it was 6am. I immediately got up with trepidation.

I had seen him enough times, I had 'travelled' with him, but this time I

141

was about to follow him. It was weird to say the least. What was weird about it was that this was a new thing I was doing, I had never once tried to follow him as I did on this day. I got to the landing at the top of the staircase, which was quite large, with the four bedrooms and bathrooms off, and I noticed the smallest bedroom door slightly move, slightly closing, a couple of inches. It was ajar by about 10 inches to a foot. This room had served as a study room, junk room, and as an 'overflow' of the kids' toy room. Occasionally, we'd also use it when friends came to stay as a bedroom.

I opened the door and all the hairs went up on my neck. John was there. Then he vanished into thin air. I sat down in this room on a chair. I rarely went into this room. The feeling I got, was 'Peace on Earth, get it for all it's worth.' I wrote lots of words, all about peace, harmony and happiness. That morning I went to the piano and played those lines, until it hit me like a bolt out of the blue.

The song wasn't to be Peace on Earth, but in fact *Love and Peace*. The words 'Love and peace, let's get the world on its knees. Share our food that feeds us across all this insanity, love and peace, peace and love.'.

ALL THE ABOVE SIGHTINGS OF JOHN LENNON HAPPENED ON AND UP TO 2nd JUNE 1994.

I WROTE MY EXPERIENCES DOWN ON FRIDAY 17th JUNE 1994.

The reason for this was that someone in the music industry wanted to look at and read all about my experiences. So rather than just tell someone a story, I sent a sealed and unopened manuscript to myself, prior to showing him. I called it Mixed Emotions, and it describes each sighting. This was the very first time I wrote about the sightings.

It must seem crazy to you, the reader, when I tell you that the following five sightings all happened in a period of 40 days, or should I say 40 nights. From 17th June 1994 until the last sighting I was to have at my house in Mold, which was on the 24th July 1994. The sightings were to continue in my next house, which I moved into in January 1996. But before that house move, I would soon feel John's presence around me, often. It felt like he didn't have to expend all his energy 'materialising' for me to have to see him, and in order for me to download his songs. It was not unusual for the hairs to be standing up on the back of my neck in these moments.

31st Sighting
Song No.57: JOHNNY AND THE MOONDOGS

It was late June, 1994. I awoke at about 1.15am and saw John sitting on a grass bank, overlooking the River Mersey. It was a sunny day. It was bitterly cold and if the words in his thoughts were anything to go by, it was January. The grassy bank where John was sitting was on the left hand side and the river was on the right hand side, sort of diagonal, and veering past this grassy area to the rear left hand side. Huge boats were coming and going, back and forth. He was sitting with his knees up and his feet tucked under his legs. His arms were crossed and he was leaning forward, resting them on his knees. He was, as always, intensely deep in thought. He appeared almost trance-like, as if he was being 'called' and 'drawn' to this foreign land called America. He looked downwards, towards the river, and I watched and I saw on this 'Sunny Saturday in January, landing stage, walking stray dogs...' He then looked up in the sky and again I watched, and I saw 'faint outline of the moon in the sky, and Johnny's on his own again...' And the song was complete. In less than five minutes, John had let me see these sights, and I concluded from his thoughts he was waiting for the band to call. He was waiting for the band to call, but they (the band) didn't yet exist. He was being called to America. He was dreaming of the day and was taking in all the surroundings in a melancholic way, he was observing his surroundings. And in that moment it became so obvious to me, looking at what I was seeing, that the line running up to the chorus in this song would be 'But wait a minute the three things that I see, the moon, the dogs, and me... Johnny and the Moondogs, well what a name for the band I say, just look at the mass of the population looking through an elephant's eye, Johnny... Johnny... Johnny and the Moondogs.' It's a melodic song that starts slowly and erupts into a powerful screaming rocker.

Another weird coincidence, when I first recorded this song at a mate's house in Mold, was that he hung a microphone out of his window to pick up noises like cars, children etc. And just on the break before the chorus, in perfect timing, to the nanosecond, in deadly silence, a dog barks. The tape machine was running and we couldn't believe it. Paul was definitely fazed. Me, I thought it was John's way of saying 'you're on the right track'. I have the original tape and I will get a sworn affidavit from my friend Paul 'Jay' Jones.

32nd Sighting
Song No.58: IT'S ALL GOING ON

June 1994. This particular sighting wasn't of John, as I've seen him normally from his outside, in whatever situation it might have been. It seemed that it was coming from the inside of him, from inside his brain. It seemed like a total calamity, chaos, things happening out of context, illogically, unbelievable – hard to invent or make up, not on this planet, and dare I say it, maybe someone who was feeling the effects of some drug or other? I've never had any drugs, so I shouldn't really say that. I can only surmise what I have heard and read on what some drugs can do to you. And I know I've said it before about other sightings but this is one of the strangest sightings of all. These images were simultaneously accompanied by John singing the song as it was happening. This is what I saw, and felt it happening, and it also happens to be the opening line of this weird song – 'It's All Going On'.

'The monkey with the fez running round inside my head wants to fly through my eyes onto the table, the white cotton glove poking through the cloud above, is the hand of a Billy Cotton Band Man...' The song was complete. It was easy to write down what I had just heard John sing, and the images were unforgettable. It was John at his brutish best, screaming this rocker out with the message it doesn't matter where you are; whatever you are doing and however you're doing it, it's all going on.

33rd Sighting
Song No.59: THE BUS CONDUCTOR'S LAST SYMPHONY

Early July 1994. This was very similar in circumstances to the above sighting (32nd sighting, 'It's All Going On'), and also happened within days of that occurrence as well. I felt like I was being shown something that John may have observed and made reference to, somewhere, sometime in his life. Was it something he'd witnessed years before? I just don't know. I can remember John singing simultaneously with the event unfolding before my eyes. It was a bus conductor jumping off the back step of his bus. He gestured with his arms out wide, had a big smile on his face, and pointed to the bus for people to get on. The people got on and the conductor started 'conducting' the passengers. The only thing that was missing was the conductor's baton. He was just using his arms and gesturing every rhythm. The passengers were not surprised at his actions, which puzzled me. They seemed to be enjoying the spectacle; it was like a treat for them. For years, this happy conductor had always lightened their days, whether they were going to work, or shopping, or visiting friends. He was clearly telling them that this was his very last trip, and that the bus route was being scrapped as from tonight.

Playing in the background was a symphony of music. It sounded like a massive orchestra, all being conducted by this bus 'conductor'. There was a crescendo of spectacular noise and a wall of amazing almost 'classical' music. It was to be 'The Bus Conductor's Last Symphony'. His route was finishing today. The area was near the Dock Road, there were vast expanses of derelict and boarded up houses. People didn't know how they were going to get to the shops some way away. One old lady in particular, I felt most sorry for. She looked lost to the world. She stared ahead looking blankly on as this music raised to a phenomenal fever pitch.

But the conductor had this smile on his face all the time. He had always worn that happy smile, but today, come what may, he wouldn't let his passengers down by being glum. On this last trip he never charged anyone bus fare, it was his way of thanking them for all the years he'd enjoyed collecting the fares, and talking daily to 'his' friends, the passengers.

All this time, John was singing this raspy song to the background of music and insane conductoring of the conductor. 'It's the bus conductor's last symphony, conducting on the bus for you and me. It's the very last trip that he will see, on the bus conductor's last symphony...'

It was sad, it was happy, it was surreal, and the music was spectacular. He, the conductor, had known all his customers for years and he said goodbye the best way he could think of.

Many years later, I pondered on this sighting. I have never given any thought at anytime whatsoever about this song or its possible implications. But what if this was John's way of saying goodbye to the people he had made music for over the years, people from all sorts of backgrounds. It was him that surely conducted the music of the masses. When he was killed he couldn't 'conduct' anymore. His leaving us when he did created a void. An emptiness that has since not been filled. Did he know what was going to happen to him beforehand, and were his last efforts a culmination, or a summing up of his talents? Was it his way of saying, hope you enjoyed the music and the ride as much as I did? Just a thought.

And why was that 'conductor' smiling all the way through, right to the end?

Around this time, I had had a response from the CEO of Capitol Records Gary Gersh (US arm of EMI). I had sent a letter to him explaining my story and a few tracks. In the first telephone conversation we had, he said he was sending me a standard letter that he has asked his assistant Craig Aaronson to send me. He phoned me several times at my home in North Wales telling me it was phenomenal and that he believed me and he was trying to get the Capitol board in the US to launch my music. He presented my music twice to the board, but they would not let him put this music out. On our last telephone conversation he went on to tell me how frustrated he was and that something 'very big' was coming out next year and that he was sworn to secrecy and couldn't tell me about it, but it is somehow linked to what you are doing. A couple of months later I tried to speak with Gary at Capitol to be told 'he has left the company' apparently there was no forwarding address/tel no for me to contact him on.

ONE YEAR LATER, THE BEATLES ANTHOLOGY CAME OUT AND GROSSED £80 MILLION POUNDS.

34th Sighting

Song No.60: SOMETIME IN THE 50s

I was awakened from a deep sleep one morning about 2am. The date was 18th July 1994.

I looked up and at the foot of my bed I saw a cobbled street. In the street, there was just one car. It was a black Ford Popular motor car, standing by the only tree in the street. It was a thin tree, about 3 inches thick, and stood about seven feet high. There were no other trees in the street. Standing side on to me, by this motor car, was a boy between about nine and 12 years old. Just then, the boy put his hand against the window, to shield the reflection of the light, and peered into the car. As he looked with his face against the driver's window, he saw shiny red seats, but he didn't know if they were plastic or leather. Then I saw an austere, solemn looking man. He was dressed immaculately. He wore a double breasted suit and a diamond tiepin right out of a magazine. The boy turned to me and he was wearing a herringbone overcoat. On that coat he wore a button badge of himself when he was old. It was very strange. I describe the badge as having bright lights around the edge, like tiny bulbs glowing, all around the face. There were about seven or eight bright lights. The face I recognised immediately as that of John Lennon.

This boy was the young John Lennon.

The next thing that happened was the boy journeying in this black car, up to Blackpool, to see the illuminations with his mother and this 'married man'. No words were spoken. The boy thought he could see the Northern Lights and asked the question, "Are they the Northern Lights?" He never received an answer to his question. All this time on the journey, the man was holding his mother's hand like they were 'on some kind of journey to the promised land'. The boy who was sitting in the back of this car was screaming inside 'LEAVE MY MUMMY ALONE, LEAVE MY MUMMY ALONE, LEAVE MY MUMMY ALONE!!' He then looked into the front of the car, and looked at his mother who was wearing a navy blue polka dot dress and high heel shoes, her Sunday best.

The man was a jeweller from London Road. He was married, and young John knew of the lies that this man carried around in his head.

When the boy asked the mother what she saw in this man, 'she said nothing'. She snapped at the boy, 'go to bed son' and turned away.

It's strange that this sighting is of John when he was just a boy. It's almost as if he'd gone back to where he came from i.e. Liverpool. Back to Liverpool, from 'whence he came'.

All the above seemed so clear, I would be very surprised if some or all of these things had never happened to John. I don't know. I am sure someone will tell me one day whether they happened to him or not! Now wouldn't that be interesting?

My journey with John didn't finish on 18th July 1994, the date of this sighting.

Not by a long stretch.

The above sighting was one of the most detailed I had ever had. It was also to be the last sighting at our home in Mold connected to John Lennon, prior to me leaving...

...**OR SO I THOUGHT...**

8

THE LAST SIGHTING IN MY HOME IN MOLD

35th Sighting
Song No.61: LOWRY COUNTRY CALLING

This was to be the very last sighting I was to have in our house in Mold, North Wales.

24th July 1994.

What was once our home, and I felt, our castle, is now sadly, just a house.

Karen wanted me out; she wanted me gone to save any embarrassment to her, and to reflect it onto me. She wanted to tell people how I had 'left' and deserted the children. Don't forget, she divorced me on the grounds of 'no emotional support' so there was a logic and a method in her madness. That way she would get the house, the kids, the sympathy, all neat and tidy. In fact, just like the house was. It was like she was wiping dog shit from her shoe without anyone seeing her do it. That's what she wanted and that's exactly how she made me feel. I had asked her many times for us to try to save our marriage, for ourselves, and most of all for our beautiful children.

She just wouldn't even discuss the possibility of us going to Relate, the marriage guidance councillors.

What beggars belief was that right up to her having these affairs we were basically happy, we never argued and used to have fun together. OK, everything changes when children come along but we both knew that, we knew we would now have to give that bit more of ourselves; it was understood. Well, I understood it. Don't get me wrong, she was a great mother to Tim and Steph, but obviously now craved the attention she used to get when she was single, and what better place to do it than on a university course with mature students, recalling events in their previous wild student days. So as the doting husband, I was to be the one to suffer. She was to tell me that her first affair happened because 'he reminded me so much of you, it was exciting, I felt flattered,

149

alive and it was just a bit of fun that went out of control'. In hindsight, I gave too much of myself. I never kept anything back in reserve, for 'me time' if you like. I worked non-stop for our future. Surely, surely, I would implore her, it's worth going to Relate, for a chance, to try and save our marriage.

Not a chance. She wouldn't hear of it, I guess her guilt was overwhelming and not for discussion with another soul, including her parents, the grandparents to our children. She just wanted me out of the house at all costs. When I told her to get out the house and go to her lover, to leave the house and I would look after the children, she was horrified, saying she was the mother and would never leave the children under any circumstances. We talked about the future of our children. She'd say, "You can still see them whenever you want," as if she had made a concession to me that I should be grateful for. Her long term plans didn't include me, which I was to find out about in the most horrible of circumstances.

It happened on 22nd December, after I had moved out of the house. I was looking forward to seeing the children over the Christmas holiday, and I spoke to Tim who excitedly said, "Dad, we are going on a skiing holiday with Mark!" Mark was the new boyfriend, an accountant and director of a large company, and I believe he drove a beautiful new Jaguar, which must have delighted Karen and her mother no end. This wasn't someone Karen had an affair with before we split up, but had met since we had divorced. I said to Tim, "Great, when are you going?" thinking it was going to be after Christmas.

Tim replied, "Christmas Eve." She hadn't even asked me what arrangements I had made about seeing the kids, their presents etc. and when I confronted her she just didn't want to discuss it. I was shattered and had the most miserable Christmas you can think of. Mark was to take the family many times over the years abroad on holidays, in the summer, and especially at Christmastime. I don't blame him. Actually, having met him in a pub called The Plough, St Asaph through my best friend, Martin, who went to school with him, he's a really nice bloke. I wished him well.

The irony is, moving on a few years, Karen had been seeing him for over 11 years – longer than our 10 year marriage had lasted – and she dumped him in much the same way as she dropped me.

Now the children have had two long term father figures that are in and then out of their life. Not for good, mind. I know Mark still sees and talks to the children as well as I do. But firstly their real dad goes, without telling them the truth about their mother, and then their other father figure does exactly the same, blaming himself and yes, crying just the way I did.

Surely to God this must have an effect on the children, or am I totally living in the past, or on planet zonk?

I digress!

I had started to tell you about the last 'sighting' I had in Mold:

It occurred in my bedroom in the same position, at the end of the bed, as the majority of previous sightings where I had seen John Lennon. What's interesting is the date of this sighting and the real life occurrences that subsequently happened to me.

The date was 24th July 1994. It was about 2am in the morning and I was awoken suddenly. The neon red numbers on the radio alarm clock that had always sat on my bedside cabinet seemed to be glowing brighter than I had ever seen before. I sat up and grasped very quickly that what I was looking at was a very steep street on a hill. A row of terraced houses were on this narrow street. The pavement was made up of wide flagstones but I didn't see any street lighting. I saw one man knock on a door at the bottom of the street and a workmate came out and joined him en-route to call for their friends. This carried on until there were about five or six men. A group of working men, going to work in some manual working class job somewhere. It was very early in the morning and they were starting the 6 o'clock shift. They wore hobnail boots and coarse old woollen clothing. As they walked I could hear the loud scraping of their horseshoe metal heels against these big flagstones. Together up this street, they knocked on the doors as they went, calling for their workmates. They got halfway up the street and knocked at a door on the right hand side. A big man came out in similar attire and said, "I'm not going in today." With this all the workmates let out a collective wince and their spokesman said, "The foreman will sack you for this." There was a whistle tooting which I think could have had something to do with a call for the workers, like five minutes before shift, or something like that. It came from the men's place of work.

On reaching this stone mill with low ceilings, the foreman out by the front gate was in a rage. He asked one of the men, "Where is he then? When you see him, tell him not to bother coming back again, he's finished!"

The men, in a true subservient working-class way, didn't have the stomach for a run-in with the foreman and acted like they had been told off, almost like 'let this be a lesson to you all, men'. The men took their jackets off in a room before getting on with their work, muttering under their breath. As they had already predicted, this foreman was a bastard and didn't even ask if there was a sound reason for this man (whoever he was) not to turn up for work.

When the shift was finished it had been extra hard and they had also done the work of the missing man. They were shattered and went straight to their respective homes, without calling to see the man in question and pass on the foreman's instructions. There were very few jobs and a lot of starving, very poor people, who all at one time had worked or been attached to the mill and had been laid off. The very cottages they lived in were all tenanted or they were being allowed to live in the house by the mill owner's good grace. In the mill yard the owner had organised a 'broth drum' with a lighted fire underneath. I could see the queue of poor women in filthy clothes and their shawls lining up, some with babes in arms, to get a bowlful of broth from their lord and master. This was a time, I surmised, when all the mills were going through a massive decline caused by either over production, under requirement, strike, or boycott from some part of the British Empire. India springs to mind.

The next morning the same routine was started by the workmate furthest from the mill. He would start up the street, walking at a pace, collecting one after the other of his mates. They were walking past the 'missing' man's door and he stepped out. He joined them in their trek up the hill and on into work. They all walked without as much as a word spoken, in army-like fashion, marching on their heels today, seeming to evoke a collective dread that was imminent and would soon be forthcoming from their foreman. Nonetheless, there was a definite 'collective togetherness'.

On reaching the mill, the foreman had waited with eager anticipation for a confrontation with the missing man in front of the man's workmates, principally to show them he was boss. And he was! He pounced on the absent worker and, like Mount Etna erupting, he bellowed, "You're fired! Why didn't you come in yesterday? You're finished!" All the other men carried on walking and went about their business instead of doing what they really wanted, which was to tear the foreman apart.

The absent worker paused and said to the foreman, "My wife was ill, and I took her to see the doctor, where she lost our baby and then died. They couldn't save her, or the child."

The foreman was lost for words; he was caught on his back foot, off guard. He had aggressively lambasted the missing worker and was trying desperately to say something. He was too proud, or stupid to back down, but could only imagine the crisis this missing man had been through. He thought showing kindness was a weakness, and that is how he had always lived his life. A life without kindness and a life full of cruelty. That moment the foreman felt a grim realisation that deep down he had always known was lying there. A tragic implosion of ill conceived, tormented, misjudged and misplaced horror. His life was false. He was brought up by a tyrant, and that tyrant had made him into a tyrant. He'd had a hard life, a life empty and without love. But he longed to be ordinary and be a good man, not ghastly and aggressive.

I thought of this man and pondered the bullshit, the inhumanity of man to man. This was his life. This was all he knew and the only way he knew how to act. He had inadequacy raging through his blood. He was weak, not strong. He had gone too far down the road of tyranny. He couldn't turn back. He would spend the rest of his life lost. Another person who thought he couldn't ask for help, another person that didn't get help.

He didn't apologise to the missing man, but said the only thing he could think of, which was, "Get back to work, and don't be late tomorrow," and walked off drowning in an ocean of guilt and angst.

The man did go back to work and carried on his wretched life, as did all the other workers in the mill, along with the foreman. And to this day I don't know why, but I wrote the song, words and music in five minutes flat. The song is called *'Lowry Country Calling'*.

In it I describe 'Hobnail boots, whistle toots, going to get back, back to my roots, this is Lowry country calling, calling me.'

9

Moving

I was to move out of the family house in September 1995. To where, I didn't have a clue at the time. All I knew was that I was moving to pastures new.

The last thing Karen and I did as a couple living in Mold was to close our joint accounts. It made little difference, as all the money had been emptied out of them that we had saved for our future together. Emptied, all gone.

When my father died in 1981, I went with my sister to close his bank account. It was overdrawn by £45.00, so we settled the debt

When Karen and I closed our accounts in 1995, one had no money in and the other account had exactly £45.00 in it.

I had made a herculean effort to hold the family together. It didn't work, and I accepted the paltry £12,000, that she had offered me to go. She just wanted me out of the house and her life. She was earning a substantial wage by then, and she told me she wouldn't ask for any money towards the children's upkeep. She was keeping virtually everything, and she knew I was only on a modest salary. It is because of this I agreed to move out. The children would stay with her, she would keep the house and all the contents 'for the sake of the children', save for 2 leather sofas, a wardrobe and sideboard. Even for those I had to argue the point even when collecting them. You see, she latterly decided she wanted them as well. The fine lead crystal set of Edinburgh glass I had collected, and a set of delicate liqueur glasses her mother had personally given me from her deceased relative, I was never to get. I remember at the time, when we went with her mother to the deceased relative's house to collect a few items I made a comment about the delicacy of the glass and the beautiful colours. At the time Karen said to me, "What do you want those old glasses for?" But that was then and this is now, and *now* she was swearing that they belonged to her. So she kept them. C'est la vie, and all that crap.

I left home and borrowed a friend's caravan in Saron, Denbighshire, for about 6-8 weeks. Heather and Allan Sherwood had finished using it for the season and I slept there off and on, over the period. It was a big old caravan and I stored all the music paperwork, my clothes and whatever other bits and bobs I owned.

For several months before I moved out of the house, I had been renting an old disused mill in Dukinfield, east Manchester, not far from Ashton under Lyne. Here, I had put a small music recording studio together. I got an 8 track machine, a mixing desk and all the other ancillaries you need to record your voice/music onto a magnetic tape. This equipment was at a friend's house in Mold until I moved it into 'The Mill'.

This mill was recommended to me by Derek Hesford, a friend whose brother-in-law owned the mill with a partner. It seems the partners had fallen out with each other, and the mill was in a terrible state of disrepair. It had pigeons in the top room where the slates were missing, stair steps missing and big holes in the floor where the boards had rotted away over the years of neglect. This was good, I reasoned, for security purposes. If someone tried to break in at night, they wouldn't know of the holes in the flooring, and... Well I did hang a sign in the entrance to the stairway, but the light wasn't working so even we had to use a torch to get in and out. I had fitted a huge metal door that was welded and bolted to the brickwork, as well as having a huge lockable metal trunk bolted to the floor in the 'studio' located on the second floor of this tired old Victorian floor mill. The mill was brilliant, I loved it. It backed onto the Manchester canal system, 50 metres from the Portland Basin, and the views were spectacular.

In between staying at the Sherwoods' caravan I would sometimes stay at the mill. I brought some of my suits and clothes in black plastic bags and slept on a porta bed, metal framed with a thin mattress, in a sleeping bag. I slept in there on my own many nights and it has to be said it was a bit scary. I would hear scurrying of rats, doors being tried downstairs, and the wind howling through the broken windows. I heard mysterious sounds from a small exterior lock up in the cellar of the mill at 3 and 4am. This used to jolt me out of a deep sleep, only to wonder where the hell I was. Very strange!

It wasn't an ideal place to doss, as to put the light on you had to walk 20 paces in the pitch black. I had an old three piece sofa, a kettle and toaster, and a bowl to wash myself - and the few plates I had. I knew I couldn't sustain living there in this damp dilapidated building for long, and a few nights I slept on the Giblins' sofa, and anywhere else I could lay my hat. Andy Giblin was our engineer, and his dad, Phil, was a print salesman. Phil had been in a 60s' skiffle band and had played at the Cavern in Liverpool a few times. His wife had left him, and it seemed he didn't have a care in the world; he was so easy going and a great laugh. He always used to frequent the Witchwood Club where live bands would play four or five nights a week. Very exciting place it was too! So I started going there!

In the mornings I would rise about 6am, have a cup of tea, shiver a little and get some toast on the go. Then I would put my suit on and go throughout the North West, conducting my business - selling print. I would eat something in the day and get to the mill, get changed into jeans and work on the next song

Eventually, I was to look for a bed and breakfast around Ashton to make my home for a few months as I had decided that with my work offices being in Leigh I might as well commute and be with the music as often as I could. I checked the local B&Bs out. They all wanted £12 per night, even paying three months up front. I asked one establishment how much per night without breakfast and the reply was £11! It was depressing. After exhausting the possibilities of B&Bs I sat in the car, looking at the list that the Ashton Visitor Information Centre had given me. I turned over the stapled sheets to the back page to write something on it only to find two campsites listed as year round caravan and camping sites.

Only the week before I had seen a close friend of mine called Pete The Meat from Shotton, who asked me if I wanted to buy his old caravan. I had said no to him, but now... I phoned him immediately and did the deal on the phone for this little 2 berth, old caravan. I thought, whatever happens, sod B&Bs, I am going to live in a caravan. I phoned the first caravan site up and it was closed for winter! I phoned the second one up. A guy by the name of Charlie Price answered and told me we could arrange terms for a three month pitch, and to come and see him first in a place called Broadbottom. I think he wanted to check me out. I had no idea where Broadbottom was, but looked on a map and found that this site was only seven miles from the mill. It was ideal. I saw Charlie and quickly we got on well, and arranged for me to move on site the following week.

I had asked my older brother Brian if he would move the caravan from Shotton to Broadbottom. He owned a transit van, which had a step cum towbar on it. This he did, and I remember seeing him pull into Charlie's place, only for Charlie to come out shouting, "We don't want f'ing tinkers here, fuck off!" I was following Brian into the site, but Charlie hadn't seen me, and soon I appeared behind the caravan in my shiny Calibra, all suited up, and saw Charlie sigh with relief. He said, "For a minute I thought he was a gypo." I assured him that it was indeed my brother who had a transit van, remarkably like the vans used by 'travellers'.

I moved my clothes and belongings out of the Sherwoods' caravan in Saron, into my very own caravan in this place called Broadbottom. I distinctly remember the very first night I was there. I took all the clothes out of the bin bags and stacked them on one of the two long bench seats. I stacked all my boxes of papers and songs onto the floor of the small upright cupboard, where an old yard brush was and, judging by the stains on the floor, a chemical toilet had once been. I laid my sleeping bag out on the other bench seat opposite for when I would be ready to 'hit the sack'. I lit the mantle gas light and it came on and then went out. I fiddled with the mantle, when the delicate fine mesh of the light disintegrated into a thousand pieces. It was probably donkeys years' old, if it had ever been used over the last 30 years! Luckily, I had a torch. I changed into my jeans and went to the local pub, The Cheshire Cheese, and as a sort of relief of completing the move, had five pints in rapid succession. I then went next door and ordered a Chinese takeaway meal. I took this to the caravan and lit a tea light candle and placed it on the stove in this quaint, SMALL, OLD, COLD 50s' caravan. I ate this delicious curry king prawn meal and climbed into a very cold, damp sleeping bag. Soon I dozed off, only to be awakened in the middle of the night by what I thought was frostbite. I couldn't feel my toes, and my nose felt like it was 10 degrees below.

I put the torch on and looked across at the huge pile of clothes stacked up on the other seat. So I climbed out of my sleeping bag and climbed under this ton weight of clothing. I was asleep in five minutes flat, and I woke up in the morning like toast, warm and rosy. This was to be my bed for the next three months, and I never woke up cold again in that caravan. It was particularly cold in November/December of that year, 1995. In fact it had snowed quite a lot. How funny I must have looked, going from the caravan across the field to the shower cubicle/toilet in my dressing gown and carpet slippers, towel, soap and toothbrush, walking through a foot of snow! I can see the puzzled faces of the serious touring caravanners, with their state of the art, fully insulated, double glazed, heated caravans. No doubt their vans had toilets and showers in as well.

It had been some 14 months from the last sighting I'd had in my house in Mold that I found myself walking down a street that I had been in before. It was very steep. It was that very street in the sighting where I had seen those workers going to work in the mill. An incredible feeling of déjà vu came over me and all the hairs on my neck and arms stood to attention, as surely as I had heard those workers marching army-like in those horse-shoe metal heels against the flagstones, 'marching on their heels today'.

I had been here before, I knew the place well, and I was here again. I had never driven anywhere near this village but there and then, at that precise moment, I knew I was going to live there.

I bought a house in New Street, Broadbottom, some three months later. It wasn't easy. This village had now become a very desirable backwater, one from which the commuters could travel into the centre of Manchester in only 20 minutes. The Manchester to Glossop railway line is one of the oldest in the world. Along with its huge viaducts, this incredible feat of engineering was built in less than two years. The reason was that the industrialists had built huge 10 storey cotton mills all around this area, and they needed to get the raw materials/finished goods off to market via the nearest main shipping port, which happened to be Liverpool. We were serving the world with our products, driven on at full throttle by the industrial revolution. Broadbottom, I was to find out subsequently, had five of these such mills, employing at its height 5000 people. This tiny village used to have 40 shops in it. Today, there is just one. This once working mill village is on the River Etherow, and that river runs from the Pennines, all the way through to the River Mersey. At the time of these mills, all power to the mills was provided by the rivers and linked and driven by huge geared and sub geared water wheels, driving all the machinery, a life-force to sustain a workforce with the mill owners as the 'tour de force' in this onward and upward progression to that thing we call progress.

We call it progress.

The mill owners called it a slightly different name. They called it profit.

I moved into the house, no. 29 New Street, and was pleased that it had a lovely feeling about it. I understand the people that had lived there had a good long life, and that they both worked in the mills. The house needed everything doing to it so I just managed to scrape a mortgage together with the small deposit I was able to put down on the house.

Sometime in early January 1996, I decided to go for a long run. It was overcast and dull. It was also Sunday morning. And I knew, come 12 o'clock, in the village pub 'The Cheshire Cheese' they were having a pound a pint afternoon on. Ed and Cath, the pub's owners, used to put a sandwich board outside on a Friday night to tempt the commuters using a short cut through the village. It was the rat run through to Derbyshire, avoiding the main Glossop artery.

I didn't know many people in the village. In fact the very first person I met was 'Little Pete'. He was in his mid-seventies and used to be a flyweight boxer, as well as being a merchant seaman all his life. He would be in the pub every night and drink like a fish and smoke like a trooper. He went away to sea when he was 15 and the intriguing stories he could tell would keep me fascinated all night. He had a lady friend who lived in the very steep street I've already mentioned. So he was my first mate in the village.

I set off that morning about 10.30am prepared for this long run I fancied doing. It was about 10 miles and it was all road work and extremely hilly. I ran up the hill to Charlesworth, over the back towards New Mills, and had a long hard descent into Glossop. And from there back up past Dinting arches, past the rugby club, and dropped down at speed from Charlesworth into Broadbottom. By this time it had been battering with rain, heavens hard, for about one hour. The run had taken just under two hours. Not only was I soaked, but I was steaming like a grand national racehorse winner. I had carried a five pound note with me in my Ron Hills, in eager anticipation of buying me some Guinness at the bargain price of a pound a pint. I entered the Cheese, ordered my pint of Guinness and went over to the roaring fireplace, peeled off my shoes and socks, hung my jacket by the fireside, and went to the loo to dry off a bit. On getting back to the fireside, still sweating profusely, one big man with a broad Lancashire accent said, "Has tha' bin runnin' lad?"

I said, "No, I've just been to the Co-op for some shopping!" With that we laughed, he bought me a pint and I bought him a pint. And we talked and drank and talked and drank. I quickly ran out of money and offered to go and get some from my house. But this man wouldn't hear of it. Anyway, the session finished about 9.30pm. We'd had a brilliant time, and I had made another friend called Crosland Ward. Crosland had been a lecturer in Manchester University until his wife ran off with a multi-millionaire. He had been devastated, and now would devote the rest of his days, or should I say her days, looking after his mother. He was a big man who, before becoming a lecturer, used to be a blacksmith. He was determined to educate himself, so he burnt the midnight oil to study and make a better life for himself and his family. He had a thick beard and was as broad as he was tall. I would say he was in his late fifties, and to be honest, he put me in mind of my dad Geo. He reminded me so much of him. He had that wild unshakable stare my dad had. He was his own man. He was eloquent and, although he hated the word, he was an intellectual, albeit a humble one. His knowledge of the area was second to none. He spoke in depth about the Romans, the Greeks, the wonders of the world, ancient civilisations. He was a philosopher, a statesman, a visionary and a great singer. He could boom out this huge voice, just when he fancied singing an old folktale, or some sea shanty, or a romantic ballad for the girls. And that's just what my dad did, the number of times I went with Geo to pubs such as Chalk Farm. He'd start singing without any thought or embarrassment. He didn't give two fucks. I'd meet Crosland maybe once a week and we'd talk about everything under the sun, each jockeying to get a word in edgeways. It was only the third time I had met him and he started talking about an artist who became his friend.

The story goes that Crosland used to deliver milk from the local farm owned by Dick Boughy.

Crosland would take the horses to the carts and deliver the milk in the village. He got to know the artist, enough to say 'good morning', and have a chat about the weather, that sort of thing. When this artist first came to the village, in 1947, Crosland was only aged six. Crosland himself was always artistic and used to enter the local village art and sculpture competitions and continued this through secondary school. It was here he used to see this artist make presentations to the winners. A village fete, a local school. He describes the artist as being a 'misty man', a man of secrecy who always wore a long overcoat whatever the weather. When he was about 18, he and the artist became friends. As well as delivering the milk, Crosland used to work for extra money, delivering Christmas post in the village. There were no computers or emails in those days, and everyone sent Christmas cards and letters. There would be a glut of mail. Crosland was delivering some mail to the artist's house this Christmas week, about 47 years ago. On opening his door he saw the artist standing there in the customary overcoat, one lapel was full of cigarette ash, and the other one was full of paint, where the artist had wiped the brushes in haste to continue his painting. He was invited in for a cup of tea. There were paintings all over the floor, on the walls, on every available space. Paintings on the table, on the sideboard, everywhere. Paintings everywhere you looked. He had his tea, they had a chat, and he was invited back any time he wanted. They became firm friends, with Cross even taking the artist to his mother's grave to lay flowers on her gravestone. The year was 1967 and at the time Crosland drove a battered Ford Cortina. Crosland was then 26 years old. He had got funding and was lecturing in various universities, so he bought this old car to make his journeys to the various universities. He used to call in and have a cuppa and watch the artist painting away. He did this for years, at every opportunity. Crosland asked if one day he could bring his son, also called Crosland (aged 5), to watch the artist. He did and the boy was fascinated, his eyes looking all over the room at the chaos in this real artist's world.

The artist died and, being a close friend, Crosland was invited by the family to attend the funeral on this dreary Manchester morning in 1976. Great people from all walks of life attended or sent bouquets of flowers. Tommy Steel sent a huge bouquet. There were so many flowers Crosland described it as being like a small florists. He also described the position of the headstone as looking directly onto the gravestone, only yards away, of John Allcock, that great pioneer of powered flight, the first aviators in the world. Great men interned, side by side, who hailed from Lancashire. 'Now that's not a bad place to be interned, opposite the founders of flight!'

Not at all as the local press at the time would have us believe. They, I understand, had their deadlines to meet and were more interested in their watches than they were to watch a funeral. They left as soon as they could and made their way across to their editor's offices in central Manchester. They never walked over to the graveside, which was some 400 yards away from the main entrance hall of the city cemetery. When the Manchester Evening News and other national papers based in Manchester came out later that day, and the following day, their headlines were saying, 'No flowers!' and 'Interned without tears'.

Crosland went on to tell me many stories about this artist. Two stories in particular that he said someone should paint for posterity, and I wholeheartedly agreed with him. One should be called 'No Flowers' and the other should be called 'Farewell My Love'. A description of these is featured in Chapter 10, coincidence number 35.

And the artist's name?

The artist's name was L.S. LOWRY.

L.S. Lowry lived at no. 23 The Elms, Mottram. This was approximately one and a half miles from my front door in Broadbottom.

Some 18 months before I had written and copyrighted the song, words and music in five minutes flat to a song. This was taken from the last ever sighting I was to have in Mold, North Wales. The sighting was number 35. The date was 24th July 1994. The song was called 'Lowry Country Calling'.

I had managed to scrape a mortgage together by putting a deposit of the £12,000 settlement I had got from the divorce and to buy a house in the village, and moved in at the beginning of January 1996. It had been virtually three months from arriving in the village, setting eyes on the place, and camping in Charlie Price's campsite. It was number 29 New Street and once again I worked hard and turned this quaint old house into a home for myself and the kids. As soon as I could, I got the building work done and I brought the children, and we had great fun. We'd walk alongside, or sometimes in the river, throwing pebbles in the fast flowing River Etherow on Broadbottom beach, or walk up Combs, which was the beautiful backdrop and view that I could enjoy from my kitchen window and rear veranda. Now obviously they were really excited about coming to their dad's house, and always they had my undivided attention. We were forever larking, playing around, drawing, singing, picnicking, meeting my new friends, playing daft games like 'The Name Game' etc.

On taking them back to Mold after the very first weekend they had stayed with me, Karen could see how overjoyed they were when we went into the house. She seemed a bit agitated, although I didn't know why.

One week later, I got a demand from the CSA (Child Support Agency) asking for money for the children. I thought, simply, this was some error and phoned Karen to get her to confirm to the CSA the agreement we had made. She seemed blasé, commenting that I had responsibilities towards the children. I said to her, "You gave me your word that you wouldn't ask for any money off me for the children's upkeep, because you said to me that you could look after them very adequately with the salary you are on, and because of the agreement for me to leave the house. That was the only reason I left the house and left you with everything. We agreed, come on Karen, we agreed."

She denied it, as surely as she had denied the affair with John Banks. Surprise, surprise, she denied our verbal agreement, and I drove up to Mold immediately that day to discuss it further with her, and make her see reason. I found myself saying the same words to her all over again. "Just be honest, and tell the CSA the truth." Eventually she told me to get out of her house.

WHY IS IT SO DIFFICULT FOR SOME PEOPLE TO TELL THE TRUTH?
Maybe seeing the children in such high spirits after having had their first weekend with me was the cause that triggered some sick thoughts. Thoughts that may have turned to actions. Whatever it was, at best it was the horrible side of human nature, at its worst, ghastly and wicked.

The children came over often, although sometimes at the last minute Karen would phone me and cancel, saying there had been a change of plan and make some lame excuse. A classic she often used was, "My mum and dad are going off to Spain next week (or worse, coming back!) and they want to see the children before they go (or drive down from

Manchester airport to Abergavenny)."
It made it all the more special when I did see Tim and Steph, and when they saw me. We always had a ball.

29 NEW STREET, BROADBOTTOM - A little old house to call my own.
I had been used to growing up in a little terraced house in Liverpool, and part of me felt comfortable because of this in this friendly neighbourhood. It was almost as if I had gone back to my roots. The neighbours were great and were there if you wanted a chat, or to borrow a cup of sugar or a spare light bulb. It applied both ways, and I felt this to be a bonus from where I had just come from in Mold, where one rarely knew the neighbours' names, let alone spoke to them.
The little terraced mill cottage I had bought in Broadbottom by now had been rewired, re-plumbed, part re-plastered and damp-coursed, and had had a lick of magnolia in most of the rooms. Part of which I had to do for the mortgage agreement in order that the company would release the £3000 they were retaining.
I had fitted a combi boiler in the kitchen as a priority, virtually as soon as I had arrived in the property and had gathered various radiators I had been given, to eventually fit into all the rooms, as and when I could. This meant that all the old plumbing was redundant.
So the house was clean, and it always gave me a wonderful feeling every time I went through the front door. There were still things to be done to it, and one day I was weighing up the bathroom that had just been skimmed ready for me to paint and tile, and glanced into the small room next to it. This 'room' didn't have a door, as the stairs up to the landing were, I wouldn't say 'open plan' onto this room, they just didn't have a wall. So in effect you could walk up the stairs and about three steps from the top take a short cut onto the landing/toilet. It was a great shortcut I always used in times of 'emergency ablutions'.
I started prodding the flimsy stud wall, immediately behind the 'open plan' part. I then found it to be made of hardboard. Inquisitively I started peeling back this hardboard with the aid of a screwdriver and pliers, and then soon with great gusto, and finally with a lump hammer! The lot came down within 15 minutes, and around me lay broken 3"x2" stud framing, old plaster, old wallpapers, big pieces of hardboard, old rusty nails and screws and a layer of dust that the Buckley cement

works would have been proud of! I was in my element.

On breaking through I found an old copper immersion boiler and an assortment of old pipes, some of which were lead. I ripped them out, laughing like a loony, simply because I could.

To my amazement, when I glanced up, I saw that there were a set of banisters and what looked like a top room. The staircase had been removed, so without further ado I ripped the entire wall down and found a galleried landing. The staircase was no longer there, and happily I continued the demolition of the 'room's' ceiling adjoining. This meant the rear room was as high as the roof, and beautiful with the sun streaming through. Needless to say, before I plaster boarded the top room, I had to clear the old mounds of wattle and dawb, lath and plaster, and copious amounts of soot that had gathered over the previous 150 years or so. This was taken, bucket by bucket, down the stairs into the backyard. There was so much debris and muck that neighbours thought I was mining, or trying to create a cellar!

I got a staircase made and fitted for £200. Then a large Velux window that was fitted to what was to become my bedroom. The pearlings (or main beams holding the roof up), were stunning beams of 12"x4" pitch pine and when I sanded them down and varnished them, they glowed a rich, warm red colour.

It was here that I would lay many happy nights and look out of 'Earth's Window' to the moon, the stars and the heavens.

There would be lots more sightings that I witnessed in Broadbottom, and many feelings of John being with and around me a lot of the time. So many incidences where I would feel his presence. Sometimes I looked around quickly as I felt he was there in the room with me, but then had vanished. Something would come into my mind, as if someone had pressed the 'download button'. There it would be. Another complete song to add to the ever expanding collection of songs from John. It is difficult to try and explain, but I never sat down and tried to write a song. They were either there, and I wrote it down and placed it in my files, or they weren't, and I didn't.

A few examples of sightings in Broadbottom are given here, with the approximate dates that they occurred. At the time I was concentrating on producing this music more than ever, and much less on cataloguing the dates specifically.

36th Sighting
Song No.62: ALL AROUND THE WORLD (A LITTLE LOVIN')

It was mid July 1996. John had been around me earlier in the day, which was becoming more the norm than not. It didn't faze me in the slightest. It had been a glorious summer's day in July. I woke up with a start, about 2am. There was deadly silence as I looked up through the newly fitted window at the night sky. Everywhere was so still and beautiful. A true feeling of peace, and I felt a oneness with mankind. In the song there is a mention of... 'a silver thread runs through us all, listen, please..' which I understood to be that we are all intrinsically linked together, as one. Also that we should all give out 'a little lovin'.

My tape player was broken, and I went over the road to a neighbour called Dave. My next door neighbour had told me Dave had a recording studio in his cellar, but thought he hadn't used it for years. He hadn't, apart from the odd dance track, and I asked him if I could record this song urgently. At this time he didn't know about John Lennon coming to me, or the amount of songs I had done. He was well impressed, and with the vocal done in one take I was in and out of his house within two hours.

37th Sighting
Song No.63: THEY GOT AWAY WITH IT

I went to bed about 11pm and had not long been asleep when I awoke and heard noises in my house that appeared to be unusual. This was in November 1996. All the time I had been in this house I heard odd sounds like central heating pipes, oven or the kettle cooling down etc. and didn't think anything of it. In this instance the staircase squeaked as if someone was standing on the stairs. There was also a 'clicking' noise coming from downstairs. Of course I checked everywhere, tried the doors to make sure they were locked and found that there was nobody there. The sounds had vanished, so I went upstairs and fell asleep almost as soon as my head hit the pillow.

About 2am I heard the sounds again and quietly asked John, "Is that you John?" There was another noise, which prompted me to get out of my comfy bed and go downstairs, check it out and have a cup of tea. When I got downstairs, the hairs were up on the back of my neck and wouldn't go down. I felt John was being persecuted, and got a weird feeling of people 'being after him'. As I sat at the kitchen table this eerie, creepy song literally fell out of me: *'They Got Away With It'*. In the song it makes references to mysterious people with 'nameless faces in flannel grey suits with glasses to hide their eyes from view...' who it seemed were constantly following John, night and day. Another line from the song goes, 'I can't escape the phone line click, or creaking floorboards, like the Titanic...' This song was sinister and I felt that at some time in his life John was genuinely scared out of his wits. Sometime later I put a new lyric and changed the title to *'John Lennon Is Back.Com'*.

But really, as the hook signifies, *'They Got Away with It'* is the actual song title. The song was complete in 15 minutes, words and music, as per usual.

At some stage in his life, he had lived with this awful 'hounding' feeling.

38th Sighting
Song No.64: CAROLINE

It was early in 1997 and my then manager, Ronan O'Rahilly, used to phone me up at all hours of the day. He would phone me on my mobile, and if I was at home in Broadbottom he would phone back on the landline. In this instance I was at home and it was around 11pm. It was unusual for me not to be at the mill, recording or starting on another song.

It was late and I had felt John's presence throughout the evening. It felt just like I was in the company of an old friend or loved one as I just went about my business. Sitting quietly I had been writing out and playing some of the songs, when the call came through from Ronan.

You see, I reasoned that John Lennon knew something none of us living mortals knew, which also meant something that Ronan O'Rahilly didn't know. Although, listening to Ronan, he'd probably even argue that toss. He always felt as if he was in the right, whatever it may have been you were discussing.

I was living on my own and didn't mind what hour he called. Always I was waiting for that magical day when he would say to me, "I've got you a deal," so every call I would hang onto his every word in the hope that he was going to get this music off the ground, for John as well as me. He continued to 'dangle the carrot' in front of me for 12 years. Musicians and friends close to me would say, "It is criminal what he is doing to you". Interestingly, they too stayed around, just on the off chance that O'Rahilly might just deliver a deal. All of the musicians I played with had their day or night jobs, so unlike me they could take or leave this 'gig'. For me, I had no choice in the matter, I had to follow it through. Now, years later, with hindsight, I felt they bought the bullshit as well as me... but the difference being not as long as I endured. Alas, I never got that call I'd longed for. But could he talk! Sometimes he would fall asleep on the other end of the phone, as I did sometimes during some of the lengthy calls. It wasn't unusual for him to rabbit on for two or three hours. Usually, he would ask how the music was going and then somehow switch the conversation to people he knew, how he had been shafted or let down. Gomelsky, clapped out Clapton, Ian Drury, Epstein... you name it, he'd been there and done it. Always these conversations would near what was potentially the finish of the call by Ronan saying... "In the meantime, how is this or that going?" I would speak for two minutes and he usually ended up talking about 'The Lady'. This 'Lady' was none other than his pirate ship — Radio Caroline, which he genuinely talked about as if it were his lover. In fact he explained what was, without doubt, the proudest day of his life. It was in Abbey Road Studios when the Beatles were recording the White Album. He was John Lennon's guest in the studio when no one else was allowed in. John and Yoko were late, as usual, and walked past everyone else and gave Ronan a brown A4 envelope, in front of Paul McCartney, George Harrison, Ringo Starr and George Martin. In the envelope was a picture of John and Yoko bollock naked, and John said to him, 'Ronan... this Is My Radio Caroline'.

When he told me this story the hairs went up on the back of my neck. It was as if he had prompted my memory to something that had happened to me years ago that I was now recollecting. I knew what he was telling me was the absolute truth. How did I know that? Because the song *Caroline* was COMPLETED IN FIVE MINUTES FLAT. I heard the complete song in a micro second, words and music together. When the call was finished, I wrote it down.

You, the reader, must be wondering why I persevered for so long with Ronan O'Rahilly. Surely, people ask, you must have known he was going to let you down? Truth is I didn't.

Listen, when I to spoke to O'Rahilly that very evening, John Lennon was privy to the call also. I categorically knew John wouldn't let me down under any circumstances. Why would he? He wanted his music out there, more than I did!

I also knew that if Ronan wasn't going to, or couldn't put this music out, or in fact there were some shenanigans, John would know, sooner or later, and find me another way to go. He would find a new direction.

At the end of the day, Ronan O'Rahilly not only let me down, but also, his one-time great friend and rock icon John Lennon. Why? I ask myself. It is a fascinating question. A question no doubt that perhaps just one or two people know about. As with everything connected with R.O.R, it is shrouded by mystery.

39th Sighting
Song No.65: AMERICA

It was late March 1998. It was about 2am and I awoke and saw John smiling, which was to say the least very unusual, as most of the time when he comes to me he is deadly serious and totally focussed, almost as if there is no time for frivolities such as laughing or smiling. There were three people standing behind him, all in 'awe' of John, but smiling also, as if he had just told them a funny story. To me he looked like he was encouraging them to sing along, or at the very least saying, "All together lads". His arms were raised openly, as if he was counting them in to some song or other, or this one. I don't know, but as ever the words and music came together as John's thoughts were immediately transmitted to me about New York and the USA. There is a line in the song that says, 'JFK, Bobby K, Martin Luther King, everyone had to hear what they say, they could see what others couldn't see and said 'why not', all they wanted to do was to find a better way...' These were the three people standing behind John in this sighting.

Five minutes later the song was completed.

Years later I painted the sighting on a big 6'x5' picture block canvas that I bought from a gift/craft shop. It already had a screen printed picture on it of a huge water droplet, which was causing a beautiful ripple effect on this 'mill pond' glass flat surface. It was a perfect circle. I painted over it, as I got it for a rock bottom price and I didn't have any canvasses left to paint on. Still, I thought it was quite apt, the fact that where there is water, there is usually life, so I didn't feel too bad about obliterating the original image, as I still have the thoughts with me of that water droplet and the ripple effect it made. Not unlike the three men mentioned in the song, and their effect on the whole world.

40th Sighting
Song No.66: IT'S BETTER TO MAKE LOVE THAN WAR

In this instance I had been running on the Fells earlier in the day for a couple of hours and was very tired and had fallen asleep on the sofa in the living room. This was in early August 2000. I awoke and saw John wearing a military shirt that was unbuttoned and a wide black flat cap. In an instant he left the room, near where the upright piano was, and went into the kitchen. I then rubbed my eyes and immediately thought of how much he, John, detested war. I then went into the kitchen to see if he was still there. He wasn't, but next to the washing machine there was a linen basket for my clothes, ready to be washed. There was an old khaki shirt I had bought from Oxfam, ages before, and couldn't remember the last time I had worn it as it was miles too big for me. It was sitting on top of the pile, which didn't make sense as all the other clothes in the basket I had recently worn, but not the khaki shirt.
The discarded shirt was John's way of saying 'Make Love, Not War'. He seemed to have disowned the shirt and what it stood for in favour of making love. Much the same way in the second verse saying people will say anything to get what they want, it's wrong. In his thoughts it's a disgrace.
The song was completed in 10 minutes flat.
I sat and played this simple tune on my guitar at about 2.30am, wrote the words and the chords, and fell asleep. In the morning I played it like I had known the song all my life.

41st sighting
Song No.67: LOVE

December 15th 2001.
John had been around me for a large part of the evening; I could always sense his presence. It was after midnight and I was feeling tired after having spent the evening searching through my boxes of songs for a particular song. Eventually I found the song I was looking for in the very last box. It was almost the very last piece of paper, but I found it.
Seek and ye shall find.
On occasions like this, sometimes I would sleep downstairs amongst the papers or music I was working on. The sofas were made in a luxurious nappa leather in a light grey colour. One was a four seater and the other was a two seater. They were so comfortable, particularly the large one, so I could stretch my body out and neither legs nor head would touch either arm. On these nights I would climb into a sleeping bag (kept behind the sofa), or under whatever clothes were downstairs, even using my old navy blue cashmere overcoat as a blanket. Old habits die hard.
Anyway, I dozed off only to be awakened an hour or so later. John was in the room with me and I looked at the piano. Right next to the piano was my guitar on its stand. The overwhelming thought was 'he wants me to do a song on the piano, not the guitar'.
As it was so late I played the piano very gently and quietly. To my astonishment, I simply played and sang in a whisper, the complete song 'Love'. I sang it before I even wrote it down, that's how effective this 'download' from John had been. The song starts with the line, 'What the world needs now is l-o-o-ove, In this wilderness, everyone looks abo-o-o-ove, searching for the answer, when there is no question, it's lo-o-ove...'
I then went to sleep and woke up early. I had a cup of tea, and sang the song as it was meant to be, and has since been recorded, with me singing it in a whisper. I believe that is the way John Lennon wished for this song to be sung.

In between all these sightings, and the times that he would make his presence known to me, something else was starting to happen to me.

171

Many, many songs would come from John, seemingly 'out of the blue'. It always feels to me, like he just has to 'jog my memory' to a song he had maybe done in the past, or even on that very day. That's all that was needed. This was happening more and more and a feeling of being on a 'creative high' for quite long periods ensued. I never looked or searched for any inspiration anywhere, it was John always looking for and finding me.

One example of this was the following song:
Song No.68: PARADISE

Excitedly, I had driven over from Broadbottom and picked the kids up from Mold and had taken them to Crugan Farm near Abersoch for a few days over the Easter period. I hired a large static caravan from Robin and Cath Jones, the farm owners who I had become close friends with over the years, having watched the children grow up over the preceding seasons and years that we used to stay on this family site. Our kids played with their kids on and around the farm and on the swings, rope ladders and the various farm equipment lying around. It was certainly a novelty for Tim and Steph. The lovely sheepdog tied up in the yard always wagged its tail and loved being stroked by all the kids and being the centre of attention. Steph used to mother the dog's head in her arms and the dog would go all 'doe eyed', lapping up the attention and slowly wagging its tail. I think it was sometime around 1996. We used to go to this lovely place year after year where the kids could pet the animals and watch them being milked or fed, or, in some instances, born. The farm was just over the road from the beach, literally a five minute walk.

It was here I walked with Tim and Steph on this beautiful, clear blue, sunny day. Not a whisper of wind in the air; perfect for making sandcastles, a swim and a picnic on the beach.

As soon as we got there I laid out the blanket and towels, sorted the food and drinks bag out, put some suntan lotion on the kids, gave them their buckets and spades and off they went to play in the sand.

I looked up to the skies and thanked God for this wonderful day.

A lone whisper of unusually shaped and feathery light cloud passed immediately overhead, and I thought of John. I watched this small delicate cloud float on by.

In the next instant I was interrupted when I heard a cuckoo, literally going cuck-oo, cuck-oo.

As with all these songs, *'Paradise'* was complete, words and music together as if, as I say, John had 'jogged my memory'. It was done in five minutes flat. The opening line was, 'Say hello to paradise, powder white beach it will entice you-oo-oo, you-oo-oo...'

42nd Sighting
Song No.69: IT'S ALL TOO MUCH

It was 2am on the 10th November 2006. I was in bed with my girlfriend Hils (Hilary), and heard a noise. I woke up to see John Lennon standing at the end of the bed. John wanted me to take the information he was giving me down urgently, as soon as possible.

John stood by the end of the bed for no more than two seconds, and then went out of the bedroom door that was always open. The room was small and somewhat claustrophobic, and if we did close the bedroom door it would catch on the duvet at the foot of the bed. The room really was that small.

This open door was on John's left hand side as he was looking towards me, and I was sleeping, if you like, on John's right hand side. In a flash I woke Hils, and explained that John had just come to me and I had to get up and write the song down. It all happened very quickly, and I couldn't have woken Hils any quicker. I wish I could have so she could have seen John as well.

As always, she was very thoughtful and supportive, and whispered, "OK, is there anything you want me to do?" I replied no and went into the lounge and regurgitated the song that John had just given me - *'It's All Too Much'*. I completed the song in 10 minutes.

Previously, I had told Hils all about my experiences with John Lennon coming to me over the years, and she never seemed phased by them but accepted them very matter-of-factly, which I was pleased about.

I got into bed and fell asleep.

In the morning Hils asked me to sing the song to her, which I did. She was amazed that I could produce a song so quickly, and even she herself felt humbled, particularly at the speed the song was done.

Later that morning I realised the significance of the words, the opening lyrics being 'It's all too much, here today, I wished I'd realised, yesterday. Telephoto fish-eyed lens, go away, living in a goldfish bowl with you this way. I didn't want to do it in the public domain, why do you have to blow it, it's such a shame. All you ever wanted was the world to know your name, now your past comes back to haunt you, and me, again and again...' This song was from John to his best and closest friend and writing partner, Paul McCartney.

43rd Sighting
The last sighting and encounter to date I have had with John Lennon was 11pm, 8th December 2010.
This sighting was brought on, I believe, by circumstances, but yet again it appeared John was showing me the way on this 'long-haul' journey. This sighting will be discussed and revealed at a later date. It has incredible implications to certain people currently living and is extremely controversial.

10

The Crazy Coincidences

I could go on giving many more incidences of the sightings, but for now it's time to turn to the amazing coincidences that have followed my every step of the way on this journey. It's a journey that me and John continue to travel on, together.

It was at the time that Ripley's Believe It Or Not!, London, exhibited my paintings in an exhibition called 'MIKE POWELL AND THE JOHN LENNON GOT BACK EXPERIENCE'. This consisted of all of the paintings I had painted of the sightings, along with the explanations and the crazy coincidences and of course, the music, as well as the old painting easel John Lennon actually painted on in the Liverpool Art College.
A well-known music writer, Jon Savage, interviewed me in front of an invited audience in Ripley's, asking questions and taking questions from the audience. I answered every one and ultimately Jon said, "Great songs, great paintings, great music – what's not to like?" I believe this was filmed by LSQTV.

The following chapter outlines the incredible, insane coincidences that have happened to me, on this journey. Some of these coincidences beggar belief, but thankfully every coincidence I have written about can be proved and quantified.
I have laid out the book and chapters purposefully in this manner rather than fitting them in amongst the sightings and dates. I think when you read about them 'en bloc' it is much more powerful, and I have cross-referenced these coincidences with the pertinent dates that they occurred.

Please note:
For ease of identification, I have highlighted each coincidence in heavy text

Number 1: FATHER JOHN LENNON

This incident preceded any of the sightings. In fact I only realised the coincidence when I was putting pen to paper sometime in 1993. Father Lennon had given me religious instruction for three months prior to my wedding. I would see him once a week, every Tuesday night, 7pm till 9pm. I had said to Karen at the time, "If we have children and you want them to grow up in the Catholic faith, then so be it, I will also get baptised into the faith." Also, Karen had said at the time it was more acceptable for the Catholic Church to marry you if you were baptised, particularly into their faith. Two weeks to go to the wedding and I asked him the question, "Father, when am I going to be baptised?" But Father Lennon told me I wasn't ready to be baptised but needed further instruction, and that he was prepared to continue with it after the marriage. I went to see Karen and said, "At my tender age of 29 years old he, Father Lennon, has told me I'm not ready to be baptised. If he thinks I am not ready now, I never will be. So that's it, I will never ever get baptised." Which has been the case. Needless to say, I never went back for any more religious instruction!

And anyway, I never even called my own father, father.

And he was my father!

At least one blessing came out of that refusal to baptise me. I didn't have to call another living being, ever again, father.

We were married on a sunny, blustery day in St. Columbus's Church, Newton, Chester.

It was 26th May, 1984. Father John Lennon presided over the wedding ceremony.

Here's another weird fact. Since the sightings of John Lennon I make reference to the number five being special for me. John Lennon's special number was nine. Add them together, and it gives you the number 14. The very number that Rose Lea said was special to me. It was our house number in Lyell Street. Eventually, when I got a photocopy of our original wedding certificate, guess what the number was?

F 021391

CERTIFIED COPY of an ENTRY OF MARRIAGE
Pursuant to the Marriage Act 1949

Registration District *Chester and Ellesmere Port*

1984. Marriage solemnized at *St. Columba's Church, Plas Newton Lane, Chester*
in the District of *Chester and Ellesmere Port* in the *County of Cheshire*

No.	When married	Name and surname	Age	Condition	Rank or Profession	Residence at the time of marriage	Father's name and surname	Rank or profession of father
5	Twenty sixth May 1984	Michael POWELL	29 years	Bachelor	Sales Manager	36 Rycroft Close Chester	George Joseph Powell (deceased)	Shop Fitter
		Karen Elizabeth GOODHEW	26 years	Spinster	School Teacher	61 Westminster Road Chester	Ashley Norman Goodhew	Author Captain

Married in the *St. Columba's Church* according to the rites and ceremonies of the *Roman Catholics* by *Certificate* By

This marriage was solemnized between us, { Michael Powell / Karen Goodhew } in the presence of us, { Denise Hetolé / Gerry Sloane } and in the presence of { *J. Kieran Priest* P.M. Chapman Authorised Person for St. Columba's Church }

I, P.M. Chapman , Authorised Person under the Marriage Act, 1949, do hereby certify that this is a true copy of the entry No. 5

in the Register Book of Marriages of the above-named Building.

WITNESS MY HAND this 26 ~ day of May , 1984 .

P.M. Chapman
Authorised Person.

M. Cert.
A.P.

Insert in this margin any notes which appear in the original entry.

Number 2: CHRIS WHARTON

The coincidences started in late 1992, in fact it was about 23rd December. It was the annual 'get-together' of the lads, my mates from the boys' pen, the corner we used within the pub in Chester called the Golden Eagle. I say it was the annual get-together: for me it was, for them it was normal routine on the town. They were out all the time, but for me it was just once a year, since I had been married in 1984. It was OK for me, to be honest; I didn't miss being on the town at all.

We started our Christmas pub crawl around all the pubs in the centre of town, about 7.30pm. As per usual I was staying at Steve's, so I dropped my bag off at his and we walked down Lower Bridge Street, and up to the Eagle. In my pocket was a cassette tape I had put together with songs on which included: *'Betcha Bottom Dollar', 'It Was You', 'Momma I'm Home', 'Yoko I Love you',* and *'Love's Twilight Hour'.* Although I wouldn't tell anyone what had happened to me, there was no harm in saying I had written these few songs. My intention was to ask the landlord to play the tape in the odd pub on our travels. Two songs, which were half decent on the tape, were done by a Jim Endemar, days before. He was a musician and I went to his house and sang *'Betcha Bottom Dollar',* and *'Yoko I Love You',* while he played guitar and put some drum tracks and a bass line down. In just a couple of hours he did a great job.

Christmas time in Chester was manic, and we started our boozing with a half a pint in each pub. Soon we were at the very centre of Chester. We got to a wine bar called 'Joe's'. I went upstairs to the DJ and asked if he could play the tape. It was loud and very busy, and when I got back to the downstairs bar the lads handed me my beer. We were chatting for five minutes and then someone said we were heading for Watergates, another wine bar in this rather salubrious town. There were about 10 of us and I downed my ale and said, "I've just got to go up and get my tape back from the DJ. I went upstairs to the DJ's bar where there was a man standing, talking to the DJ. I apologised to them for butting in, and I asked the DJ for my tape back. He said OK and went across to the tape machine, at the back of his area.

Just then the man standing there said to me, "What's on the tape?"

I said, "If you heard it, you would think it was Beatles' songs."

To which the man laughed out loud, and said, "Give over."

I replied by saying, "You asked didn't you, I'm just telling you."

He replied, "Seriously?"

I said, "Yes!"

He started writing something on his cigar packet and asked if he could have a listen to the tape in the New Year. I said, "OK, if you really want to." He then gave me the cigar packet, where he had written the address and telephone number of both his home and his business. As I left him standing by the DJ he laughed and said, "Music like the Beatles? Yeah, right!"

So January came around and it was the second week and I was in Chester on business. So I decided to phone this man up called Chris Wharton. It turned out he owned a business selling microwave machine to caterers, right in the city centre, and I arranged to call to his offices early afternoon, that day. I had brought a copy of the tape so we had a coffee together, listened to the tape and I left it with him. It had my name and mobile telephone on. As I was leaving he asked if I had any of the lyrics of the songs with me. I went to the car and pulled out a wodge of lyrics and sorted out the ones pertinent to the tape. We photocopied them and I passed the copies to him. He then said, "Have you copyrighted these songs?"

I said, "Yes," and told him how I had done it.

He said, "Good, that's all you need to do to prove you wrote the songs."

The very next day he phoned me and asked when I was in Chester next. I told him it would be Friday of that week. He asked me to call and see him, and I put a time in my diary to see him.

It was 2pm on Friday afternoon when I called to his offices. His secretary said, "Go right through Mike. Would you like a coffee?"

I sat down with Chris, we were having coffee and biscuits, and he asked me a question. "Who has written these songs Mike?"

I told him what I had already told him in the wine bar. "I've written them." He asked me how long I had been writing music. I replied, "About six weeks."

He burst out laughing and said, "You're taking the piss, Mike."

I asked him what he meant. He said, "The song writing is just too good. You couldn't have done it if you've never written a song before, there's no way you could have written this quality from scratch in just six weeks." He produced the lyric sheets from his desk I had left him, then went on to ask questions about some of the songs: how did you arrive at that line, what made you write that, etc. etc. He asked me again, "Do you honestly expect me to believe that you have written these songs, Mike?"

I was getting a little agitated, to say the least.

He kept me under pressure, and on one song, *'Momma I'm Home'*, he held the sheet to me and asked about 'Voorman standing in the doorman' and said again, "Where did that come from?"

I relented and said, "You really want to know the truth?"

He said, "Yes, I do!"

"OK," I replied, "John Lennon has come to me several times and given me these songs. The questions you ask I can answer, starting with 'Voorman standing in the doorman'. This was the moment John was shot and killed. The second he was hit, he somehow 'transferred' his thoughts onto me. He ended up back in Liverpool with a family waiting for him, and in the background I saw a 'doorman standing in the door man'. It didn't make sense to me, and with the speed of light (literally one or two seconds), I found myself saying that doesn't seem right. And proceeded to go right through the alphabet, ending up on Voorman. If you can imagine Aoorman, Boorman, Coorman, Doorman, Eoorman, Foorman, Goorman, Hoorman, etc. etc. All in split seconds. That's how I arrived at that line." I answered all the questions he had asked.

He didn't appear shocked, but went onto tell me that he and his wife believed that such things were possible.

This unknown stranger called Chris Wharton was to tell me that he used to go to The Star Club in Hamburg and a guy called Klaus Voormann used to also go to the Star Club, and he occasionally 'worked on the door' as a bouncer. This amazing coincidence made me feel I was on the right track, or being guided some way.

Chris had also made reference to something his wife had seen but glossed over it, feeling slightly embarrassed, I guess. But over the last couple of days, he had phoned a mate who was a saxophonist and seasoned session muso, who had incidentally played and recorded with the Beatles. He wanted an opinion from someone 'still in the business'. The guy was living in London, so during their phone call Chris arranged to fax the lyrics to him and asked him the question, "If you had to make a stab at who has written these songs, who would you say?"

The guy had phoned him back within the hour and said, "John Lennon. No question, John Lennon. It's got John's fingerprints all over them. Where did you get them from?"

Chris told him about me, he said, "I met this guy called Mike Powell when I was in a wine bar in Chester, it was my staff's Christmas Party and I talked to him, not the other way around. He's claimed he's written these songs and I've asked him to come in to see me again."

The saxophonist was fascinated and said to Chris, "Let me know what happens."

Then Chris went on to tell me about his background. **He was from Liverpool and had been a good friend of John Lennon's, as well George Harrison's.**

He told me how they used to go out drinking and 'crash' at John's flat in Gambia Terrace, and told me that the flat was literally only yards from the Liverpool Anglican Cathedral. (This was the same cathedral where, before anything happened, I had asked God for help.)

At the time, Chris's parents were quite wealthy and had a chain of butchers' shops around the North West of England. They also had a large commercial garage, where their fleet of butchers' vans would be serviced, repaired and sprayed.

He told me that when the Beatles came back from Hamburg, John didn't like his 'blonde' Rickenbacker guitar, and wanted it spraying black. He asked Chris if he would do it. Chris went into the garage one night, took all the knobs off the guitar, sanded it and sprayed the guitar with several coats of gloss black paint. He left it overnight and replaced all the bits the next day. Then John went on to do his next gig that night, which Chris thinks was Litherland Town Hall. Well, did Chris get a lambasting from John. John said to him, "You fucked my guitar up Chris, the volume control, you turn it up, the fucker goes down, turn it down, the fucker goes up." Chris fixed it and they eventually laughed about it. That same guitar was the one John became famous with. He (and the guitar) starred with the Beatles on the Royal Variety Performance – Remember that RVP where John says, "Will the people in the cheaper seats clap your hands? And the rest of you, if you'll just rattle your jewellery."

Chris also told me that he and George Harrison were both car freaks, and drove down to the Motor Show in Earl's Court in George's Zephyr 375. On the way, they stopped in a café, George wanted to know how their first song *'Love Me Do'* was doing. He came back from the phone all excited, they had a coffee, and George told Chris, "I've just phoned Eppy (apparently all the Beatles used to call Brian Epstein that) and he's told me that *'Love Me Do'* is at No 17 in the charts. At this rate Chris, I'll be able to buy myself a new car, and I'll give this one to my dad."

I was sitting in an office in Chester being told by Chris Wharton he was a good mate of John Lennon's. Chris carried on this fascinating story of his life in Liverpool. He had owned a club called Mardi Gras with a partner who was called Billy Butler. All the popular 'beat' groups of the time played there. Chris reckons 'The BIG 3' were the best band he had ever seen play live in his life, closely followed by the Beatles. Chris and Billy also had a radio show, playing all those groups' hits of the time. Chris hated the adulation that the radio show brought and left show business, and they also sold the nightclub. Chris went into the catering supplies industry, Billy Butler put all his efforts into the radio, and right up to today he is the most famous Liverpool DJ there has ever been.

Chris told me of another mate and DJ, Bob Wooler from the Cavern, who was very good. Alas, he and Billy had both seen Bob recently and he was suffering from extreme ill health. To this day, Chris and Billy remain firm friends.

Chris then offered to take me to see some other friends in Liverpool, he wanted to get their opinions of my music. Billy Kinsley and Tony Crane were the front men for the Merseybeats, and latterly Billy Kinsley was the front man in Liverpool Express, who had the number one years ago called *'You Are My Love'*. Together they also recorded *'Sorrow'*, the track made famous by David Bowie.

We arranged to go over the next week so I met Chris and dropped my car at his office in Chester. I put my guitar and some music and lyrics into his car and we headed through the Mersey Tunnel. We got to Goodison Park, home of Everton Football Club, parked off a side road and went into a small and very secured lock-up business on a small industrial estate. We got inside and I was flabbergasted. It was a 72 track state of the art recording music studio. It was dark and had moody lighting. Chris introduced me to Billy Kinsley. But first they had a good old chinwag, catching up with the news the way old friends do. Chris said to Billy, "Did you have a good Christmas?"

Billy said it had been mad. He had been very busy gigging, saying he'd done more gigs than he'd ever done in his life. "And you know how many we used to do in the 60s!" Billy went on to tell Chris that he went to Mike McCartney's New Year's party. He said, "We were all there, and Paul McCartney and his family were supposed to be coming as well. We played our guitars, and Mike got a call from Paul about 11.30pm, saying they were snarled up in heavy traffic in the centre of London (Paul, Linda and the kids). Paul had said, 'We're still coming, but we'll be hours yet.' A disappointed Mike told the other people at the party the news. One minute later there was a knock on the door. It was Paul, Linda and their family. They all shouted 'Surprise, surprise!' and that was it," Billy recalled, "we played and sang and drank until 3am. It was brilliant."

After hearing that I felt somewhat awkward, or overawed maybe. After all, I couldn't play the guitar that well. Anyway, I played the songs to him. I had sung about three, then I played *'Love's Twilight Hour'*. Billy was dumbstruck. He said, "That's the one you've got to do, it's brilliant, and that will be a hit." He then said, "My partner Tony Crane was coming in shortly, when he does, play that song and see what he says."

Tony did come in, and I played the song for him. He looked at Billy, Chris and then me and said, "That's brilliant, are you going to put that out?" meaning release it.

"I told you it was a great song, Mike," Billy retorted. He showed great enthusiasm for my songs – praise indeed!

Then I told them both the story. They both believed me and wanted to help in any way they could.

I remember Billy saying he and his engineer were mad busy with a band recording at the time, they had booked a block of several months to produce their album. But still, Billy generously offered his facilities, a separate recording room, and his four and eight track systems for me to use at no charge. What an opportunity. But as I mentioned earlier I am not a technical person and hate anything that requires technical know-how. How crazy is that? A golden opportunity wasted. With hindsight I should have found an engineer and taken up Billy's kind offer.

Number 3: JUSTIN NICHOLLS

Justin was a work colleague of mine in the late 80s. He was 18 years old and had worked on the manufacturing line. He had also done a stint in the general office and display work in the field. He came into my office to see me. He had told me that he had been fired for stealing. He had actually spent more than he should have done on a hotel, so his expenses were questioned by the owner's son, who deemed it necessary to fire him. What he didn't tell the MD, his father, was that he fancied Justin's girlfriend, also a company employee, like rotten. He was jealous of Justin and his frustration led him to jump at the opportunity to get rid of this thorn in his side, this direct opposition.

Upon hearing this, I asked Justin if he would like to come and work for me in the Marketing Department. He said yes so I went to see the MD, told him the truth about his 'wonderful, jealous' son. I also said I would take full responsibility for Justin and would put him on a three month probationary period. This the MD agreed. I went and told Justin that with immediate effect he worked for me. Any communications that the son of the owner would make to him, I insisted that he referred straight to me. This he did.

I then went and saw the owners son in his office and said, "Justin is working for me, stay away from him. Do you understand? Stay away from him, otherwise you'll have me to answer to, not Justin. Do you understand?" He understood and kept well away.

I think it had been the first time anyone had ever stood up for Justin.

The company eventually closed down, but Justin and I remained friends and kept in touch

It was Justin's house, in the conservatory, where I had the 'Nescafe coffee cup release'.

I had been playing Justin some of my songs from literally when they came to me but I had never told him of the sightings. I confided in him all about Karen and he empathised. Sometimes I would call up with my children to see him and he'd take photos of the kids in sepia in the back garden. He was quite a talented photographer.

And then after hearing the songs, just like Karen had, and Chris Wharton, and the saxophonist, he started saying to me that they sound like Beatles' songs.

I tried to act surprised at what he was saying to me, in fact almost dismissing his comments. Obviously, I knew why they sounded like Beatles' songs Also, he had never seen 'the letter' I wrote on 3rd December 1992, about my John Lennon experiences to a third party. This was towards the end of 1993, so almost a year had passed.

Eventually, I told him the story. He was amazed, and immediately volunteered the following information. He told me that when he was a kid, a relative of his knew Cynthia Lennon and how Cynthia and Julian used to visit his parents' house and he would **play games with Julian Lennon.** He said Julian used to get bored easily and never finished a game off. I think he was a bit spoilt. I am not sure whether the relative was an uncle or cousin, but I believe his name was Jim Christie. What is weird about this is that Justin only told me about him after I had told him about a sighting I'd had of John Lennon, in fact sighting No. 10 called 'I Wish I Could Fly'. There was a bald-headed man standing in the shadows of this sighting, which I painted and felt really uncomfortable about. I tried to explain how ill at ease this 'person' had made me and could only describe him as 'Christie' or 'Crippen' – both murderers. He also told me that when he was 10 years old in 1980 he had a bad dream and went into his parents' bedroom. **He said to them, "I've just had a dream that John Lennon is dead."**

The parents put him back to bed and said it was only a dream, try and go back to sleep. The date was 8th December 1980, and it was very early in the morning. The following day the tragic news was all over the media: JOHN LENNON SHOT DEAD. I spoke to his parents about what Justin had told me, and they confirmed this story to be true.

I would eventually appear on the television show GMTV (7th February 1994) and Justin was to travel down with me, but bottled it literally the day before. The TV company had the hotel rooms booked for both of us, the train journey paid for, and the hotel food. Sadly he made up some excuse, so trivial, I can't even remember what it was. I can only surmise that he was frightened of any backlash, being associated with this 'nutter' called Mike Powell. Whatever it was, he never told me the real reason. We had typed up a contract, with me and him managing me! He promised me that he could get me a recording deal through his friend Mike Connaris who owned Macasso Music, and would introduce me to the very talented jazz singer, Ian Shaw.

Nothing happened.

We fell out when he couldn't deliver his side of the bargain, although I gave him ample opportunity. The saddest part of all of this was that Justin was my best friend and we had known each other for years. He was beginning to let me down over a couple of business dealings and to add insult to injury, when we fell out and I cancelled the management contract with him he'd told Billy Shears (the Lennon soundalike on 'It Was You') that I had made the whole story up and all these songs had been written "not by Mike, but by his father".

He let me down once at a TV show we attended in Scotland that was all about body builders. We met the Gladiator called Hunter, who was on TV regularly at the time. Instinctively, within seconds after meeting him, I said to Justin, "We'll manage Hunter, we'll get him a fashion clothes deal and I'll do a song for him as well." I asked Justin to go back and get Hunter's phone number, and we would make an appointment to meet him in more appropriate circumstances

Justin got his phone number.

Justin got a management contract to manage Hunter, but on his own.

Justin got him a contract with a leading national fashion clothes outfitter, Cirrio Cirratta.

Justin got him a contract for an album deal, the first single planned for release being 'Shakaboom' The music was produced by his friend, Mike Connaris.

Also, there was a local boyband Justin had heard of, through a friend who knew them. They were called Ecos. He asked for my opinion of them. He said he had the chance to co-manage them and he would like me to be their marketing manager, eventually buying out the other partner, and I would co-manage them. I gave him the marketing support and suggestions.

The other partner had a double glazing company and had been funding the band for about 18 months and his son also sang in the band. His son was the least talented, but the other three were superb. I wrote a song for them that they sang at 'Children in Need', in Birmingham. The song was called 'Help the Children in Need'. I told Justin to lose the weak singer and we'd concentrate on the main three. Justin kept them from me and eventually fell out with the other manager. The band went underground only to pop up a year or so later as a band called BBMak.

They were playing on Radio 1 and 2, and appeared on Top of the Pops. And the band consisted of just three boys, the three talented ones. I understand Justin was going after damages as he was claiming something connected with management, ownership of some existing recorded songs and marketing. He said he should be able to get me some money, when they settled. I never heard from him again.

Number 4:
GMTV, URI GELLAR AND THE POLYDOR CONTRACT

I had been on GMTV. It was 7th March1994. They played *'It Was You'* whilst they were showing footage of the Beatles in various locations, as well as showing the grieving in New York on the news of John Lennon's death. The big question that Eamonn Holmes was asking that morning to the nation was: "Listen to this music Mike Powell claims came to him from John Lennon. Is this the music of John Lennon, or not?"

Prior to going on air the producer told me I was going to see someone who would ask me several questions. He reiterated that if I was making this whole thing up I would be exposed by this person. Next thing I remember was being taken into a tiny windowless room, just off from the main studio, and then Uri Gellar came in. The producer introduced the two of us, and left the room.

Straight away, without any big introductions, Uri got straight into me, asking lots and lots of questions in no time at all. I don't know whether he was trying to trick me, but as quickly as he was asking the questions I was giving him the answers without any thought or pondering, but straight away. After about 25 questions we left the room and he told the producer, "Yes, Mike is telling the truth, I believe him."

Within two minutes of that conversation, we were sitting side by side on the GMTV couch. Eamonn Holmes and Lorraine Kelly were the presenters, and the interview commenced.

Uri told the viewers that he knew John Lennon, and John was always talking to him about his fascination with the afterlife. The interview went well and I got the train out of Euston and back to Crewe, where I had parked my car, and drove back home to Mold.

It had been a tiring day and I went to bed at 10pm. At 10.30pm there was a knock on my bedroom door, it was Karen holding the phone with a puzzled look on her face. She said, "It's Uri Gellar on the phone for you."

I spoke to a very enthusiastic Uri, and the conversation went something like this:

(UG) "Mike, Mike, I have not thought about anything else all day. I believe you totally, John came to you. I have got some ideas, and I would like you to come and visit me ASAP."

(MP) "Great, what about?"

(UG) "I want to use the song that came from John to you called *'Everything's In Reverse'*. I want to use it as the main music title track in the film I am doing about my life."

He said that we would need to talk about a contract, and how he wanted to manage me. He went on to say, **"What you don't know Mike is that the day before I met you in the studios, I was on the phone to Yoko in New York, asking her permission for me to use John's song *'Imagine'* as the music title track to my film, 'Uri'. She turned me down, and then, right out of the blue, the producer phones me and asks me to come into the studio and meet you. You have all these fantastic songs coming from John Lennon. Talk about a coincidence, or synchronicity."**

We arranged a time and date for the following week. I'll never forget the visit.

I arrived in Sonning on Thames at about 1.30pm. I buzzed at the intercom and looked toward the cameras overhead. There was a high wall of thick, neatly trimmed hedges, about nine foot high. Hannah, Uri's wife, answered the intercom and said, "Come through Mike." I went through the gate, another two walls, and another two gates, along the stone chipped path. I parked right opposite the rather grandiose main entrance. I got out of the car and started walking towards this main door. Just then, barking and snarling as furious and as loud as I have ever heard. From round the corner, hurtling at full speed towards me, came three of the most enormous King Doberman dogs I have ever seen in my life. I was halfway from my locked car, to the main door entrance, in no man's land. I dropped my overnight bag and sprinted as if my life depended on it towards, I hoped, an unlocked front door. As I sprinted I left a bald path in my wak, where the loose stone chippings had been, as you might well imagine Steve Austin the Bionic Man would have done. As I was getting nearer to the door these 'growling monsters' were getting nearer to me.

Just then, at the last second prior to impact, a man came to the half glazed fine Edwardian door and opened it in the nick of time. I was about 8 foot away, and by the time I put the brakes on I was 15 feet inside the grand foyer. That's how fast I was going. Well, the man was Uri's manager and Hannah's brother, Shipi.

He was crying with laughter and said, "That must be a world record sprint." It took him some time to stop laughing, and me to stop shaking. He said, "I'm going to let the dogs in now to meet you Mike, they are OK, just be friendly towards them." He opened the door and these bastard dogs came straight over to me and were sniffing all around my feet and my privates. They were obnoxious, and what made it worse was the way that their dog owner thought nothing about their dogs invading my space. "They are only playing, they won't harm you," or some shit like that. The bastards were sniffing my bollocks and I was trying to act normal, you know, pushing them away. They had a vicious look about them, and I wondered if this was the way you would have to live if you became famous. I think not!

I met Uri after freshening up. I stayed in the lodge by the swimming pool. We had a bite to eat then we went for a walk, out of his rear garden and through his back door that faced the River Thames. We walked for about five miles along the river pathway, enjoying this green and pleasant backwater, which was some 40 miles or so from London Town. That evening, another coincidence was to occur. One of Uri's friends and his girlfriend arrived and joined us for the great dinner we were to have in Uri's huge conservatory.

Uri asked how long the guy was in the UK for, and he replied, "We flew in this morning, and we fly out tomorrow evening." Uri asked him what he was doing in London, this time. This guy and his stunning model girlfriend were very well-heeled; they oozed success and money from every pore. The guy said, "Oh, we've been over to look at a mansion for sale in Virginia Water, in Surrey. It was John Lennon's house."

Uri looked at me and said, "Has Mike got a story to tell you. But first, are you going to buy the house?"

The guy said, "No, it didn't feel right. I didn't get a good vibe in there."

I went on to tell him my story, and he wanted to stay in touch with me. Uri quickly moved in to say, "I am going to be managing Mike."

Still the guy said to me, "Keep in touch Mike." I didn't get his card, Uri made sure of it. After they had gone Uri told me that he was the guy who put up the seven million (dollars, I think) for the film 'Uri', the film that Uri wanted my song, *Everything's In Reverse* for.

We talked about this song, and all the others, and some sort of ideas Uri had about launching me onto the world stage. He said he would speak to the record company Polydor and get back to me within a couple of days. We had lunch and I drove back home to North Wales. Two days later and Uri faxed me a 'heads of agreement' contract for me to have a look at and a think about, stating the terms he wanted. He was asking for 50% of everything, on songs done and not yet done. He told me his close friends were the Bee Gees and Mungo Jerry. They lived close by and would help produce the music in their studios.

I thought at the time he was being greedy and I said I needed some time to think about it. I would get back to him inside two weeks. We agreed, and I put the phone down and pondered what might be in the future. Strangely, I also thought of those King Doberman dogs.

Number 5: RONAN O'RAHILLY, RADIO CAROLINE AND ALL THAT

A day or so after receiving Uri's faxed contract I got a phone call out of the blue from Ronan O'Rahilly, founder of the pirate radio ship, Radio Caroline. I had been inundated with calls from all kinds of people, from BBC'S Dominic Savage, who wanted to do a BBC 'Forty Minutes' programme about me. The programme was based in BBC Bristol. There were interviews with several radio stations, Argentinian TV did an interview with me at the Rock Circus etc. etc. There were also a few calls from 'spiritualists' and other people, all inviting me to give a talk to their 'flock'. All of which I said no to. I had so many calls via the GMTV studio that in the end I phoned them up and said, "Don't give my number out to anyone else." They agreed. And days later, I got this phone call from Ronan O'Rahilly. I asked how he got my number, and he told me that he'd done a rare telephone interview with the researcher, who had been trying to speak with Ronan for ages. It was over a famous jazz/blues player that had just died, and Ronan had known very well in the 60s. He gave the researcher the interview on condition he got my phone number.

We talked for one hour. **He told me that he was one of John Lennon's best friends.** Apparently he booked John, Yoko and himself into one of Ireland's most exclusive and private hotels. The three of them were also photographed on the tarmac at Shannon Airport, on the front page of the Irish Times, and other newspapers of the day. Yoko had a word in Ronan's ear as they crossed the tarmac about how worried she was for John's safety as he was getting involved with the John F Kennedy assassination conspiracy theories, something Ronan was making a film about. John and Yoko wanted to buy a small island off the west coast of Ireland. So Ronan chartered a helicopter and they set off to the island. John had a tape recording to two brand new songs no one else had yet heard – 'Come Together' and 'Number Nine'.

He told me that after Brian Epstein (the Beatles' manager) had died from a 'suspected' drug overdose, John phoned Ronan immediately and said, "I want you to manage the Beatles, you are the only one in the world I trust." Ronan did meet Sir Joseph Locke, head of EMI at the time, and over lunch told this man that if he did take over the Beatles' management, the first thing he would do would be to get them a serious pay rise. The guy said, "They are all millionaires." Ronan said that they should be multi-millionaires. Ronan spoke to John days later and told him how flattered he had been at being asked, but he had decided not to manage the Beatles, purely because he could see years of difficult litigation ahead, which proved to be the case. The interesting thing is that Ronan reckoned that John was orchestrating the whole thing from 'the other side', saying, "John wanted me to manage the Beatles, and now I am managing you, who is receiving songs from John."

There are literally hundreds of stories Ronan told me over the years. Like when he re-opened The Cavern Club in 1966 and got Harold Wilson, the then Prime Minister, to do the official opening.

I will tell you just a few stories, in short detail, so you can get a flavour of the man, Ronan O'Rahilly.

One story he told me:

He flew up to Newcastle on a tip off about an up and coming group. He watched their gig at a local club and realised he had found a brilliant group with a dynamic singer. The first words he said to them after seeing them perform was, "You're a bunch of animals, I'm going to call you 'The Animals'," and agreed on the spot to manage them, under the group name he had just given them. Nothing was signed at the time, but he had arranged for them to play at his club in London called The Scene, and of course sort out the contract. Working in his club at the time was a failed guitarist from Australia, who was more or less down and out. He used to brush and clean at The Scene for a few bob, and would sleep on the club's tables. The particular day that The Animals came into the club it was early in the day, Ronan was at meetings somewhere in London, and the only person there was this cleaner, this failed guitarist.

The group set up their gear and started to play. The cleaner saw this amazing talent and its potential, and he nicked the band from under Ronan's nose; he signed them up. He got a contract, a record deal, and their first world number one smash hit was called 'The House Of The Rising Sun'. And the guy's name who went on to manage them and own his own record label? It was Mickey Most. Ronan used to say to me, "No favour goes unpunished," in reference to the double crossing by The Animals and Mickey Most.

To date, the only person in that whole scenario to really apologise to him was the group's bassist, Chas Chandler. He is the person that found (and later managed) Jimi Hendrix. He'd found Jimi performing in a café in downtown New York and brought him over to London to appear at the Bag O' Nails club. It was a hip place where everyone who was anyone went. Present that day were the Beatles, the Rolling Stones, Eric Clapton, Jimmy Page and of course, Ronan O'Rahilly. Ronan was Radio Caroline owner, night club owner, record label owner, entrepreneur, former manager of The Alexis Corner Blues Band, Eric Clapton, Rick Mayall, The Rolling Stones, The Blockheads and Georgie Fame. Actually, the list goes on and on. Ronan recalls the reaction of all the guitarists and everyone in the room present when Hendrix performed. They were speechless. They all wanted to throw their guitars away. They had become instant guitar 'also rans'. He was sensational, a true genius had been found. No wonder Clapton made friends with Jimi as soon as he got off the stage! "Jimi Hendrix was doing something new," recalls

Ronan, "and by the way Mike, you are going to have that same effect on people, not with a guitar, but with your voice."

Another story he told me:
The Beatles were making the White Album in Abbey Road, London. At the time the Beatles had become the biggest band in the world, and the world's press would gather from morning till nightfall, just to be able to take the odd photo of a Beatles' band member getting out of or into their blacked out stretch Limos. No one, but no one was allowed anywhere near the studios other than their producer, a guy called George Martin. There was one exception.

Ronan O'Rahilly.
John Lennon's best friend.

At this particular time, over a three month period, Ronan practically lived with John and Yoko.
One morning in a recording studio in Abbey Road, standing around, leaning on a piano and talking to each other in anticipation of John and Yoko's arrival, were several important people. They were George Martin, Paul McCartney, George Harrison, Ringo Starr and Ronan O'Rahilly.
When they did arrive, John walked straight towards Ronan with Yoko following in quick pursuit, taking her small but nimble steps; as always she was inseparable from her lover.
John gave Ronan a brown A4 envelope and said, "Ronan, this is *my* Radio Caroline."
Ronan opened the envelope and pulled out a naked photograph of John and Yoko. John said, "This is going to be the cover of our album," meaning his and Yoko's album that they were currently putting together called Two Virgins. Ronan's reaction was to say, "Fuckin' brilliant." On looking around to see the other people's reactions, Ronan looked at George Martin, who had turned as white as a ghost. Paul McCartney turned red as a beetroot. George and Ringo were to remain silent, which spoke volumes. George Martin said to John, "I am not sure whether EMI would want to put that photo/album cover out."
Ronan interjected, "Hey John, if they don't, I'll put it out." There was an embarrassing few moments for everyone except John, Yoko and Ronan.

It was one of the proudest moments of Ronan's life. John was telling him that he'd recognised Ronan had striven to do something different, to make a difference. And that's what John and Yoko were also doing, hence the first words in the studio that morning John uttered: "RONAN, THIS IS MY RADIO CAROLINE."

When Ronan relayed this story to me, I wrote a song almost instantly called *'This Is My Caroline'*, and it's all about that studio session.

And finally, another story he told me. Ronan went into his club, The Scene, unexpectedly one morning and heard someone singing and playing a Hammond organ. He couldn't see the person who was on the stage but behind the stage curtain, which was down. Ronan thought it was the voice of a brilliant black singer. He opened the curtains to find a small, northern Lancashire lad, playing the keys and singing. He asked what his name was, and the reply was, "I am Clive Powell."

Ronan said, "Clive, you're a star mate." This time Ronan took no chances, he signed Clive up right away and touted his music around the record companies in London. No one wanted to know. One record company said, "Black music isn't in at the moment, we're not interested."

Ronan said, "But he's not black."

The reply was, "Well he sounds black, it's the same difference."

It was so obvious to Ronan that this guy was a star. So he set his own record company up called Island Records. He started managing him. He changed his name from Clive Powell to Georgie Fame and promptly had his first number one hit with the single *'Yeah, Yeah'*.

Ronan said to me, of everyone he had ever met in the music business, only two people were genuinely honest and decent human beings. One was Georgie Fame and the other one was John Lennon. He then referred to me as being only the third one he had ever come across. Praise indeed!

There is another coincidence in this little story that beggars belief.

Sometime in April 1994 I had been asked to gather sworn affidavits of people who were close to me, friends growing up, work colleagues, etc. The affidavits related to the person stating that to their knowledge I had never written any music or sang etc. before 16th November 1992, the day of the first sighting and the first song I had ever written in my life.

One of the affidavits was sworn by Mike Travers, a good friend and the owner of the print company Collins & Darwell, based in Leigh, Lancashire. I had known him for 12 years and the last few years I had a desk and my own phone line in his print works. I put all my print work through Mike and he didn't charge me for 'my office', which gave me credibility and a base from which to work from. It was May 1994 when I asked Mike for the affidavit. He signed one in the local solicitors and I also videoed him more or less stating what he had just signed. I went on to tell him about the person who I had met called Ronan O'Rahilly who started Radio Caroline, and mentioned to Mike some of the pop stars he had managed over the years. **To one of the names I mentioned, Georgie Fame, Mike replied, "Bloody hell, you mean Clive Powell, George's real name?"**

I said, "Yes, that's him."

Mike said, **"Clive used to work for us. He used to deliver the Leigh Gazette, the local paper we used to print, years and years ago. In fact, Clive used to sit at that very desk that you're using now. Bloody hell Mike, that's *some* coincidence isn't it?"**

Ronan O'Rahilly on one occasion told me that when he wrote his biography, he was going to call it **'FROM CLIVE POWELL TO MIKE POWELL'**.

Sadly, that was not to be the case.

Number 6:
MY DAD BOUGHT BRIAN EPSTEIN'S CAR

My eldest brother Brian told me of the time in the early 60s when he was working with our dad, George, in a Ford main dealers in Liverpool called SLS Motors. They had a commercial vehicles dept, and George and he were signwriting a van. Dad saw this car in the showroom, it was less than one year old and was 'like new'. **It was a gleaming bottle green Ford Zodiac and it had just one previous owner, Brian Epstein, the manager of the Beatles.**

Number 7:
GEORGE BRIAN POWELL, MY ELDEST BROTHER

When Brian left school at 16 he got an apprenticeship with a well-known ophthalmic manufacturing company in Old Hall Street, Liverpool.

The company's business was to make lenses for people's glasses. **The year was 1965, Brian was 16, and I was 10 years old.**
I was getting an affidavit and a video from him in May 1994, during the course of which he informed me that he had worked on a pair of spectacles which were like 'milk bottles', which were for John Lennon.

Number 8:
JOHN LESLIE BEAUMONT, MARRIED MY SISTER
He told me that he was in the same class as Paul McCartney at his junior school, which was called Stockton Wood Road School. John was a general builder, and was doing work for many national celebrities, including Ken Dodd, Jimmy Tarbuck and Johnny Hackett who all lived in the North West of England.
He also did a lot of building/extension work for Brian Epstein, the Beatles' manager.
Brian Epstein lived in the fifth house from the roundabout, at No. 275 Queens Drive, off the junction of the Childwall Fiveways.

Number 9: THE SONG PENNY LANE AND THE BARBER'S SONG
There is a line in the Beatles' song *'Penny Lane'* that says, 'Penny Lane there is a barber showing photographs, of every head he's had the pleasure to know...' During the mid/late nineties The Beatles Anthology was brought out, along with a couple of John Lennon's previously unreleased and unfinished tracks. One of the tracks that featured in the anthology, that the remaining Beatles played on over John's haunting vocal, was called *'Free as a Bird'*. The backdrop of the video for this song was shot in Penny Lane. On it, it shows you the barber's shop called Tony Slavin's. That very same barber's shop in Penny Lane had the signwriting done by my dad Georgie Powell. **My dad wrote the sign for the barber's shop in Penny Lane; very strange!**

All change: the home of Paul McCartney as it was in the Sixties and (above right) with modern alterations which have to go

A cut above: the Penny Lane barber's shop

Number 8; The song PENNY LANE, and the barber shop

There is a line in the Beatles' song 'Penny Lane' that says, .. 'Penny lane there is a barber showing photographs, of every head he's had the pleasure to know..'. During the mid/late nineties, The Beatles Anthology was brought out, along with a couple of John Lennon's previously unreleased, and unfinished tracks. One of the tracks that was featured in the Anthology, that the remaining Beatles played on, over John's haunting vocal, was called 'Free as a Bird' The backdrop of the video for this song was shot in Penny Lane. On it, it shows you that Barber's shop called Tony Slavin's. That very same barber shop in Penny Lane was signwritten by my dad Georgie Powell. My dad signwrote the barber's shop in Penny Lane,.. very strange !

Paul, Ringo and Tony Slavin

UNLIKE drums emblazoned with the word "Beatles", scribbled John Lennon lyrics or cast-off Sergeant Pepper clothes, buildings make less than perfect pop memorabilia because they are so notoriously unportable — you can hardly set them up in the corner of your living-room as talking points.

That has not stopped pop's responsible for this morning's controversial sale of Fab Four memorabilia at Bonhams in Knightsbridge, London, from including a couple of buildings.

The Penny Lane barber's shop and the two-up, two-down terrace house in Toxteth, where Ringo Starr was born, sit at a little unerasily alongside Paul McCartney's gold-plated guitar, not to mention an avalanche of otherwise worthless clobber.

Paul, for the Beatles fan who has

everything, the barber's shop might appeal. It is definitely the one immortalised in the song and has been included in the sale at a guide price of £190,000. The Toxteth birthplace of Ringo Star could be yours for £10,000–£15,000.

If there was ever any doubt that it is the tune that makes a song and not the words, then *Penny Lane's* lyrics demonstrate the point. But the auctioneers hope the new owner will soon be wondering about his or her new domain humming: *"There is a barber showing photographs/Of every head he's had the pleasure to know".*

Tony Slavin's Ladies and Gentleman's Hair Stylists is the salon of which the Beatles song, although, technically, it is in Smithfield Place. There can be little doubt that this is "the most famous barber shop in

musical history", as the brochure floridly describes it, but can its price really be justified?

Penny Lane's non-Beatles-related businesses have been in decline for years, as the area has had to compete with the larger shops and facilities of nearby Allerton Road. What would someone do with the shop?

Gary Murphy, the auctioneer, argues that it is unique and impossible to value accurately. "It could easily go to double our estimate," he says.

A too-up, two-down terrace house in Toxteth is, on the face of it, a much more affordable souvenir, although it suffers from not featuring in any Beatles' songs (as well as being in a state of near-dereliction). It did, however, produce one Richard Starkey, later Ringo Starr, into the world and was his home for the first three years

of his life. Although it is part of the Magical Mystery bus tour, which operates for Beatles devotees visiting Liverpool, it does not have the same pilgrim status of Penny Lane monuments.

Murphy is quick to point out that it is the area and condition of the house, rather than the link with Ringo, that makes the guide price relatively low. "The property is in Toxteth, which has its own history," he says. "No one's pretending it's a great house, least of all Ringo."

And if they miss this opportunity, those with an eye on the market for increasingly tenuous examples of pop memorabilia could do worse than buy the house-next-door-to-the-one-where-Ringo-Starr-was-born. With luck it could be even cheaper.

Tom Rowland

Tony Slavin

Article from the Weekend Telegraph, 22nd March 1997, about the auction of the Penny Lane barber shop.

Number 10: THE STRANGE TRIANGLE

There is a strange triangle if you look at a Liverpool suburb street map. It's only strange to me, given the circumstances of me seeing John and other coincidences that have occurred. I visited my brother after not seeing him for years to tell him my story of my John Lennon experiences. When I had finished telling him, he took me in his car to three places very close by. He took me to Paul McCartney's house, John Lennon's House, and Strawberry Fields and said, "Fancy me living near where the Beatles lived."

When I got home I looked at a Liverpool street map and found my brother was inside of a strange triangle connecting these three places.

Look at Forthlin Avenue, this is where Paul McCartney lived.

Now look at Menlove Avenue, this is where John Lennon lived in a house called 'Mendips'.

Now look at Strawberry Fields on Beaconsfield Road, this was a nursing home that John wrote about.

Now look at Moorcroft Road, this is where my brother Brian lives within this triangle.

Number 11:

THE TURKEY HOLIDAY, WITH MY MATE STEVE ASPLET

It was in or around September 1996 and I was living in Broadbottom. I still kept in touch with my best mate, Steve Asplet, from Chester. I was stony broke when Steve phoned me to ask how I was doing in my new house. I had moved from North Wales and hadn't seen Steve for ages. Truth is, I was still getting over the divorce and I was missing my beloved children like mad. Every time I saw the kids then bade them farewell, I would get knots in my stomach and feel sick to my guts.

Steve's reason for the call was to ask me if I fancied going away for a break to Turkey, to the resort of Marmaris, in fact. I hummed and aahed, but Steve said, "It will do you good, you need a break and it's only £125, all inclusive, food airfare, hotel, everything."

So I decided to go with him.

It was a real tonic, and at the end of it I felt so refreshed. I was ready to continue where I had left off. I was still picking songs out of my box file and getting them copyrighted, and recording them down onto tape. I was still working nine to five so any music was done in the evening to early morning. As you can imagine, my days were quite long. This break was just what I needed. Then, as we were standing in the huge marble floored airport lounge, in readiness to leave, I thought about John Lennon. I wondered if he knew where I was, and how happy and refreshed I was feeling, ready to get stuck into his songs again, as soon as I got home.

We checked into the departure terminal, got our boarding tickets, and all I remember doing was walking through to the departure lounge on my own. I don't know where Steve was, but I remember hearing loud shouting voices. And they got louder and louder until I turned around and two police/army personnel grabbed me by my arms and frogmarched me to a silent area of this big complex, away from the public. In all the commotion, Steve came to within about 15 metres of me and the guards, as near as he dared. We both had no idea what was going on. One guard said to me, "Don't move!" and he spoke in Turkish on his intercom. I was by a wall that had a ledge running around it that was about half a metre wide. It looked similar to a coffee/snack-to-go type ledge you see in the likes of Starbucks or Costa coffee bars. The floor was immaculate gloss marble. There wasn't a speck of dirt anywhere. There were no other people about, there was nothing of any description I could recall. Then I decided to lean my arm on this 'ledge', which was about the same height as you would do on an English pub bar.

I looked to where I was about to rest my arm and lying there flat was a gift bag. It was totally out of place, there was nothing else anywhere on this ledge, just this small white paper bag.

I picked the bag up and was astonished to see the word IMAGINE. This was a gift shop bag from somewhere in Turkey.

This, I believe was John's way of saying, I do know where you are.

Bizarrely, the guard told me I had walked through to the departure gate before we had been called. Nothing more than that! And Steve and I were walking to our departure area within five minutes. If I didn't know better, I'd say John 'orchestrated' it so the guards would take me to that very spot where the paper bag was to let me know, that John knew and experienced my enjoyment of this overdue break from all the insanity. Also, a few days before leaving Marmaris, **I had bought a thick** pair of brightly coloured hand knitted woollen socks, to use with my walking boots when I got home. On arriving home I unpacked the socks only to find the initials J L in the general pattern, running through the whole design, which I hadn't seen at the time of buying them.

Number 12:
PETE THE MEAT, MY FRIEND FROM CONNAH'S QUAY

Peter Wynne Jones was a butcher who was married to Maggie, a school teaching colleague of Karen's. We would regularly go to each other's houses and eat and drink, and have a good laugh. That was in the early days, before Karen started carrying on with her shenanigans. This was a bit of a one-off and we were both putting on a brave face to our friends, and they still didn't know what had happened to me, with these John Lennon sightings. **The year was 1993, Pete and I had left the girls at home having a good old natter, while we walked the 200 yards from my front door to Mold town centre. We nipped out for a couple of pints before the meal was ready, only for about an hour or so. We were in the Kings wine bar, when right out of the blue, Pete told me about how the Beatles used to play in the big pub on the high street, here in Mold.** It was the black and white building, mock Tudor, and it used to be the main pub in Mold. It was no longer a pub, it was now trading as one of these cheapo discount pharmacy type outlets. We walked to another pub, and as we walked by we stopped at this black and white building, **and Pete reminisced about the good old days in the 60s and how he and his friends from 'the Quay' used to drive up to Mold in an old banger to see the Beatles whenever they played here. He told me how the band used to play two sets, and at the break the band would nip out of the back for a fag, or maybe more. Pete told me that where my house was now standing, at the time there were no houses, just trees and allotments, a place where courting couples would go!** The large house where we lived had been built in the early 70s, so that makes sense. Then I thought Pete has made reference to where my house was now standing, in the same breath as insinuating that the band courted the girls from the pub. When Pete said 'out the back', that is exactly the direction to get back to my house. Then Pete recalled the sheer amount of girls around the Beatles at this time, throwing themselves at these four Scouse lads collectively known as the Beatles. Pete was about 10 or 11 years older than me, which meant in 1960 he was an underage drinker. Tut tut Pete, shame on you!

What was weird about the night, was that I never knew that Pete had ever seen the Beatles, and I never knew they played in Mold. And I never knew that courting couples used to go amongst the trees, where my house was now standing.

Then an incredible possibility hit me between the eyes.

What if John Lennon had 'courted' someone on the very spot where my house now stood?

What if he'd just walked to this very spot for a bit of peace and quiet, a break from the loud noise and the screaming?

What if he had done it several times, and always went to the same place?

What if, after he'd died, he went back to his favourite old haunts, and what if one of those favourite places was here, on the spot where my house now stood? Then another weird thing hit me. We had only recently extended and built our brand new bedroom on the house.

Did John come back to this spot after his death to reminisce and found Mike Powell there, a man who had asked for God's, and his mum and dad's help? Perhaps John found me by accident?

And after all that, did he like the idea of coming back to this spot and sharing his music still inside him with me? Was it therapeutic for him? Did we help each other over the biggest tragedies in our two lives? It's got to be a possibility, if you can 'think outside of the box'. The only thing we know for sure is that we are all going to die. What we don't know is why we only use 10% of our brains when we are alive. What about the other 90%, is it used afterwards, in some release from shutdown mode? During my sightings I have experienced vast quantities of information being downloaded through thought transferral from John to me. That being the case, logically that would have to mean that you can still function/reason on the other side of life, in death.

'Makes you thinkx, stink bomb stinkx, booboo and jinks, pour the drinkx, remember me!'

(This is a line from the song called *'Chimney Pots'*, from the 6th sighting.)

Number 13:

SONIA SELIGSON, BRIAN EPSTEIN'S BEAU

My friend Steve Asplet bought a second home in Spain in spring 1997. I remember him showing me the details of this flat that he bought for £36k. We were sitting in his house in the centre of Chester, and he knew exactly what he was going to do regarding extending and opening up the rooftop. I thought at the time it seemed a bit expensive and the way property moved, and with Steve's vision, that same flat was nearer £200k in 2006. His instincts to buy were dead right, despite the short term financial hardships it brought him, he was right on the money.

I went to his apartment to help paint and modernise it. He also opened up the rooftop and created the most beautiful terrace I think I've ever seen. The views over the Aloha golf course and the mountain range dominating the skyline in the west and the north of Marbella can only be described as spectacular. I went several times with him over the years, the first time being in 1998. We used to drive to old Marbella town and walk along the seafront promenade, past Sean Connery's fabulous old house in its own grounds. Stopping off every now and then for a café con leche, maybe a beer, or if it was near lunchtime a menu del dao. This usually consisted of a bottle of tinto, a starter like paella, main course like pork chops, potato and vegetables, followed by a sweet, ice cream or coffee. Three courses and a bottle of wine for about three pounds.

And come early evening, say seven or eight o'clock, we would prepare something like a chicken dinner, roast potatoes, fresh vegetables, with all the trimmings and lashings of gravy, all washed down with of bottle of fruity tasting, tremendous Rioja. We would then drive down to Puerto Banus and walk the walk, see the sea, drink the drink, view the views, in this plastic and solid gold millionaires' paradise, where size counts for everything; size of your boat, size of your car, size of your apartment, size of your label on your designer clothes and sunglasses, size of your bank balance. It was pure horrendous bull-one-up-man-shit, but nevertheless fascinating to visit and great to leave.

On one occasion, in 2001, Steve and I called to see an older lady nearby, whom Steve had helped in the past. As we drove down towards Puerto

Banus we called in to see her and Steve introduced me to Sonia Seligson. I think that originally there was a problem with her plumbing, and Steve had sorted it out for her. In return she took him for a meal, and thereafter they'd see each other for coffee. He had made a good friend in Sonia, who offered him intelligent conversation. She was an ex-pat who had moved over from the UK in 1994. She was from Liverpool.

We called to see her and had a coffee, and I find out the following.

She was from an affluent family in Liverpool. Her father had the biggest jewellers in the north west of England. She was courting Brian Esptein at the time, also affluent, and also Jewish, whose father owned the huge store in Liverpool centre called NEMS. This is where Brian worked, managing the record department, when one day he was inundated with requests for a record from an unknown band called Beatles. They were local boys and had just come back from a long stint in Hamburg, Germany. This is where they would play music for up to eight hours a night in the Star Club. Apparently, they became very good. Out of curiosity, he was to check the band out at a local dingy cellar club called The Cavern, and the rest is history. **There is a photograph of Sonia and Brian in evening wear, pictured in the Adelphi Hotel, Liverpool. In the book 'The Brian Epstein Story' the caption that accompanies the picture says, 'Brian Epstein, accompanied by his beau Sonia Seligson', inside the grand Liverpool Adelphi Hotel.'** This was the upper classes at play. At the time, in late 1950s' England, the Adelphi catered for the world's richest and elite upmarket passengers, either waiting for or arriving from their round the world cruise. The stopover in Liverpool, if you were anyone of any substance, would have been the Adelphi hotel. Liverpool was a thriving port, chock-a-block with ocean going liners that would transport them, first class, anywhere and everywhere in the world on the huge passenger liners such as the Mauritania, Lusitania and Queen Elizabeth.

The photograph of Brian and his beau was taken when he had started to manage The Beatles, and before his personal and private life became common knowledge, that is to say his attraction towards men.

Another coincidence, apart from Sonia being the girlfriend of, and going out with Brian Epstein, was that Sonia's father was the biggest jeweller in Liverpool. I make reference to the song *'Sometime in the 50s'*, the 34th sighting. The song was copyrighted on 18th July, 1994, seven years before I meet Sonia. In the sighting I see a man with 'diamond tie-pin, right out of a magazine'. Also a line in the song that says, 'he was a jeweller, had a shop in London Road, didn't come from round our way.' Another question raises its head. Did Sonia's father, brother, or anyone male connected with the jeweller's business take John Lennon's mother out, when John was aged about nine years old?

Another coincidence was that Sonia had introduced me to her friend called Nigel Mallinson. I told them about the John Lennon sightings and they were blown away. In fact Nigel wrote me a letter, saying how privileged and humbled he had felt at being told this amazing story. He lived in West London and frequented the Oriel Brasserie. A place I knew well and a place O'Rahilly used to call his 'office'.

He told me he knew and had had dealings with Ronan O'Rahilly, apparently, a couple of years earlier Nigel had spoken to O'Rahilly about his friend who was a scriptwriter. Ronan had promised the earth, so Nigel got the script to him, and upon reading it Ronan started promising fantastic things, only to let them down. Ronan was living on his past Radio Caroline days and that credibility but was now full of 'hot air', I think was the expression Nigel had used.

Number 14:
MEETING CHRIS WHARTON'S SISTER-IN-LAW

I was on holiday with my girlfriend, Hilary, in January 2006. We were in Bangkok, in a little restaurant cum bar that served organic vegetarian food. There was a couple close by, and probably only about six people in total in the restaurant. Apparently, the man had said to the woman, "I bet he's from Liverpool, I can tell by his accent." The woman who was born and raised in Liverpool, disagreed. They asked me and Hils the question, "Excuse me, but are you from Liverpool?" I said I was, and we started chatting, **only to find out that the lady we were speaking to was the sister-in-law of Chris Wharton.**

I gave her my email to pass to Chris, and pondered on another weird link, to another friend of John's.

Number 15:
MIKE McCARTNEY AND THE DISAPPEARING SIGN

In early 1994 I had called to Mike McCartney's house. (See between the 22nd and 23rd sightings.)

I asked for his opinion on some of my songs, which included the track *'Abbey Road'*. (See 19th sighting.) He said he would give me an honest opinion but three weeks later said, "I can't give you an opinion on the songs," but admitted, "it's all rap in the charts now", and he said that my songs "were songs just like 'our kid' has written", meaning Paul McCartney, and "he was just waiting for the right time to release them". He also said to me, "don't give up the day job".

Two weeks later, the street sign for Abbey Road in Liverpool, that I sing about in the song, disappeared. There was nothing in the press to do with the Beatles, over the previous few weeks, all was quiet. But the sign went, and another weird coincidence had occurred.

Number 16: IT'S YOU FRANCAIS

In May 1993 we had holidayed with the children in Northern France, around Normandy. (See Déjà vu.)

I had this incredible feeling of déjà vu, the hairs on my arms and neck would stand on end.

At the time I wrote a song called *'It's You Francais'*. I write about 'the marketplace, piano player in Honfleur, the harbourside, no wonder Monet came here, primary coloured houses, all along the quay, it's you, yeah you, Francais...'

I got back home and copyrighted this song, and another song called Etratat. They were done within three days of getting home from France. Moving forward three weeks, and now well and truly back into the routine of working again, I was on business in Hipperholme. It was about lunchtime, I had seen my customer and I called into the post office for some stamps and a sandwich. I opened the post office door and directly in front of me was a greetings card display 'spinner'. Every greetings card on the spinner was black and white. Except one, right in front of my eyes at eye level, in the centre of all these black and white cards. I saw a coloured greeting card, hitting me in the face. A blind man on a galloping horse couldn't have missed it. Instinctively, I picked it up.

I looked at the picture. It was a painting with a girl sitting at an upright piano, in a town square or market place. I flipped the card over to see if it described where the scene was painted. I was again shocked at this coincidence, **it said 'the Piano Player In Honfleur', a line from a song I wrote three weeks beforehand! Needless to say, I bought the postcard.** This said to me that all the powerful déjà vu feelings I had in France were either relating back to my ancestry and that of my great grandfather, La Vash, or, John Lennon had been here before.

The question is, who visited the places I had visited? Was it my great grandfather? Did he live or ever visit this part of France before? Or was it John Lennon? Did John ever go to France, in particular, this part of Normandy? I don't know.

Number 17: THE BRIT AWARDS

It was only days after my GMTV television interview, in early February 1994.

I was in Mold and got a call from my friend, Steve Asplet. He said, "Let's go to the Brit Awards next Tuesday, they are being advertised on TV and are to be held at Alexandra Palace."

I said, "We don't have any tickets."

Steve said, "Don't worry, some way we'll get in."

We got through three tough security sections with me in my dress suit and Steve in a morning suit, posing as my manager. The premise was that we had an interview with Sky News, and as we were walking up the steps, past the first security section, we had a bit of luck. A GMTV presenter, with his camera crew, was walking ahead of us. He turned around and saw me and said, "Mike, how's it going?" I started talking to him as if we were old friends and Steve talked to his crew, and we walked effortlessly past the second security section. The bouncers must have thought we were with the GMTV crew. Then we went into the press office, where we had to make up a story of 'Sky TV interview'. We were told to sit in a spot, when someone went looking for a Sky manager. We decided to take the bull by the horns and walked the 50 paces into the Brit Awards, being held in the main hall of the Palace. As we walked on ahead and towards the main entrance, the last remaining security checkpoint was nearing. I was in front of Steve and I walked past a guard pretending to be on my mobile to someone. I was using expletives and as I passed him, I heard the security man say to Steve, "Have you got your passes?" I remember thinking, just keep walking. I looked at Steve, who gave a gesture to the guard as if to say 'go away'. It was a dismissive gesture that could have tallied with my irate phone call.

Anyway, we got through the door and into an incredible night where the tickets, if we'd had any, would have cost us £400 per person. We stood for a while, near the stage side, talking, making out that we were both old friends and we'd just bumped into each other. Just then two waitresses came up to us and asked us if we wanted to buy a £5 raffle ticket. We said we would after we'd had a drink. One of the waitresses said, "No problem sir, what would you like to drink? There's wine, spirits, champagne?" We said red wine, at which point she lifted a bottle off the nearest table, gave it to us with two glasses, and said all the drinks were free. We bought a raffle ticket each, and just then a stunning, 6 foot, young, olive-skinned beauty came up to us and asked if she could join us, saying that we looked like two interesting men. She was 18 years old and owned up to having gatecrashed this Brits ceremony. We offered her a drink and she joined our company. We then walked diagonally across the magnificent hall, amongst the tables seating 10 people each. There were hundreds of tables and we were walking right through the middle of them, behind this stunning young beauty. All eyes were focussed on the girl and her two men friends.

We saw lots of music people and celebrities as we walked. We were right in the centre of the hall, when a striking black man stood up and said to me with deep dulcet tones, "Hey, my man, come and join us." We joined his table and I sat chatting to him, Steve and the girl, listening, smiling and also joining in the conversation. After a while, Steve whispered in my ear, "You know who he is don't you?" I told him I didn't have a clue. Steve said, "It's Seal!"

I said, "Seal who?"

Steve said, "Fucking hell Mike, you're going into the music business, and you don't know one of the main singers around today?" (Seal's No 1 single at the time was 'Kissed by a Rose') Seal ended up with the leggy beauty. Steve and I moved on to different tables throughout the night talking to people, drinking with people and eating with people.

One table we were sitting at had a few people on and a German girl who took us on the rides downstairs. Downstairs in the Palace, they had constructed a fairground, with a full size merry-go-round, and swings, spinning cars, waltzes etc. I remember going on the ride, flying high and having an absolute ball. It was fantastic!

When we got back to the table, she introduced us to Geoff Baker, Paul McCartney's publicist. He did give me his card at the time, saying he was interested to know more about my story. I still have the card somewhere.

We were the last two people in the whole of the Brit Awards, in Alexandra Palace. The cleaners were tidying up and the security man said, "Come on boys, haven't you had enough? You're the last two in here and it's quarter to three in the morning." We agreed and bid him good night, or should I say, good morning?

On the way out, I had collected a full size cardboard cut-out of the Brit Award. It was my height, a silver sculpture in thick cardboard. Waiting outside in near freezing conditions outside in his car was the John Lennon sound-alike, Billy Shears, and his wife, Trish. It was seriously cold and they had been there for hours. Steve climbed in the back of the car with Trish already sitting there. I opened the front door, climbed in, and slammed the door on the Brit Award cutout. Its head came clean off. I giggled as we drove along with this decapitated six foot cardboard cut out lodged between me and Billy.

Within two minutes I threw up all over the dash. It was disgusting. Billy shouted, "You dirty bastard!" We all tried to clean it up but Bill said, "Leave it; I'll clean it in the morning."

Then Trish said, "You dirty bastard!" Then she said to Billy, "Yes you will clean it up in the morning, because I'm not." This made it even more hilarious, in a 'sick' kind of way. Then Billy dropped us of at my friend's house in Shepherds Bush and he and Trish went on to their home near Heathrow.

We met the next morning and told them of the contacts we had made. They were much happier than the previous night. I did apologise to Billy saying I couldn't find the window handle in the car last night. He said the car was filthy and needed a good cleaning. They had a huge Afghan hound and with all the smoking they used to do in the car, the interior was shaped like an ashtray! I offered to pay for the cleaning, but bought lunch instead. He and Trish accepted my apology and we had lunch, then Billy drove us around some of the sights of London, including the famous Abbey Road Recording Studios where the Beatles recorded all their hits, Camden Town, and the usual tourist attractions. We, Steve and I, left them early evening. We got the train to Henley on Thames where we met a girlfriend of Steve's and stayed the night there. During the course of the evening the girl had told us that George Harrison lived literally around the corner from where she had a flat. Steve suggested that I "just call to George's front gates and see if he will see you."

Number 18:
TREVOR LLOYD, GEORGE AND HARRY HARRISON

The following morning at 9.15am, two days after the Brit Awards, I found myself walking up a country lane at the top of the high street in Henley on Thames, towards George Harrison's home.

As I walked, I remembered a friend of mine called Trevor Lloyd. He had a garage, virtually opposite Vauxhall Motor Plant in Ellesmere Port. He used to service Vauxhalls, and I had been going to him for years. We were good friends and when he had heard of my story seeing John Lennon he believed me implicitly because he knew me well. I remembered a distant conversation we'd had in his reception. **There was a picture of him and Paul McCartney, taken years ago, alongside Paul's Lotus. Trevor used to service his car, and Paul's brother's too.**

Trevor told me how he was friends with and knew George and Harry Harrison. So I phoned Trevor as I was approaching George's home, 'Friargate'. I told Trevor where I was, and asked if he could give me any information that George might recall. He told me a host of things, and said Harry (George's brother) was still the handyman for George; he might well answer the intercom. After five minutes chatting to him, I buzzed the intercom. "Hello?" a voice answered, in broad Liverpool Scouse.

I said, "Is that Harry?"

He said, "Yes, who are you?" I explained about my friend and his, from Ellesmere Port, called Trevor Lloyd.

He replied, "Trevor! How is he?" I told him and talked about my sightings of John Lennon. He said, "I'll come straight down to see you." Within a minute, the tall commanding wrought iron gates opened slowly and silently and Harry came out to meet me. I told him the whole story. He was fascinated and said that he couldn't wait to tell George. I had two cassette tapes of my songs, and I asked him to give one to George, and see if George could get one to Ringo Starr. He said, "No problem, I'm sure George would love to hear the stuff." He also said, "Mike, I don't need to phone Trevor," as I had suggested, "I'm sure you're his mate, and I believe what you are saying." He then said, "Look, George is late for a meeting in London, and his car has been running for 10 minutes. I can't promise anything, but I will tell him you are here, and about John coming to you, and that you know our old friend Trevor Lloyd. He might stop and talk to you." I thanked him and he went back up the drive.

Five minutes later, the gates slowly opened, and a big black Mercedes Benz drove through the gates, pulled over towards me, and the driver's window opened. It was George Harrison and his wife Olivia. George said, "Who are you?"

I said, "I am Mike Powell from Liverpool, I am also a friend of Trevor Lloyd, who I believe you were friends with." George nodded in agreement. I then told him that John Lennon has come to me several times and that he had given me songs, all complete with words and music. George's hairs went up and I saw he was visibly shaken. Just then, Olivia leant forward to have a closer look at me. Then George said to me, "Have you got the songs with you?"

I replied, "I have given two tapes to your brother, Harry, one for you, and one for Ringo, if you could please pass it to him."

He said, "Yes, I'll listen to them." Then he drove off, and I never heard a dickie bird from him after that meeting.

Trevor told me that Harry, George and Patti Boyd used to go around to his parents' house and have Sunday tea. They used to visit quite a lot, and they all stayed friends. He also told me Andy Fairweather Low, who was in the Eric Clapton band and played on George Harrison's 'Live in Japan' double album, was his cousin. Small world isn't it? When I was talking to Harry, he recalled the days to me when he used to be a lorry driver for Burmah, the giant Petrol terminal, based at Stanlow, nr Ellesmere Port. (The same refinery I mentioned earlier, where my dad had painted the Shell and Burmah refinery tanks.) He also confirmed Trevor's story of them always having Sunday tea at the Lloyds'.

Number 19: TIM AND MARGARET HOLMES

I was advised to look for someone to give me piano and singing lessons. This was in May 1994, after I had been on GMTV. As I didn't have a clue where to look, I phoned Mike Clark up to ask him. Mike had given me some guitar lessons, and had advised me to stop wasting my money on lessons because I never used to practise. He told me of a brilliant operatic singer turned voice trainer in Chester. He said she was brilliant. I phoned Margaret and arranged to have a lesson the following week. I arrived at the small, neat semi-detached house in Hoole, Chester, and was invited into the front parlour. There in the parlour, was a gleaming grand piano dominating the room. She asked me some questions like, did I want to learn to sing and play, to go around the clubs as an entertainer. I laughed and told Margaret, "I just want to sing and play my music."

She then said, "There's no time like the present, play and sing me one of your tunes." I did, but didn't expect the response I got from Margaret, the first person to actually see me singing and playing. She said, "That was a lovely song, with nice lyrics, and some very interesting chord movements and structures. And your voice isn't bad at all, considering you have never sung before. Did you write this song?"

As I had never played to anyone before, I guess my ego was flattered or something. Because something made me tell her the whole story about me and the John Lennon sightings, all in about two minutes flat.

I watched Margaret's face turn slowly but surely beetroot colour and as she walked out of the door, she said, "I won't be a minute Mike."

I thought, I've blown it, she thinks I'm a nutter, probably gone in the next room to call the police. **The next instant she brought in an old school photograph. It was of a class that her husband Tim Holmes was in during the 1950s. He was a pupil at Dovedale School, off Penny Lane in Liverpool. I thought that in itself was a coincidence, until she pointed to someone else in the school photograph, and said this was Tim's best friend in his class. It was John Lennon, and I was yet again, amazed.**

John Lennon, 2nd row from top, 3rd from the right, at Dovedale Primary
School in Liverpool

She asked me to come for my next lesson, and made sure her husband,

Tim, was there. He told me of his friendship with John, and how John could be nice one minute and awful the next. He told me a funny story about how they used to have boxing lessons in school and one day he was boxing John. Well, John didn't wait for the whistle and boxed Tim's ears. Tim recalls the last time he saw John in the late 50s, he asked John, "What are you hoping to do for a job?" John said, "I've got this group, I'm hoping to make records for a living, and what are you doing?"
Tim replied, "I've got an apprenticeship as a trainee draughtsman."
They said their goodbyes, and each went on to their respective successes, within their chosen field.

Number 20:
MIKE CLARK AND THE PEACE OFFERING
The guitar teacher Mike Clark was the person who I had some lessons from, and who gave me Margaret Holmes' telephone number. One day, he phoned me up out of the blue and said something very weird had happened to him. He said an aunt had fallen out with him years before over something very trivial. **They had never spoken for an age. Then apparently the aunt had bought Mike a 'peace offering'. It was a book all about John Lennon.** Mike asked me, "What's going on Mike, do you have any idea?" I said I didn't and advised he just accept it graciously. To this day, they have remained firm friends and Mike is still mystified as to why she should buy him a book on John Lennon, because neither of them were fans. Join the club!
I got him to swear an affidavit about my total lack of musical knowledge. At the same time I told him that John Lennon had come to me. That was a couple of years before the above incident happened, but only days after I had asked Mike for Margaret's phone number in 1994.

Number 21: NICK MARLAND
I was introduced to Nick Marland by my friend Jay in Mold. It was sometime in 1994. I had been recording some of the music with Jay at his house, where he had my studio gear set up (I had bought an 8 track analogue recording machine along with all the bits to record this music, to the best quality I could afford). Jay had his mind elsewhere at the time, so eventually I got together with Nick. I hired a run-down mill in

Dukinfield where we recorded and videoed a lot of the music John Lennon was giving to me. I was taken with Nick's guitar playing. In fact I used to call him the guitar man extraordinaire. We had some great laughs at the mill and a lot of serious work was done there. (There were more than 30 serious musicians over this period that played and recorded with me, all of them had been told about my John Lennon encounters.) Initially, when I told Nick about this incredible story of John Lennon coming to me, Nick replied, **"That's weird, the guitar technician I use in Manchester was the Beatles' guitar technician." When I asked what does that mean, Nick said, "He used to get all the guitars on stage for the Beatles, tune them up, re-string them, service them, keep them clean and generally look after them."**

Number 22:
THE NEW 'BEATLE' or 'BEETLE' SIGHTING

The year was 1993. I had been awoken by a strange sighting of John with the other Beatles.

There was no song to this sighting, but it made me sit up and take notice, all the same.

(See 18th sighting.)

I had seen and heard John say to the other Beatles, "There's the new Beatle." They were sitting in an old Volkswagen Beetle, with its rear window removed.

So convinced was I that there was going to be a new VW Beetle built I phoned up UK Head Office of VW (VAG) and spoke to their UK marketing director, Paul Buckett. He denied that one was being built, and asked me, "Why the interest?" I told him what I had just seen and the sightings of John Lennon. **He told me he was the biggest John Lennon fan in the world.** He asked me to send a tape down to him with the music coming from John. He said if it was good, he would put it to the board with a view to using the music in one of their VW adverts. He got back to me and said the board didn't want to use the music, but to keep in touch with him. A week later, a VW spokesman on a Radio Four programme, presented by Brian Hobday, denied that there was a new Beetle about to be produced. **But the following year, they produced one!**

Number 23:
MICHAEL JOSEPH AND THE LADY DIANA BOOK

During my very first meeting with Ronan O'Rahilly, there were two other people present. One was Katherine, Ronan's wife. The other was Michael Joseph, a descendant from Mike Joseph of publishing and print dynasty. I told these three people the whole story of how John Lennon came to me. I was having regular dialogue and mailing Michael with my work, accounts of what I had seen and the songs coming from the sightings. Michael, as well as Ronan, knew the ins and outs of my story, better than anyone else.

Six years later, after several meetings, letters, correspondence, telephone calls, and sitting in on studio sessions with me, Michael Joseph 'miraculously' produced a book of 'how Lady Diana came to him' called Love From Diana, Michael Joseph. Now I was also told by Ronan that he thought Michael had nicked the idea from me and my sightings of John Lennon.

Ronan said 'At the very least, if Lady Diana did come to Michael after John came to you, it would be 100 miracles, and probably 100 billion to one.

Number 24: MARTIN GEORGE FEARNLEY

Martin Fearnley has been my best friend since 1990. I met him when he was a buyer for a company I was dealing with, two years before my sightings of John Lennon. He had taken over from another buyer and he was in a different league. Martin was premier division. Needless to say, my prices were inflated somewhat and fair play to Martin he could have kicked my company out of the door in favour of an existing printer he had been using at his previous employment. But he gave me a chance to re-present all the print prices again, giving me the nod when a suitable price was reached.

He had lived in a village in North Wales for years, since he was a small boy with his family. He was born in Manchester and was a huge Manchester United fan. I had moved over to North Wales from Chester, two years before I met Martin, in 1988 I believe. We became firm friends and I introduced him to circuit training. Before that, Martin just played football. I say just played football, he was consistently the players' player of the year and his house was adorned with medal upon medal and trophy upon trophy that he had won for his beloved Trefnant F.C. All the trophies and medals were engraved with Martin's name on as Player of the Year, Captain, and so on. We would go circuit training twice or three times a week, and we'd have the odd pint after work or the odd meal out somewhere.

Then my marriage started to collapse. I eventually told Martin I was trying to keep it alive and he knows the efforts I went to to try and keep it all together. It wasn't to be. But when I did get around to telling Martin about the John Lennon sightings, he said, "That's weird."

I said, "What is?"

Then he told me. When he was born, his mother and father were huge Beatles fans. So they called their newborn son after the Beatles producer, George Martin. Only they turned the names the other way around. That is Martin George Fearnley, born in 1963.

Number 25: MY TEACHER FRIEND, ALISON

After the break-up of my marriage, which ended in September 1994, I met a teacher through a mutual friend of ours, Steve Asplet. I would see her every so often when I was in North Wales, and continued to see her for a time, when I moved over to Broadbottom. I remember one day I arrived at her house and asked how her day had been. She told me it had been very good. **She mentioned that the school where she worked in Chester had just taken on a new member of staff. She'd spoken to this new member in the staffroom and she was very nice. Her name was Julia Baird. She was John Lennon's half-sister.**

Number 26: SHARWOOD'S SPECIALITY FOODS

I was a Territory Manager for the speciality food company called Sharwoods, part of the international food giant, Rank, Hovis, McDougal (RHM). My territory was Liverpool, North Wales, and the Isle of Man. In the year 1978 I was asked to do a caretaking role in Devon and Cornwall for a period of six weeks. On that territory, I discovered Poole in Dorset and thought that it was the most beautiful place I had ever seen. I envisaged a beautiful mansion just overlooking the Sandbanks ferry, thinking that if I had the money I would build a mansion and live there.

In fact, I asked my then Regional Manager, Gerry Sloane, for a territory transfer to this region. He refused and told me that my Merseyside territory was the best performing in the UK, and he needed my input to keep it that way.

Moving on to 1994, I had long since left Sharwoods and I was dealing in print in the North West of England. At the time, I had told the printer Bill McNab, Pentagon Print, all about my John Lennon sightings. He was a big John Lennon fan, and believed what I had told him. At the time, Radio One did an interview with me. Emma Freud was the DJ, and in Bill's printer's all the staff listened to the interview with the radio on full blast. **I got a phone call from Bill in April 1994 saying that there was an article in the Liverpool Echo stating how a developer had acquired a property, a run-down bungalow where they were planning to build a mansion. It had sea views, and was overlooking the Sandbanks ferry. As Bill told me about this property, I remembered back to when I had been down there in 1978, and thought it a strange coincidence to me; the place, the mansion, the views. Not connected with anything, just a coincidence. Then, wait for it, Bill continued reading the article to me over the phone. It said John Lennon had bought this bungalow for his Aunt Mimi to enjoy in her latter years, and described the place as 'the most beautiful place on earth'!**

Aunt Mimi was the aunt John lived with, in Menlove Avenue in Liverpool, prior to becoming world famous. When he did make it, he repaid Mimi with this gift of a bungalow in Poole, for her to enjoy in her retiring years.

Numbers 27, 28 & 29: THE PAINTING EASEL

It is now 2001. I am working in the North West, with my office still in Leigh, Lancashire at Collins & Darwell's the printers. I have my house in Broadbottom where I live a few days a week. The rest of the time I was staying at my friend Martin's house in Trefnant. We would go circuit training a few days a week and go out to the pub, usually on a Friday night, to the local called The Plough, in St Asaph. On one such occasion, I met a girl there called Jackie and we got talking. We started to go out for a while, and sometimes I would see her before going home for the weekend, or stay on the odd night in the week. It was flexible and suited us both. One such day in May 2003, I was lying in her bed on a bright sunny bank holiday Monday morning. I was planning to go to my office in Leigh on the Tuesday morning, directly from my house in Broadbottom, so I had said to her I was going home early on Monday morning to see Ian, a running friend, for a run on the Pennines, and no doubt a few jars afterwards.

I wanted to leave Jackie's about 10.30am, but Jackie had told me there was a car boot sale near her house, in a small village called Llanasa. I didn't want to go, and reiterated my fell run, etc. She coaxed me to go, or rather I went to placate her, if I'm honest.

So we had breakfast and set off for this quaint village and a rummage through the junk. Deep down I've always liked mooching around car boot sales for the odd bargain. We got to the site. It was a farmer's field and all the tables were set up on a gentle slope. There were probably about 100 cars there, so it was quite a big sale.

I looked across the whole site and in the far corner of the field, about 100 yards away, one tall art easel caught my eye. It was a big, studio easel and, as I had just started painting these sightings, I thought that if it was cheap enough it would be ideal for me to paint on. We didn't rush to the easel, but at the same time I didn't hang around. Soon I was at the stall with the easel on sale. I couldn't believe my eyes when I read what was on the easel. It was a framed A4 certificate stating: 'Certificate of this 'PAINTING EASEL PROVENANCE – EX- Liverpool College of Art'

THIS EASEL WAS USED BY JOHN LENNON

Below is that Certificate of Provenance, as supplied by Derek Hodkin:

PAINTING EASEL PROVENANCE – ex-Liverpool College of Art

I attended Liverpool College of Art, Hope Street, Liverpool from September 1957 to July 1962. John Lennon began there the same day as me. I had completed my National Service commitment in the Royal Air Force prior to going to Art College so that I was 20 years of age to John's 17 at that time. I was with John Lennon every day (except of course the days when he 'bunked off') for three years, firstly in the Intermediate Course in Arts & Crafts which lasted for two years and then, for the first year of the National Diploma in Design course. I became a close friend of John Lennon at one time, mainly I now realise owing to the fact that I had a reel to reel tape-recorder in 1957 . . . John of course, used people constantly and saw a golden opportunity to record himself and his friends, Paul McCartney and George Harrison playing in their group. We are now in 1958 when I became particularly close to the three of them. Paul and George were pupils in the adjacent building to the Art College, the Liverpool Institute for Boys school in Mount Road. There was a door connecting the canteen of the Art College with the school yard at the back and Paul, particularly, would use this to come into the Art College and meet up with John.

After the first two years Intermediate when I studied Lithography and John, quite stupidly studied Lettering and Graphics (owing to the fact that Cynthia Powell his future wife was on that particular course). Here I do have to point out that I 'went out with', that quaint old-fashioned phrase, with Cynthia early in 1958, long before John did! In September of 1959 I began the NDD course in Painting (Special) and, as I recall, John returned to the College having failed his Intermediate exam that summer! It was possible to retake the examination once only and I believe it was at this time that he left the College en route to Hamburg and his future, whatever that may have been! I did visit Paul's home in Forthlin Avenue and record them playing for over an hour when we decided to call them the 'Jaypage 3' as in John, Paul George. I booked them in at La Scale Ballroom Runcorn for a trial playing in the interval of a dance and at several other venues around Widnes, effectively, I was their first manager therefore. The point of all this preamble is that the painting easel 'acquired' by Brian Hughes my one-time teaching colleague was taken by me from the painting studios at Liverpool College of Art in 1960 or 1961 when I completed my course. These studios were additionally used for life drawing classes for the Intermediate groups and as there were only about 12 of these older-type easels, it is 100% certain that John Lennon used this particular easel on many occasions. The letter 'P' painted on the easel denotes that it belonged to the painting studios, which are on the top floor of the hope Street building.

This is simply a certification of the provenance of this particular painting easel, which many other students and I used from 1957 to 1961.

Derek Hodkin
11th June 2001

Needless to say, I bought that very easel and am using it to paint the various John Lennon sightings. Now how weird is that?

I met up with Derek, who had moved over to France to be with his childhood sweetheart.

He had been married to someone in the UK for 40 years, which was finished, and decided to find his former French girlfriend on the internet, just a couple of years before I bought the easel from his friend and artist, Brian Hughes. It was Brian who made it possible for me to meet up with Derek. Miracle of miracles, Derek found his sweetheart after all these years, and she had recently lost her husband to illness. So he moved fast, over to France, taking only his computer and a few clothes, and of course, giving the easel to his best friend, Brian. She also was friends with John, Paul and George, and when Derek showed me a photograph of the two of them taken in the 50s, they looked like film stars. Really cool, they both could have been Vogue models, and best of all, for a Scouser like Derek, she was the real deal, she was French.

Now this fantastic coincidence and story doesn't end there.

My father was a signwriter in Liverpool, 'the best in the business', to coin my father's rather modest phrase.

When I read in the provenance certificate that Derek studied Lithography 'and John quite stupidly studied Lettering and Graphics', again, I couldn't believe my eyes.

My father George Joseph Powell went to the Liverpool College of Art, in Hope Street, Liverpool when he left school. He also studied Lettering and Graphics and no doubt used this very same easel on many occasions. As Derek told me there were only 12 such easels of the older type, and they were the best ones to use. The fact that my father did go on to use the skills gained at the college, namely lettering, proved how worthwhile it was for him to pursue his great artistic talent, that of signwriting.

THIS EASEL WOULD UNDOUBTEDBLY HAVE BEEN USED BY MY FATHER

And the third coincidence connected with the easel:

I was short of money, and put the easel into a London auction house called COOPER OWEN. They sell pop memorabilia and the easel duly went into the catalogue. This was in October 2005. I went down to London to the auction to see if it would be sold. To cut a long story short, it failed to reach its price and was automatically withdrawn from sale. A couple of days went by and I was speaking to Cooper Owen. They asked me if I wanted to put the easel in their next auction, which was in December. I decided that I should keep the easel and continue painting the John Lennon sightings on it. After all, this easel had been used by John himself, and almost certainly my father, George. There in those two coincidences, I knew that I had to keep it and continue the work on it. I needed the money, but money isn't everything. I decided to struggle on regardless. And anyway, I believe it was fated not to be sold. The easel only missed its auction price by £100. I could have let it go, as they asked me on the day did I want to sell it at the lower price? But I didn't. It was too special and I had realised that during the auction. I happened to be talking to one of the owners of the auction house. **It was Cliff Cooper. I told him about my experiences with the John Lennon sightings. He was amazed. He told me that he set up and owned the Beatle Museum in Liverpool.** He went on to tell me that it was their company, Cooper Owen, that sold the piano at auction, that John Lennon wrote *'Imagine'* on, to George Michael for a staggering £1.45million. The piano, apparently, was for some time on display in the Beatle Museum in Liverpool. We are going to see each other, when he is next up in Liverpool.

Number 30: MARK JEPSON

In January 2005 I went to work for a marketing consultant called Simon Morris. His business was seeking grants for businesses and marketing grant work, and the company was called Lugeilan. His office was based in Rhewl, near Ruthin, North Wales. I remember the first day I went to work in the offices. I was given a specific desk, a laptop, and a phone. We went through the customer base and I familiarised myself with the accounts we were currently dealing with and any new enquiries that had come into the office recently.

About mid-morning I had a coffee with the office manager, Angharad Jones, and Simon, the director. Simon told us about the former director, Mark Jepson, who used to work for Lugeilan. He said his only claim to fame was an interesting one. He went on to say that Mark had been given the task by the headmaster when he was at Ruthin High School for boys in the 1980s to mentor one of the new intakes of freshers (first year pupils). Mark was in the second year above, and each new intake was designated a mentor to settle in, and hopefully become friends and form an integral part of the Ruthin School scene.

He became great friends with the new pupil, and soon, they would be at each other's houses, playing, laughing and joking, meeting parents, etc. **Although Mark met the mother of the new intake, he discovered that the father and mother had divorced, the mother was living on her own with her son, and the father was now living in New York. The boy's name was Julian Lennon. The mother's name was Cynthia Lennon. And the father's name was John Lennon. Mark and Julian were to become great friends over a period of four years.** Simon's final words on the subject were even more of a weird coincidence. **He said, "In fact Mike, you're sitting at the very desk that Mark used to sit at."**

I was dumbstruck again. (Although by now, I'm surprised that I'm surprised anymore!)

What Simon never knew, or anyone there, was what had happened to me and the John Lennon sightings.

I met Mark Jepson several times at the office, and he remarked, "How are you settling in at my desk?" He told me all about Julian Lennon and how they were always at each other's houses. He told me one story, which I don't think you could make up, when he was at Julian's playing Monopoly. They were in the lounge and the telephone rang in the hallway. Cynthia, Julian's mother, answered. She spoke for a while, and then called through to Julian, "Julian, your dad's on the phone for you." Julian went to the phone and chatted with his dad for about 15 minutes. Then Julian said to his dad, "Will you speak to my friend please, his goldfish had died and he's very upset. His name is Mark." John Lennon, the boy's father, agreed, and Julian handed the phone to Mark. This is what Mark told me, and I quote:

Mark: "Hello."

J.L.: "Hello, is that Mark?"

Mark: "Yes."

J.L.: "I'm sorry to hear that your goldfish has died, but everything has to die sometime. The goldfish is dead, so why don't you put it in a liquidiser, and eat it with some salad?"

Mark couldn't believe his ears, but he told me that he and John went on to talk for a little while longer, and Mark felt a bit better, in a strange kind of way.

And that was Mark's claim to fame, and yet another strange coincidence for me.

Number 31:
TRIATHLON WORLD CHAMPIONSHIPS, 2003

I met Hilary on August bank holiday Saturday, 2003. I remember a band was playing in the local pub, The Plough, and I was with my friend Martin. I had been to the loo and on the way back to the room where the band was playing, I saw this striking lady standing by the doorway of that room, watching the band.

I had seen her here only a week before, when she had been with her friends at the time, and was wearing trousers which accentuated her slim figure. I couldn't take my eyes off her whilst I was talking to my friend that night. She then left the pub with her friends, and a week later I saw her again.

So, as I passed her I said, "Come on let's dance." So we did. And could she dance. She was brilliant, and I could see she loved music. She was a physiotherapist and she had represented Wales in the Home Nations, at Triathlon. That, I assumed, was the reason why she looked so fit and always had a glow about her face. Her beautiful smile would light up any room.

Shortly after that, we started going out with each other. It soon became mid-September and Hils (as I affectionately call her) was attending a World Championships Triathlon Age Group Qualifier in Bala. She asked me if I wanted to go and see her compete. I jumped at the chance and as I watched, I was excited but frustrated at not actually competing myself. After she swam 1500m, rode her bike 40km, and ran 10km, I was exhausted just watching! It was great, and I felt very proud of Hils as she qualified for the World Championships to be held in Madeira in March 2004. So we went and I watched Hilary compete on the world stage in Madeira. She trained every day except the last day before the competition.

One day, we walked the two steep miles into the town centre Funchal and along the seafront. The weather was fantastic, and there were several cruise and restaurant boats moored on the front, bobbing up and down in the sunny shimmering crystal clear waters. The backdrop all along the front was adorned with the World Triathlon Championship flags and banners. Television crews from all over the planet had descended on Madeira and there was real energy in the place, what with all these pumped up athletes, the doting relatives and friends, the triathlon elite (the pros) the reporters and the media circus. There was a carnival atmosphere, certainly for me, although Hils was starting to get focussed on her race, so she was more reserved. She had worked hard for her place and she deserved it and did well, in her age group.

We walked up the ramp and onto one boat that caught my eye. It was a medium size vessel, and it was very clean. As it was a restaurant I thought cleanliness is next to godliness, so this one was as good as any we had seen that day. It had a good vantage point, literally yards from the start line of the following days races. So we went up to the top deck and ordered a couple of cappuccinos and a gluttonous cream cake each, yummy!

The coffee and cake were delicious. We found the ambience glorious.

We didn't pick the menu up when we ordered as we knew we were not going to eat, just have a drink and a snack. After we had spent a pleasant half hour or so, I picked up the menu to find out what the bill would be.

I was amazed, again.

There was a picture of the Beatles, and a paragraph of text about the boat. It said that in 1966, the Beatles had bought this very boat and had visited this very place, partying on this very vessel. It went on to say that the Beatles had bought the boat for tax reasons and gave a date when it had then been sold on to the present owner who had acquired the boat in the late 70s.

The boat was called 'Vagrant'.

Number 32: HILARY AND A CHANCE MEETING

It was in spring 2004. I was with my girlfriend Hilary, visiting friends in Machylleth. We called in to the co-op to buy a couple of things. So we were waiting in the queue at the checkout to pay for the wine and flowers. Just then, an old friend of Hils' came up behind her and said, "Hello stranger!"

We went through the checkout and we were properly introduced. It was a girl called Roxanne, and she was a vocal voice trainer, in the main, for children. She worked all over the UK and it had been some five years since she and Hilary had seen each other. Hils introduced me to Roxanne and she asked me what I did with my time. I recall I said, "As little as possible, and I write and sing." **She asked me who I sound like. I replied, "People I have been with in the studio think I sound like Paul McCartney."**

Right out of the blue, she said, "Don't tell me, John Lennon came to you in a dream?"

Hilary looked at me and we seemed to laugh it off, but why on earth did Roxanne say that? It was definitely a chance meeting in a supermarket queue of two friends who hadn't met or spoken for five years.

Number 33: DANE CHAFLIN

Moving on to December 2004. I was in Broadbottom with Hilary for the weekend, having a drink with some good friends of mine, Graham and Kate, in the pub called the Cheshire Cheese. It was a Friday night, and although we'd planned to go back to North Wales sometime Saturday, Graham told us that he and Kate had been invited to a party Saturday night in the village, and he would like us to join them. He assured us that it would be OK, and told me I had met the couple who were having the party before. We decided to go. We arrived at a beautiful old cottage at the bottom of Moss Lane, near a tributary that ran under a charming stone bridge and into the River Etherow, 100 yards or so further on. Once inside, there was music, food, a lot of people I knew, conversation and an all round 'good crack'. I remembered the couple throwing the party, I just couldn't put a face to the name Graham told me on the Friday night.

During the evening we mingled with the other guests and got talking to a couple called Dane and his wife Beth. Beth was a physiotherapist and she and Hilary talked about their jobs. They were both physios and both worked for the National Health. I spoke to Dane. He told me he was a vocal trainer, saying he was in fact a 'certified speech level singing instructor'. We chatted, and I asked him if he could give me a couple of lessons. He agreed and gave me his telephone number. I phoned him on the Monday and arranged to see him towards the end of the following week. I got to his house in the village, on the row near where the cenotaph cross stood, just adjacent to the railway station entrance. It was the house where my friends Dawn and Steve 'Downsy' used to live. I had coincidentally been to many a party in that house.

Once inside, Dane stood by his piano and told me that we only had one hour before his next client was due. As I had told him at the party that I had written some songs, he asked me to sing one of my songs to him. I sat at the piano and played and sang. After I had sung, he said to me, "Wow, you sound like Paul McCartney, is that your own song Mike?" I said it was, and he told me how impressed he was with my voice and the song. I guess he wanted to know more, but it wasn't forthcoming from me. I told him nothing about John Lennon or the sightings, and besides, we had time constraints. He then explained how the lesson would go, and then he contorted his face and was 'sloshing' his words, saying, "Try this, don't worry if you sound stupid or babyish, can you do it?" I did, and during the course of the hour, he commented on how well I was doing, saying, "I wish all my pupils were as good as you." At the end of the lesson, I booked another one for one week's time. Same time, as he couldn't do the Tuesday that I wanted. I asked him was he fully booked that day. He said, "No, I have another job, my real job where I make my money." I was curious and asked what his real job was. He went on to tell me it was exactly the same job i.e. speech level singing instructor. **But it wasn't in this village called Broadbottom, he told me, it was in Liverpool.**

At the Performing Arts Centre.

The one that has Paul McCartney as its patron.

He had met Paul many times. It appeared that this Dane Chalfin, who was from the USA, was a serious player and 'big hitter' in the world of vocal excellence.

Number 34:
PICASSO'S DEAD HIS MEMORY LIVES ON

See sighting No 28: 18th February 1994

I wrote the song *'Blindman'* after seeing John in the 27th sighting in February 1994.

I saw John for a split second and the word Picasso came into my head. I don't know why. The song all came at once and I was physically sick with the sheer excitement of it all. I didn't try to write words or music, they were all there. The hook was 'a blind man sings so sweetly', and on the very last chorus of the song 'there comes a time in every man's life, a man must cook, art's not dead, Picasso's dead his memory lives on'. It was a very unusual finish to a song, but that's how it was.

Two years later, all the press, local and national put out a story (see Daily Mail cutting, dated January 24th 1996, page112) saying 'Unveiled after 35 years, pictures from Liverpool's lowly arts club band.' The article goes onto say that when building work was being done on a small coffee bar in Liverpool called the Jacaranda that they uncovered murals on the wall painted by John Lennon and Stuart Sutcliffe. They were in 'THE PICASSO STYLE' and should be preserved for the nation. They were in a sorry state and a Liverpool Artist, now Chairman of the British Art and Design Association, was brought in to carry out the restoration. That person was Terry Duffy, who incidentally also went to the Liverpool College of Art.

Number 35: L.S. LOWRY

The last sighting I had in Mold, North Wales was not connected to John Lennon in any way. At least I don't think so.

But the coincidences make it important enough to link in with the story. Please refer to the 35th and very last sighting in my home in Mold, North Wales, which was on 24th July 1994.

In the sighting I saw an old street, with people of a bygone age.

Some 14 months after the sighting and writing the song 'Lowry Country Calling', I found myself walking down that very street. I bought a house there. I met a man who was one of Lowry's closest friends and confidantes, called Crosland Ward. He told me Lowry lived one and a half miles from my front door. He told me he was at the great artist's funeral as a friend. He told me that the national and local newspapers misrepresented Lowry, with headings in their newspapers like 'No Flowers for Lowry' or 'Lowry interned without tears'. But no reporter was at the graveside, just in the entrance building some 400 yards away.

On 22nd June 2006, I travelled to the top end of the United Kingdom to a place where my girlfriend, Hilary, was working as a locum. A place just 12 miles from John O'Groats called Wick. The journey by train was 15 hours long, but I made the effort to go as it was Hils' birthday, and I wanted to be with her on her special day. I had gone up for a long weekend that ran from Thursday to Tuesday. I'd set off from North Wales at 7.30 in the morning and Hils picked me up at Wick station at 10 past 10 that night. The views from the train had been spectacular. The following day, Friday, it was Hils' birthday, so she had arranged to take the afternoon off. It was 7.30am, I give her the birthday presents, we had breakfast, and we walked the mile or so to her place of work, Wick Hospital, for the half day's work prior to celebrating her birthday properly. Then I set off to explore Wick. I also had a drawing pad and some oil chalks and some water in a backpack, in case I was inspired to draw anything I saw. After a couple of hours walking around the town and its surrounding area, I walk towards a café in the town for a bacon sandwich and a milky coffee. As I came out of the café I walked up the high street and turned left at the traffic lights.

As I walked past yet another charity shop the sun was hitting my face and I thought to a time in days gone by when there were no charity shops, only the odd second-hand shop and the bulk of charitable or junk items were traded door-to-door by the rag and bone men. These 'tatters', as they were called, would buy or exchange goods from their handcarts as they used to walk around the streets of Liverpool when I was a kid. I remember sometimes I would get a tin whistle or yo-yo in exchange for some old clothes that the tatters would trade. I wouldn't ask Mum, as she used to think that it was common to associate oneself with the rag and bone men, but I would take some of the hand-me-downs, old jumpers and the likes. Stuff would disappear and really, no one would be any the wiser.

Then I thought again about charity shops. When I moved to Broadbottom, and lived for three months in a caravan prior to buying the house there, I started buying t-shirts and shirts for 35 pence or so. This meant that it was cheaper to buy a few shirts per week, use each one for two or three days and then throw it away, rather than washing, drying and ironing it. Much better and quicker and more fun than going to a launderette and pondering about the washer, dryer and all the comforts you had been asked to leave behind in your former home. I understood why these type of shops always seem to flourish in run down areas. They don't have rag and bone men anymore to take the junk away.

I passed one charity shop, I passed the post office, I passed another shop, a sort of local information/council pay-your-bills type shop with an A1 art poster in the window. **It had two Lowry paintings. I did a double take. I back tracked and stared at the paintings in this window. I thought why on earth are two paintings by L.S. Lowry in a window in a shop 500 miles from Manchester? I walked into the shop and asked if the poster was for sale. The lady told me it wasn't for sale. I asked her why it wasn't for sale and she told me the poster was commissioned to promote the Wick festival, and she'd had a few people asking if they could buy it. I asked, "Why would you choose Lowry to promote Wick?"**

She then said, "Because Lowry painted these two paintings in Wick." I was flabbergasted and asked for directions to the sites of the two Lowry paintings. One site had long since been knocked down and new, more temporary, housing had replaced it. Some 'arts granted highland programme' redeveloped, or more to the point destroyed if the painting is anything to go by, this wonderful historic range of buildings. I walked to the other site and couldn't believe my eyes. There, facing the docks and its range of single storey Victorian warehousing, was none other than the famous 'Black Steps' that Lowry immortalised. His painting had children playing on and around the 31 steps, and had a cheeky dog in the foreground. I was sure that this scene was from a Manchester town that Lowry had grown up in and around. Salford, maybe? It wasn't. It was here in Wick. A place I travelled over 15 hours to, to celebrate my girlfriend's birthday. But Lowry? Here? Why? How? When? I sketched the scene with my chalks and sat for an hour, pondering, yet again, another absolute amazing coincidence.

The following week a friend of mine called Fred from Broadbottom asked me if I could spare a day or two to help him move some rubble from his house. Fred had retired early on the grounds of ill health, so I duly obliged. Because I was up there, so soon after Wick, I contacted my old friend Crosland and arranged to meet him that night in the Cheshire Cheese pub in the village. We obviously got onto the subject of Lowry and Crosland said to me, "Someone should paint those two scenes I have told you about Mike." These were the two scenes he had told me about before, and not the ones I had seen in Wick. One of the scenes he had witnessed was at Lowry's funeral when the newspapers had reported, 'No flowers for Lowry', or 'Lowry interned without tears'. Wrong on both counts. Crosland Ward was there at the graveside.

He said the painting should have, "enough flowers as you would find in small florists. And there were tears all around, from everyone at the graveside."

The other scene that should be painted for posterity, Crosland explained, was a true story Lowry told him about. You have to understand that Lowry never married. He lived with his domineering mother all his life. He wasn't worldly wise when it came to women. But he did have 'a love, the love of his life'. She was young compared to Lowry's age, 55. It would have been a shocking experience for the whole neighbourhood, had Lowry ever 'gone out' with this girl. He longed for her and would draw her, either while she was sitting with him or from his memory of her. And then came the day she told him, "I am emigrating to Canada." He was devastated, but had never shown his feelings or the real affection he had for the girl. She didn't know the real feelings he had for her. She had told him the times she would be getting the trolley bus from Ashton to the centre of Manchester. She had no idea and was taken by surprise when Lowry turned up at the trolley bus depot at Ashton to wish her farewell. The scene was a bustling market town, buses coming and going, on the platform people were moving forward to board the bus. When she got onto the bus, at the rear door she turned to say her goodbyes and thanked Lowry for seeing her off. Lowry was holding on to the chrome pole from outside. Just then he leaned forward to kiss the girl's cheek, and as he did so the trolley bus pulled away. And Lowry missed the only chance in his life to kiss the love of his life. And even as he tried to kiss her, she wasn't even aware of that as she had started to turn towards the front of the bus in readiness to take her seat. He uttered the words to her as the bus pulled away, 'Goodbye my Love'.

As Crosland had said to me, "Someone should paint those two scenes, if not I'll have to try."

My reply to him was, "I will paint those paintings, sometime, I will paint those scenes, and they will be titled, 1: No Flowers For Lowry and 2: Goodbye My Love

We said our goodbyes, and I am sure we will see each other again, no doubt, in the future.

I said there was no link to John Lennon or the Beatles with Lowry. At least, none that I know of.

However, if you look at the Daily Mail on Saturday 26th August 2006, there is a four page article, written by Hunter Davies with extracts from his book – 'The Beatles, Football and Me' by Hunter Davies. In the article he says he was the one with the idea to write a book about the Beatles' lives, a serious attempt to get it all down, once and for all. He had spoken to Paul McCartney who had said, "You have to speak to Brian Epstein, he's the one who will decide." Hunter spoke to Brian and arranged to meet him at his home in Belgravia. I quote:

"Brian agreed to see me at his home in Belgravia. He kept me waiting so I mooched around his drawing room, admiring his two fine paintings by Lowry…"

Number 36: HUNTER DAVIES - 'JOHN AND JAGGER'

In the eighth sighting I'd had, and the subsequent song to come from this called *'Crazy Lady'*, I saw John handing a piece of paper to Mick Jagger. At the time I didn't know if they knew each other or whether they were friends at all, and wondered why John should be handing this song to Mick.

I quote Hunter Davies again, taken from the same four page article as mentioned in coincidence number 35:

"I was with the Beatles in Bangor, North Wales, in August 1967, when we heard the news that Brian had died of a drugs overdose. On the train journey down from Euston I had been in their carriage along with Mick Jagger and Marianne Faithful, all of them in flower power clothes. **It was interesting to watch John and Jagger together. They seemed wary of each other, respectful but distant."**

Number 37: MARTIN BOARDMAN

I started going to a pub nearby where I was living called the Mountain View from September 2007. It had just had a major refit and a new owner had taken over and was serving food, getting new customers in and having musical acts performing. Hils and I would go sometimes for 'early doors', or sometimes to watch an advertised band. I would acknowledge the owner, and he me, but we never introduced ourselves or in fact talked to each other. There appeared to be a mutual respect between us.

On 23rd November 2007, we went to the pub about 8pm as a local duo were due to perform, which they did. The pub was chock-a-block that night. There was a child's confirmation party and buffet, as well as the growing number of customers enjoying the huge portions of honest to goodness home cooked food. About 10pm a member of the bar staff went around the tables offering food from the buffet that was left over from the party. About 10 minutes later I walked into the room where the food was laid out, and the room was empty, except for the owner and myself.

He said, "Hello, please help yourself to the buffet," and he got himself a plate. We introduced ourselves. His name was Martin Boardman, and we started talking as if we were old friends. I was curious to know why he had moved to the pub. His reply was strange: "I don't honestly know why I moved here."

Absurdly, I said, "I do!" He told me he didn't have any kind of reason for this large investment and the move to this place. We talked about the musicians he had on, and he said they were all his friends – he made guitars as well as collecting them, and had a great collection. I was clearly taken with his honesty. So much so I told him I was in the process of getting a band together, and he instantly said he could recommend good musicians that I could see. He told me he could get probably six or seven musicians gathered on the following Monday, to which I initially laughed, as musos are notoriously difficult to get together at one time. So we arranged for a meeting on the Monday at 2.30pm in the pub. The meeting took place when the pub was closed, and every one of them turned up and the music was played. Everyone was impressed, and asked who has written this music. One or two said it was very much like the Beatles, and a few others agreed. One guy said, "You have copied a Beatles song," although everyone disagreed. Another guy said, "You sound like Paul McCartney." Another one said that the words and music were very Lennonesque. They all agreed that the music was very good indeed. I didn't tell them the story, as I didn't want them joining just to jump on the Lennon bandwagon. They were interested and were asked to think about the possibility of forming a band around me. After this, I got Martin to sign a confidentiality agreement and told him the whole story. He was blown away with the John Lennon sightings, and slowly but surely it began to dawn on both of us that our paths had crossed, unknowingly, over the past few years. IN FACT, KNOCK ME DOWN WITH A FEATHER!!!!

I found out that he was from Glossop and knew Broadbottom very well. I had moved up there in 1995 and had lived there until 2003. It transpired that at identical times he was going to buy the pub in Broadbottom called the Harewood Arms and I was going to sell my house there. At that time, my friend Adam and his family owned The Harewood Arms. Martin then told me he went to the pub/restaurant five times from Llandudno, and decided at the last minute not to buy it, but couldn't explain why. At the same time I had taken my house off the market and decided not to sell it, only to reverse the decision last minute, and decided to sell, and I couldn't really explain why.

Martin instead then moved and bought a pub in Meliden, North Wales, called The Miners Arms. Now although I didn't sell my Broadbottom house until 2003, it had been on the market for nearly a year. At the time I was working and virtually living up in St Asaph, North Wales, and going to Broadbottom at weekends. I was seeing a girl from Dyserth, who always, always used to say to me, "You must go to the Miners Arms, they have live music, you should go." I never did, but had I done I would have met Martin Boardman years earlier than I did.

Then Martin moved to Mocdre, where I was living, and finally we met. I showed him the website, and he was aghast as he saw a video clip of Times Square, NY, which incorporated the time that John Lennon was shot - 10.51. Martin told us that that was his date of birth. He then went on to tell me the first time I walked into his pub in Mocdre I was followed by a white aura that stayed with me. He also said that when we left the pub on this very Friday night, one of his staff members asked him if the pub was haunted. He said, "No, why do you ask?" She said just after I left the inner double doors opened, and then the outer double doors opened. Martin replied, "Oh the back door must be open, and it's probably windy."

She replied, "There is no wind about at all," and the young waitress was spooked at this occurrence.

I had mentioned my L.S. Lowry encounter to Martin, and he told me

Lowry came to Prestatyn when he was alive. The story goes that Lowry got off the train in Meliden, thinking it was Prestatyn, and went straight to the nearest pub (The Miners Arms), had a drink, and drew the pub. A copy of that very drawing hangs in the Mountain View where I usually sit. So what do I deduce from this encounter?

1- I moved to Broadbottom and reluctantly decided to sell – Martin went several times to Broadbottom and met with my friend Adam (landlord) with a view to buying the Harewood Arms (my local). Very undecided, at the last minute decided not to move to Broadbottom.

2- I move to St Asaph and Martin moves to and buys The Miners Arms in Meliden, some five miles from St Asaph.

3- Martin puts live music on at The Miners Arms, and my then girlfriend implores me several times to go to The Miners Arms in Meliden, as they have fantastic musicians playing. I decline the offer.

4- I move half a mile from Mocdre, and Martin buys the Mountain View, Mocdre.

5- Fate makes us enter the buffet room together, alone, and we introduce ourselves, and finally meet. THIS MEETING WAS PRE-DESTINED TO BE, AS IT WILL UNFOLD BEFORE YOUR VERY EYES.

6- ONCE AGAIN it would appear that JOHN LENNON IS HELPING, EVEN AT THIS STAGE, TO PICK AND FORM THE BAND. Martin arranges for me to meet seven musicians at the pub. We play them some music and all seemed impressed. After a week, a few of them are humming and harring – will you phase us out and get a new younger band around you, what is this all about, we will record the albums for you but we won't be doing any touring etc. Then I got a phone call one night at 12 o'clock from Martin, saying he was restless and had found the answer to the problem. (I made the decision not to tell the musicians anything about JL, because they would all come, just to get on the bandwagon.) He then mentioned someone he had known for years called Simon who had a studio in Llandudno. Of course, you the reader might think this is just a few coincidences, and coincidences do happen. But, ay ay? What's going on here?

7- We meet Simon at his studio in Llandudno. I recall his face from a band I had seen playing in Llandudno years earlier called Dare. It was Darren Wharton's band. Darren had been keyboard player in the world famous Thin Lizzy. I wonder if Darren Wharton is in any way related to Chris Wharton (as mentioned in coincidence number two)? I was to go on and record with Simon and a talented guitarist called Andy, and we struck it off instantly. They loved the music, and too were blown away by the story.

Number 38: NEW YORK CUP AND SAUCER SET AND THE IMPENDING DOOM

In 1997 I had bought a bronze lady statue from a shop in Glossop. On my many previous visits to the shop for over a year (1996) the owner had repeatedly told me the statue wasn't for sale. Eventually succumbing to my pestering, or persistent enquiries, she sold me the statue. The shop was just off the high street in Glossop, in the square, by NatWest Bank and right next door to the Oxfam charity shop, where I used to buy my clothes from. It was an old antique cum bric-a-brac shop and it was from here that I also purchased an old oak drop leaf table, some chairs, and on one of my visits there I bought two cups and saucers.

I remember the occasion of that visit vividly. It was a Saturday morning in July 1998 about 10.30am. It was a glorious sunny summer's day, and I fancied a walk from Broadbottom, over the tops to Glossop, some four miles away. I could have driven, got the bus or the train, but what with the spectacular views over the countryside, the vivid heather almost glistening on the Pennines in the distance and everything looking so inviting, there was no contest. I would soak up the warm sun's rays, breathing in country air, and generally rejoice in life itself. This is one of the times when I felt John was with me, so really I wasn't walking over to Glossop on my own, if you like, I was walking with a mate.

I walked up through Charlesworth, passing the two main pubs on the junction, and the greengrocers, Peaches and Greens.

Usually, Saturday was a hive of activity in Charlesworth, and this day was no exception. Shoppers would flock from the surrounding countryside to the shop called Peaches and Greens. It always had a tremendous stock of every fruit and vegetable you could think of, and a superb selection of fresh fish. The owner would open the shop at 8am, close it on a Saturday at 1pm, and if you got there just before 1pm you could come out with baskets of fruit and veg for a fraction of the normal price. It was so popular because everything they sold was fresh. There was also a choice butcher's that specialised in homemade exotic savoury sausages. There was a newsagent that stocked milk, papers, cigarettes, coal and wood, groceries etc. There was also a little garage, right next to the square, that wasn't self-service but the owner actually serving you! In fact the only thing the village lacked was a bakery.

I continued up the next hill, past the old stone terraced cottages with their minute front doors and tiny windows, all neat and tidy, and extended to allow for modern facilities to be added, such as bedroom, bathrooms and toilets. Over one of the doors was a stone that was dated 1775. Many of these quaint houses had their stonework blackened with years of coal soot, which, looking at the surrounding countryside, made it somewhat incongruous.

Tommy Docherty, the former manager of Manchester United, had lived on this very road before recently moving. It brought a smile to my face as I passed the house and thought of one of his famous sayings: "As one door closes, another one smashes you in the face."

This real estate is now highly desirable and very much in vogue for the upwardly mobile set. The views here are spectacular and the house prices even more so.

I climbed out of the village and onto the road over the tops, looking down across to the fields of one of the oldest clubs in England, Glossop Rugby Club. A club where many a good day and night was to be had by Graham, Martin, Paddy, myself, and others.

I started singing some of the songs that John had given me, in particular, a song done three years before called *'Nature As Intended'*. The opening line was 'The sun is shining, it's a beautiful day, the river's flowing and I'm happy to say, the birds are singing oo oh yeah, the insects playing oh yeah, but I'll never know, why people never go, and I'll never say, this is mine today, this is nature as intended...'

In the distance, Glossop was beckoning, nestling snugly in what looked from here to be the lea of a large shallow valley. Here I saw the main through-road, the artery road, climbing up through Glossop towards the Pennines. The properties thinned out to virtually nothing, apart from the golf club, then suddenly in stark contrast one could see, immediately above this line, the heather and bracken and areas of barren land, interspersed with areas of dark peaty soil: the Pennines. Glossop itself was dominated by a huge old derelict 10 storey mill at the foot of the high street and, a relatively new edition to the skyline, a massive great big tower for some chemical works or other.

Looking behind me I could see Manchester shimmering in the distance. The most noticeable thing recognisable from here was the reservoir reflecting the sun off the water to everyone glancing in its direction. This was probably Denton, midway between here and Manchester, some six miles away.

Overhead in the clear blue skies I saw the gaseous trails and the logos of the BA and EasyJet aircraft making their descents, bringing the holidaymakers back from foreign climes. Their route would be virtually signposted from the skies by a huge 'bowl' carved out of the landscape caused by a glacier which was known as Combs. This is where the pilots could identify a clear natural landmark and start their ark left, towards their descent and landing on the tarmac at Manchester airport.

I arrived in Glossop feeling on top of the world. I had taken my time and thoroughly enjoyed the experience. I was on a high by the time I got to the charity shop, whereby I bought a few T-shirts. I went next door to the antique cum bric-a-brac shop still feeling on top of the world.

On looking into the shop window, everything changed.

My heart sank, and an overwhelming state of impending doom hit me straight between the eyes.

I saw a matching pair of cups and saucers, white, with a big red apple on. On top of the red apple was a green leaf. Written in gold within the red apple was 'New York', as well as buildings painted from part of the New York skyline. The centre being the Twin Towers. All the buildings were in black and immediately my attention was brought to and focussed on the Twin Towers. I felt physically sick and an incredible, nauseous feeling came over me. John was telling me that the Twin Towers were going to be destroyed, and thousands of people would die. These cups were not nice, but I felt compelled to go in and buy them. This I did, and couldn't bear to look at them. In fact to this day they have been wrapped up and put away, out of sight.

What could I do? Who could I tell? What proof did I have? I knew I had the proof in these very cups and saucers, as surely as I had the proof of the songs coming from John Lennon. This feeling of guilt racked my brain for weeks and weeks. I think I bought the cups and saucers for no other reason than to take them off sale, away from and out of public view. This feeling of helplessness and sickliness stayed with me for ages. Moving on nearly three years to 11th September 2001 and the Twin Towers were destroyed, and thousands of people lost their lives.

I cried because I had told no-one. I didn't know which way to turn. I had no one to help me through this knowledge that John had given me. Had I let John down, and all those people? Should I have gone to the police or government and told them what I knew? And that the evidence was there on those cups and saucers? Was I afraid they would think, what with the Lennon sightings as well, that I was some kind of nut?

Would it have mattered what they thought? If I had told someone I could feel that I had tried my best to deliver this message from John Lennon from 'the other side'. Looking back, it felt like a step too far for me to take. I still don't understand why I didn't speak out, just as I had done on GMTV when John Lennon came to me and I told the whole country.

Number 39: THE NEW YORK POSTCARD

In 2007 I called to the YMCA in Colwyn Bay with my brother-in-law and saw an acquaintance of ours called Ray. The place was up for sale and Ray was getting rid of items in readiness for the building to close down.

Ray had retired. He had been the chief steward and main trainer for British Airways, and told me some incredible stories of his flights all around the world.

This day, he had given us hundreds of old plastic bags that were used to wrap items in that the customers bought and were now of no use. Ray ran the charity stalls there for no money, giving the proceeds to Colwyn Bay Football Youth Club.

We took the huge box of old plastic bags and within the big box was a smaller box of bags.

On getting home I opened the box to see all kinds of different plastic bags. I probably had about 70 odd bags. Not your normal Tesco bags, but some were from up market places like Marks & Spencer, Thorntons, John Lewis etc. Out of curiosity I sifted through the bags when out between two of the bags fell an A5 size postcard. It was an old postcard of New York City. But what was strange was that there were no Twin Towers, and again the hairs on the back of my neck stood on end. On checking the rear of the postcard I found it was from the 1950s before the Twin Towers were built. Instantly it took me right back to the Glossop cups and saucers, and of course 9/11.

Number 40:
SIMON GARDENER, RAY GARDENER AND JOHN HAGUE

It was early 2008. I was in the studio with Simon and Andy laying down some tracks, as Simon was looking at my lyrics and asking questions about how John Lennon came to me and gave me this music. I was explaining it to Simon, when he told me there was a coincidence to all this that really surprised even him.

He went on to tell me that **his dad's best friend, John Hague, was a close friend and went to art college with John Lennon.** John Hague used to drive to Liverpool Art College every day in his auntie's old Ford Popular. Also Simon's dad, Ray, had also met Lennon, through John Hague, both here in Llandudno and in Liverpool.

Simon then pointed to a painting on his studio wall, saying, "That was painted by John Hague, and is supposed to have John Lennon painted in it somewhere." The painting was abstract. So close were these two art college friends that when John Lennon made the big time and John Hague asked him for some money to start a business, John wrote a cheque out there and then for £20,000.

Number 41: ANDY MOORE, GUITARIST EXTRORDINAIRE

Andy was the guitarist mentioned above who put the guitar tracks down, who incidentally had also been in Darren Wharton's 'Dare' band along with Simon Gardener.

In between breaks from the intensive studio atmosphere we would kick a ball around the garden for 10 minutes or so. Andy is from Birkenhead, so we had an affinity with each other. He started telling me how he was really spooked when I told him the John Lennon story, and as Simon had done previously, he asked me many questions about these sightings.

He then went onto say, "What's really weird Mike, is that I transcribe

music for a living. I am working for a company in the United States."
He went on to tell me what this transcription entailed, by what means, and how he did it. He said, "Guess which book of music I have just finished before starting this project?"
I answered, "No idea."
He said, "John Lennon: The John Lennon Guitar Collection." He went on to tell me that he had also transcribed the Beatles' Let It Be and Hard Day's Night books for the same American company. The company that distributed the books was called Hal Leonard, but the music publishers were EMI MUSIC PUBLISHING.
When he told me I wasn't remotely fazed, and I told him I wasn't in the least bit surprised as John Lennon had been guiding me through different situations all along. And also he was guiding me to different people, but it was nonetheless great news. It was John telling me, yet again, I was on the right track. It is situations like this (or as Uri Geller once told me, "it's synchronicity") that just keep me going.

Number 42: CYNTHIA POWELL MARRIES JOHN LENNON
Cynthia Powell marries John Lennon, August 23rd 1962.
As far as I know, I don't think Cynthia Powell and me are related, just a coincidence of names...maybe?

Number 43:
CYNTHIA LENNON'S BOOK 'JOHN' PUBLISHED IN 2005
Cynthia Lennon wrote a book called 'John' in 2005. Its publishers were Hodder & Stoughton. On the rear page of the book is a description about Cynthia's journey and is probably written by the publishers themselves. Amongst other things, it says, quote, 'For the first time Cynthia presents not just new and fascinating insights into those legendary times, but also tells her full and compelling personal story of marriage to a man who was to become the most idolised and admired of all the Beatles.' It also goes on to say, 'Since John's assassination in New York in 1980, Cynthia has retained her silence about many of the subsequent events.'
My girlfriend Hils bought me this second-hand book in 2006. We were walking along the front in Rhos on Sea and came upon an old book shop,

next door to a cafe on the front, and we started mooching about. I think I was looking at the car books.

I read the book, and two things jumped off the pages to me.

1 – A picture that Cynthia had drawn of the wedding to John Lennon. Apparently there were no photographs ever taken at this wedding. She draws the scene in the register office. In the background can be seen a worker with a pneumatic drill outside the window.

Going back to the 10th sighting of John on 8th February 1993 and the song *'I Wish I Could Fly'*, I describe vividly this navvy standing between John and me, holding what I describe as an industrial size brace and bit with which he was digging a hole to hell.

In it there is a line that says 'Standing on a corner watchin' a man digging a hole to hell, wonderin' why all the fuss, when Isaac Newton said, yeah, this is the apple that fell...' The hook was, 'All I see is the sky around me, and I wish that I could fly, I'm so lost and all on my own, like a bird in empty skies...'

I had painted the image I saw even years before I had met Hils.

John's overpowering feeling to me through thought transferral, and the crystal clear images at the time of this sighting, was that he wanted to get right away from where he was. He was screaming inside his head.

Interestingly, there is reference in the song to a 'granite quarry lorry, making a delivery, dropping a pile on me...' This was actual sounds of a lorry passing on the main road, about 100 metres from my home at the time of the sighting at 4am. The road in Mold was Ruthin Road. The town of Ruthin is about nine miles from Mold. I believe Cynthia once had a café there, as she says in her book she got the news of John's assassination while she was in her café/home which was in the high street in Ruthin.

2 – A photograph showing John Lennon, Tony Carricker, Cynthia Powell and John Hague

This photograph is very interesting to me because of three things that are significant.

(1)

These four people are sitting on an old Ford Popular motor car. John looks like a Teddy Boy, as does his friend behind him. In the sighting *'Betcha Bottom Dollar'* I describe how John is dressed like a teddy boy with three other men, going out 'on the town'. The image I had painted years before is of 'this John Lennon' but in other clothes (and possibly these two men and one other).

(2)

The car they are sitting on is an old Ford Popular. In the sighting *'Sometime In The 50s'* I make reference to a 'Ford Popular motor car, it had shiny red seats, but I didn't know whether plastic or leather...' I also painted the scene, which had a black car in a street, with a young 9- or 10-year-old John Lennon looking in. On the boy's overcoat was a badge with lights all around of himself, when he was older and a star.

(3)

In 2008, John Hague is brought to my attention by Simon Gardener as being his dad's best friend, and a good friend of John Lennon. I'd had this book for two years, and of course, before Simon told me the connection, this man called John Hague was of no significance to me, nor indeed, his auntie's Ford Popular.

Number 44: RICHIE 'DE WALT' VAUGHAN EVANS

Richie was a chippie, or joiner, who I had known for quite a few years. When we needed some joinery work doing, his name was at the top of my list as his work was always first class and, because he had all the proper 'De Walt' gear, he was fast. He had helped with various things including building a car port, and subsequently a loft conversion.

As he was packing up to leave, he made a comment about my rather small old piano, saying, "It's a pity I don't have the old piano I got years ago, that would have fitted there perfectly."

It was one of those moments when I could have gone on to the next subject, but I asked him what happened to the piano. He then went on to tell me he sold it for £3500, and that was 12 years ago! "How come you got £3500 for an old piano?" I asked.

Wait for it...

The piano was from Quarry Bank School, and John Lennon was not only certified as playing on the piano, but he had also scribed his name on the inside top of the piano. This too was independently certified.

When I asked him why he had only told me this now when he was leaving, I realised myself that I had told him absolutely nothing about my experiences with John Lennon. There was no reason for him to tell me. Why would he?

The year he came by the piano was 1989, and Quarry Bank School was being pulled down to make way for a new superstore – Tesco's. When Quarry Bank School was being demolished, as one of the demolition party he was given a choice of one piece of furniture from the school that would have been thrown away. Richie chose the old upright piano. When he got it home, he looked inside it and found John Lennon's name scratched inside it. This was the piano that John Lennon used to play on in Quarry Bank. John had scratched his name on the inside lid. A crazy coincidence, if ever there was one!

Number 45: RICHIE LLOYD JONES

Richard Lloyd Jones was a graphic designer who worked for Laurence Nicholls at Nicholl's Print in Heswall. I used to get various printing jobs done there. It was Richie who had produced the artwork for the Mike and Rowena McCartney official invitation card to the opening of a new maternity wing in Clatterbridge Hospital. The full story is mentioned previously under the title Mike McCartney, the tape, and the World Beatles Song.

Richard eventually went on to University in Liverpool and did a degree in filmmaking and media and worked on the likes of Brookside, Merseyvision.

I worked again with Richard around 1997. Rich had been in the studio when my band were recording two tracks. He videoed the event on my camera, meeting and filming Sylvan Richardson, Ronan O'Rahilly, and the rest of the band.

It had been years since I last got in touch with Rich, and when I did it was to see if he would paginate this book. I wasn't quite finished and said I would be in touch in a couple of months time.

Moving on, I spoke again on the phone to Richard.

He lives in London now, and was enthusing over the birth of his beautiful baby girl and how marvellous being a daddy was. After general chit chat, he told me his partner's parents live in Caernarfon, North Wales, and they had travelled up to see them when the baby was born. He had tried to get me, but didn't have my current mobile number. After discussing my project, he then went on to say, "I told you about the video and artwork I worked on in Liverpool three years ago didn't I?"

"No," was my response, I remember him being all loved up and talking only about the impending birth of his first born!! He went on to tell me he had just moved down to London and he got the call: "Do you want to work on a video and artwork for Yoko, in Liverpool?" **It was for eight days work, and this company wanted Richie to work on the track *'Working Class Hero'.* Yoko was putting together a DVD of John Lennon's tracks and wanted the Liverpool/local influence.** Richard jumped at the chance, as his all-time heroes are the Beatles. Weird isn't it?

He went on the next train back to Liverpool and duly did his proud eight days work. Needless to say, the highlight of his career to date is those eight days, and obviously the finished result: the DVD. The DVD was produced in 2004 and was called *JOHN LENNON – LEGENDS*.

Number 46:
JOHN LENNON – MICK JAGGER TRACK 'FOUND' IN 2007

It was revealed in 2007 that Mick Jagger and John Lennon had collaborated on a track called *'Too Many Cooks'*. It was a previously unheard track that was thought to be just hearsay. When it came to light, from Ronnie Wood, Jagger decided to put it on his then latest album – The Best of Mick Jagger. (This album was a compilation of his solo albums.)

This is relevant to the sighting No. 11 called *'Crazy Lady'*. I didn't know why in the sighting John was passing Mick Jagger a piece of paper with a song on. Now it is obvious that they had actually worked together before!

Number 47: ROCKET MAN??

It happened on November 23rd 2007. It was 4am and I was awakened by a loud sustained 'rocket' type noise outside the bedroom window. As I was lying there, slowly coming round for two or three minutes, I realised that this loud sustained sound was still there and not disappearing, as the normal overhead aircraft would have done. I asked Hils if she was awake and she replied that she was, and that there was a sound coming from outside that was very unusual. I immediately got out of bed and went to the window, which was already open. I opened the window, fully leaned out and looked up to the sky to where this very loud and close rocket sound appeared to be coming from. It sounded as if it were very much overhead. In fact looking back towards the woods and the mountainside beyond, the noise appeared more prominent from that direction. There was a very heavy, thick, dense low cloud, which was virtually touching the top of the trees; again very unusual. So this meant I couldn't see whatever this 'thing' was. Hils got out of bed and looked with me. She too could not make out what it was, nor see anything. I stayed at the window for about 15 minutes, some considerable time, and the noise was still there. I was drawn someway to go outside. I don't know why I had this 'pull', but I decided not to go, thinking instead that I would check out the area in the morning. I then got back into bed and listened for a further five minutes or so, and began to realise that slowly but surely, this noise was abating, or moving away. I got out of bed and had to look again to where the noise had been coming from. The noise wasn't in the same place, but seemed to be further to my right, which was in fact, a northerly direction. After a further five minutes there was a break in the clouds and very high up, travelling away from me at a slow pace, and with this noise, I saw four bright lights close together. It appeared to have one large light and three smaller lights to one side of it, not unlike a dog's paw. By now it was very high in the sky, and through a break in the low lying cloud I saw a clear starry sky. This craft was high in the heavens. I drew the image. This image was not an aircraft, but more squat and rounded without wings. In the morning I phoned a neighbour and asked if they had heard any strange noises. They had, so much so, that they had got out of bed and checked their house out, as they thought this 'strange noise' which they had never heard before was coming from somewhere in their own house. They confirmed to me that this strange noise lasted at least half an hour, from about 4am.

This date – 23rd November 2007 – was the 15th anniversary of the second sighting which included an out of body experience with Yoko Ono on 23rd November 1992.

The following day, at about 8am, I walked up the lane and I saw four military helicopters flying just above the trees, but no noise was coming from their engines. They were sinister looking, and I had never seen helicopters shaped like this before. They had no markings on, but were dark/black in colour. It was surreal. Not a sound came from them, and everything felt as if it was in slow motion. They separated and as they did I hid in the trees and took photographs of these helicopters. They appeared to be looking for something by the way they seemed to be methodically 'sweeping' this area, all at very low level. What was spooky was that on the tops of the helicopters was a big bulbous thing, a bit like a squashed ball, attached to the rotor blades. Eventually, after about 20 minutes, they left the area with their engines really loud and deep, sounding like jet engines. It was as if they had been able to switch their engines from a silent mode onto a 'normal sound mode', if that makes any sense to you.

Number 48:
ELECTRICAL COMMUNICATION AND TEDDY DAN

Other weird things were to happen several times over a three week period, leading up to this rocket noise occurrence, which I began to think about.

How can I describe this weird thing to you? A month or so before I had caught a cold, and was having severe coughing fits, particularly at night. In the dark, these coughs caused like a circle of jagged white lines, which caused headaches after 10 or 15 minutes continually coughing. Moving on to the three weeks before the strange noise my cough had long since gone, and I was relaxed, lying awake, in the early hours of the morning. What happened next was what appeared to be some sort of electrical current in the form of a straight jagged white line in my head. It appeared to travel from the right hand side of my brain to my left hand side. It would last for no more than two or three seconds. Always at the end of this period, and immediately when this white jagged line disappeared, I would hear a sound or a movement in the house. Maybe I'd hear a cupboard door closing, a creak, or an unusual noise.

WHAT IT FELT LIKE WAS SOME SORT OF ELECTRICAL COMMUNICATION. The video clock would flash, and the hi-fi would be switched off or on. Also, a Rastafarian figure I had that was a wine bottle holder would be turned around in the mornings, on these occasions. I would ask Hils if she had moved it, or she sometimes asked me if I had. Neither one of us had ever moved it, only to turn it back to its normal position. Also within this period I was searching through the songs when a postcard fell out from a wodge of songs. It was a postcard from my Rastafarian friend called Teddy Dan. I had met him years ago in Oxford, where I sometimes met Mr O'Rahilly. The coffee shop in Oxford was called CoCo's. Ronan gave Teddy his usual spiel, Radio Caroline etc. etc. I became great friends with Teddy, and this Jamaica postcard brought back fond memories of him. He was a musician who wrote his own songs. One single that was quite popular he did was called 'The United States of Africa'. He had recorded over five albums, and was travelling the world to exotic places recording and gigging. It also made me remember what Teddy had said on one of the days I stayed at his gaff. He said, "Mike, don't wait, record an album and put it out now." (This was probably about 1995/96) He said, "Ronan is living on dreams of his past. If you wait for him, you will wait forever, he's just living on dreams."

How right he was!

11

There is not a day goes by when there isn't an article or piece written in one of the newspapers, somewhere, relating to the Beatles, or John Lennon, or the other members of the band. Such is the incredible popularity and intrigue surrounding this pop phenomenon; people are fascinated and read with interest every scrap that is written about them. As I have said before, this journey I have been on with John Lennon has continued for over 20 years, and there is clearly no sign of it stopping. It is an ongoing, fluid movement of thoughts and music and art from John to me. There is a power at work, which I believe is outside the realms of our knowledge or indeed our comprehension.

The times, I think, they are a changing. A few years ago, if people couldn't understand the unexplained, they ridiculed it. I think people are starting to consider the possibility that there must be more to life than this, *even if* it can't be explained.

But think on, we, the human species, are still busy plundering the Earth's riches and fighting wars all over the planet.

There are still millions and millions of starving people.

There is a tiny percentage of the populous that own a massive majority of available wealth. Robbing from the rich earth to take for themselves. In fact, the rich become richer, while the sick, starving and the poorest of this globe watch on in disbelief.

There are people I know who know the cost of everything and the value of nothing.

Now is it just me, or are we on a self-destruct mode? Why does life have to be like this?

It's weird but we 'normal' human beings seem to accept everything that is going on around us, which in fact we could actually change but choose not to. Or perhaps we continue to follow like sheep? The few who can take control, and the consequence always seems to be that it's never enough – they want more. Ugly greed and lust for power and fame sets in.

And the latest phenomena to add to this race for riches is the celebrity culture.

It seems a lot of ordinary people are in awe of their heroes, craving, wanting and trying to live their lives vicariously through their own hero 'celebrity', whilst texting and tweeting everyone they know to let them in on their important life. No wonder so many people on the planet are trying to become a celebrity, but for all the wrong reasons. They want money, people to love them, adulation, and lots of it in abundance. But what must they do to get it?

Actually, it doesn't really matter if they have no talent whatsoever. All they have to do is go out wearing next to nothing, go to the right clubs, parties, award ceremonies and so on, and do their thing.

Be it swear, do drugs, blaspheme, take their clothes off, be as crude as possible, get drunk and go with someone who is already a celeb. Hey presto, a new minor 'Z' lister has been born and the tabloids are on your case.

Nothing else matters as long as they make the morning headlines in the papers, and the TV networks, and paparazzi are chasing them all over the place to get the whole sorry, sordid story.

The more you think about it, the more absurd it becomes.

The majority of normal human beings just want to go about their business and not be on some sort of crusade or masquerade. On that I agree. But the world is changing. In this instant media focussed frenzied world, it is becoming more difficult to be normal, to be yourself.

Clever marketing techniques by media moguls via the TV box sitting in every home in the country continue to add to the pressures of everyday life. More and more people are finding it difficult not to envy and want the facelift, or the Ferrari, or what the neighbour has got and you haven't. This is a culture of instant gratification.

None of it is real. It's plastic and it's short term. But most of all, it won't stand you in good stead on life's journey.

THAT IS ALL I CAN TELL YOU.

OH YEAH, AND... THERE *IS* MORE TO LIFE 'THAN THIS'.

In the meantime folks, I think...

YOU JUST HAVE TO DO YOUR BEST.

YOU JUST HAVE TO TREAT PEOPLE AS YOU YOURSELF WANT TO BE TREATED.

GOODNIGHT AND GOD BLESS XX

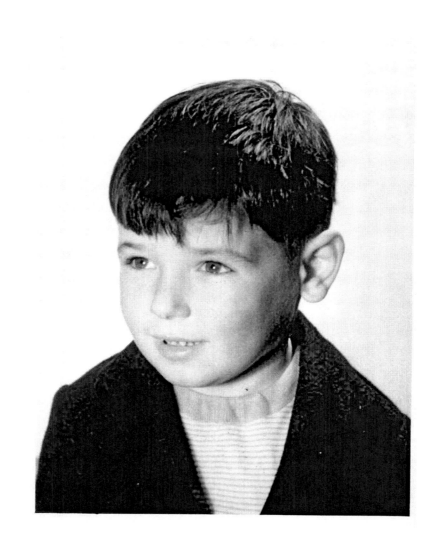

Top Left: Kicking a ball outside No.14   Top Right: On the trusty scooter
Middle: Aged 14, ACT, RAF Woodvale
Bottom Left: Fooling around in my jim jams.
Bottom Right: 1966 School football team (top R)

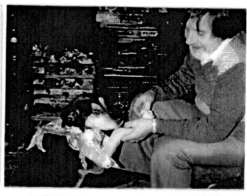

From top L to R clockwise
1. Mum – Gwen – pictured with 'Gebaron' in back yard
2. Dad – George – pictured with 'Handel' in kitchen
3. Mum and Dad – only picture of them together that exists
4. 1980 – Mums funeral – Brian, Jayson, Diana and me
5. 1972 – aged 17, my first sales role with Unilever
6. Dad – with his Zodiac in front of caravan in Silver Bay

Top: Me with Ronan O'Rahilly and Nick Marland
Bottom: In Whitezone Studios, with band – Sylvan (bass and producer) Nick (guitar/vox) Kareem (piano/keys) Me (vox) Ronan O'Rahilly (manager) Missing from pic – Simon Moore (drums)

Top: Rehearsing in 'The Mill' with Beau Jangles bass, Simon Moore drums, Nick guitar
Middle: Me at the start of another long session at 'The Mill'
Bottom: Me and Nick fooling around with one of the guys filming our antics!

Lightning Source UK Ltd.
Milton Keynes UK
UKOW02f0302050716

277720UK00002B/36/P

9 781911 113287